HOW TO PROMOTE YOUR BOOK

A PRACTICAL GUIDE to PUBLICIZING YOUR OWN TITLE

DR. JAN YAGER

SQUAREONE
PUBLISHERS

T0013622

Cover Designer: Jeannie Rosado
In-House Editor: Joanne Abrams
Typesetter: Gary A. Rosenberg

Square One Publishers
115 Herricks Road
Garden City, New York 11040
(516) 535-2010 • squareonepublishers.com

Publisher's Cataloguing-in-Publication Data

Names: Yager, Jan, 1948– author.
Title: How to promote your book : a practical guide to publicizing your own title /
    Dr. Jan Yager.
Description: Garden City, New York : Square One Publishers, [2023] | Series:
    Square One writer's guides | Includes index.
Identifiers: LCCN 2022028661 (print) | LCCN 2022028662 (ebook) | ISBN
    9780757004742 (paperback) | ISBN 9780757054747 (ebook)
Subjects: LCSH: Books—Marketing. | Authorship—Marketing. | Authors and
    publishers.
Classification: LCC Z285.6 .Y34 2023 (print) | LCC Z285.6 (ebook) | DDC
    002.068/8—dc23/eng/20220722
LC record available at https://lccn.loc.gov/2022028661
LC ebook record available at https://lccn.loc.gov/2022028662

Printed in the United States

10 9 8 7 6 5 4 3 2 1

Contents

Acknowledgments, v

Preface, vii

A Note on Gender, x

Introduction, 1

PART ONE. **BOOK PROMOTION BASICS**

1. You and the World of Bookselling, 9

2. Know Your Audience, 21

3. What Is Traditional Media?, 31

4. What Is Internet-Based Media?, 49

5. You As the Author, 73

PART TWO. **WHAT TO DO BEFORE YOUR BOOK IS PUBLISHED**

6. Setting Up Timelines, 87

7. Getting Advance Blurbs or Endorsements, 109

8. Getting Reviews, 121

PART THREE. **WHAT TO DO AFTER YOUR BOOK IS PUBLISHED**

9. Launching Your Publicity Plans, 159

10. Speaking Your Way to More Sales, 185

11. Exhibiting at Book Fairs and Trade Shows, 201

Conclusion, 219

Glossary, 221

RESOURCES

Audiobook Reviews and Promotion, 234

Author and Publisher Groups and Organizations, 235

Book Fairs and Events in the United States, 238

Book Fairs Around the World, 241

Book Fairs—Companies That Display Authors' Books, 242

Book Promotion and Marketing Information Websites, 243

Book Publicists, 244

Book Reviews from Fee-Based Services, 244

Book Reviews from Prepublication Trade Journals, 245

CIP Data, PCIP Data, LCCN, and ISBN Information, 247

Companies that Imprint Promotional Materials, 247

Crowdfunding Platforms, 248

Email Management Programs for Sending Out E-Blasts, 249

Foreign Rights and Translation, 250

Free PR Leads, 251

Freelance Editors, Proofreaders, and Other Publishing Professionals, 252

Media Outlets, 253

Online Services For Sharing Digital Review Copies, 254

Online Sites Where You Can Sell Your Books, 254

Press Release Distribution Services, 256

Social Media Websites, 256

Training in Media Skills, 258

Training in Speaking Skills, 258

Website Builders, Do-It-Yourself, 259

Sample Filled-in Timeline Table, 261

About the Author, 264

Index, 265

Acknowledgments

I f I were to list all the people who have contributed to my knowledge of book publicity, or who have helped me promote my own books or those of my publishing company's authors or other book clients over the years, I would come close to filling up a book with just those names! So let me instead express a heartfelt general thanks to all of those dedicated book publicity professionals based in New York City and throughout the United States and internationally, as well as those associated with my book tours in the UK, Sweden, Australia, and New Zealand. I am so appreciative of all the numerous book publicists I have worked with, as well as the bookers; the hosts and hostesses at TV shows, radio shows, and podcasts; and the book reviewers, book review editors, bloggers, staff and freelance journalists, feature writers, and so many others who write about, and care deeply about, books and their authors.

A shout out to my readers and fans who have bought my books or borrowed one of them from the library, written reader reviews, or attended one of my workshops or online book talks, as well as to those who have sent me emails expressing appreciation for my work.

I also want to express my gratitude to everyone who contributed to the research for *How to Promote Your Book* by filling out an extensive survey just for this book; by completing a questionnaire for my previous books, which included questions about book promotion; or by providing information through interviews. Whether or not you were quoted in the final book, you have my deepest gratitude for the time you took to share your book promotion experiences as an author, publicist, media trainer, or media representative.

Finally, thanks to my husband, Fred, for reading an earlier draft of this book, as well as to the staff at Square One Publishers, who worked so hard to help me finalize it, especially editor Joanne Abrams, marketing manager Anthony Pomes, and publisher Rudy Shur. Thank you also to those at Square One who worked on its predecessor, *How to Self-Publish Your Book,* particularly editor Michael Weatherhead.

Preface

My earliest education in the ins and outs of book publicity began when I was twenty-five years old and was fortunate enough to work at Grove Press, Inc. Among other responsibilities, legendary founder and CEO Barney Rosset tasked me with publicizing Irish poet Ulick O'Connor, as well as a controversial memoir. I was also responsible for publicizing the nonfiction books I had acquired: sending books out for pre- and post-publication review; booking magazine, TV, and radio interviews; and organizing an author tour. These were just some of the numerous book promotion activities in which I was engaged.

After I left Grove Press and was finishing up two books I was writing on vegetarianism, I received my second training in book promotion, this time, as a published author. Grove Press was publishing one book, a celebrity interview cookbook called *Meatless Cooking, Celebrity Style*; while Scribner was publishing a history entitled *The Vegetable Passion*. Since the two books were on a related topic, I negotiated a unique arrangement in which the two companies co-sponsored a cross-country author tour. We agreed that they would pay for my airfare, and I would pick up the tab on the hotels and meals. All the arrangements were made by the head of publicity at Scribner, Susan Richman, and her staff. Later, when I published two additional books with Scribner, I learned even more about publicity by watching Susan and her team do everything that a proactive book publicist should do, first sending a book out to trade journals for pre-publication reviews, and then pitching it to magazines and newspapers for reviews or features as well as to TV and radio for author interviews. Susan and her team also set up author events and local newspaper interviews in each of the cities on the cross-country tour. For two of the books, the tours began with an appearance on the *Today* show.

A few months before my first two books were published, I stopped by a new restaurant in Manhattan and told the owner that I couldn't make any promises, but if he sponsored a publication day party, I would try to get the media there. He agreed. (My friends and I prepared a lot of the food by cooking up several recipes from my new cookbook.) A reporter for *The New Yorker*'s "The Talk of the Town" showed up at the party and wrote a full-page story on the event, as well as on me and my books. I had learned a very important book promotion lesson: Yes, it's great when others help with some or most of the tasks related to book promotion, but authors can do a lot on their own as well.

Over the decades that followed these major book promotion experiences, I went on to publish more than fifty books in a range of genres— mostly nonfiction, but also fiction, poetry, and illustrated children's books. My publishers included such commercial houses as Doubleday, Wiley, and Prentice-Hall. Then, in 1996, I decided to take more control of the publishing process, so I founded Hannacroix Creek Books, Inc. At Hannacroix, I am the Director of Publicity. I also continue to publish books with other houses.

In my years of working with other authors and of speaking to numerous authors at book fairs, conventions, and workshops, I have learned that many writers do not know what I discovered early in my career: Regardless of who publishes a book, promotion needs to be part of the process even while the book is still being written. Moreover, authors are usually the best advocates for their own book. And although promoting a new book is normally where all the focus is—especially if you are published by a commercial, hybrid, or academic house—it is also vital to keep a book alive once it is no longer new and becomes a "backlist" title.

That is why I decided to write *How to Promote Your Book*—not only to tell authors like you what you need to know about book promotion, but also to convince you that your promotion of your title can make the difference between your book getting the attention and sales it deserves or having it fade into obscurity. In researching this book, in addition to drawing on my own professional and personal publicity experiences, I surveyed or interviewed more than a hundred authors who have written in a range of genres. I learned what they had done to promote their books and how their efforts either succeeded or failed in getting them the results they wanted.

Yes, book promotion is hard work. It is also true that it benefits from developing and maintaining relationships with the media, which takes time. But, whatever the subject or genre of your book—and whether your book was produced by a commercial, hybrid, or academic press or you are self-published—*How to Promote Your Book* was designed to guide you through the process of getting your book noticed by reviewers as well as the media, librarians, educators, booksellers, and readers.

There's a lot to cover so let's get started. Happy promoting!

A Note on Gender

In order to avoid awkward phrasing within sentences while acknowledging both genders, the publisher has chosen to alternate between the use of male and female pronouns according to chapter. When referring to someone in the third person, odd-numbered chapters will use female pronouns, while even-numbered chapters will use male pronouns.

Introduction

You have just written the best book in the world, but what good does it do if few people know it exists? When it comes to book publishing, the writing—as challenging as it may be—turns out to be the easiest part for many authors. Book promotion is often the more difficult task. However, it is also what separates the books that sell from those that collect dust in warehouses, in garages, and on bookstore shelves.

If up to this point, you have not given much thought to what book promotion includes, it might be helpful to define what I mean when I talk about promotion. It includes announcing your book on social media; getting it reviewed in trade journals as well as general or specialized magazines, newspapers, and newsletters; securing interviews on network or cable television shows, radio shows, and podcasts; taking part in author events at bookstores, libraries, schools, or association meetings; exhibiting or speaking at trade book shows and public book fairs; and much more. Book promotion and publicity involve everything you can do to make people aware of your book and to persuade them to buy it.

There are situations in which being interviewed on even one show or written up in even one article can catapult a book on to the bestsellers list. But in most cases, promotion involves a steady, often slow effort, in which you build upon each success. A good review in a small newspaper might not result in a flood of sales, but if that review lands you an interview on a local radio show, and a podcast host hears the show and decides to feature you on his podcast—which is a *perfect fit* for your book—all this exposure might lead to sales as well as additional publicity opportunities. And as word continues to spread about your book and about you, the sales can become significant.

The results of book promotion are unpredictable, but I can make one prediction: If you do nothing or next to nothing, your book is likely to fade into oblivion before it has a chance to find its audience and become the success that you believe it could be.

What is exciting about book promotion today is that there are so many ways to gain attention for your book. Although it has become more difficult for self-published and relatively unknown authors to get booked on national television and radio shows, there are still many local and regional traditional media outlets—such as local television and radio shows, local newspapers, and specialty publications—as well as national podcasts that may be happy to give you and your book a chance. And, of course, social media has opened many doors that didn't exist even a few years ago. You can pick and choose among the many promotional possibilities, channeling your time and energy into the opportunities that seem most appropriate for your particular book and for you as an author.

You can also decide if you will take a DIY—do it yourself—approach to book promotion, with you sending out emails, crafting pitches, and mailing out review copies and press kits; or if you will hire a professional book publicist to handle most of the promotion for you. But even if you're lucky enough to have your book published by a commercial publishing house—in which case, your title should be promoted by a dedicated publicist—you will want to work with your publisher to maximize the staff's promotional efforts. Just as important, unless you are a celebrity or a best-selling author, your publicist will probably have to move on to other authors and titles after three to six months. The bottom line is that if you want your book to be a success, in most cases, it will eventually be up to you to pick up the book promotion ball and run with it. And unless you have worked at a book publishing company or successfully publicized previous books, you will need to learn what book promotion entails and how you can make it happen.

Whether you are an aspiring author, a new writer, or even a seasoned wordsmith who is looking to brush up on your promotional skills, *How to Promote Your Book* will help you get the word out about your new title. It begins by filling you in on the world of publishing so that you will understand your place in it, and by examining the various marketplaces and media outlets you need to know about. It then helps you plan and carry out a promotional campaign, step by step, from creating a smart and realistic timeline to publicizing and selling your book at various venues.

Chapter 1 starts the ball rolling by looking at how the media and booksellers will see you as an author. Was your book published by a commercial, hybrid, or academic house, or are you a self-published author? This chapter explains how your answer will affect the challenges you are likely to face as you work your way through the various marketplaces, from traditional bookstores to online retailers. It also helps you understand which marketplaces would be most appropriate for you and your book.

One of the secrets to achieving the sales and recognition that help you get a greater commercial return on your book is recognizing who would most likely have an interest in a particular book, and how you can reach that person. In Chapter 2, we look at the various factors that can help you zero in on your book's audience so that you can get the word out to your potential readers.

Once you have identified your audience, you are ready to explore the many forms of media available to you. Chapter 3 fills you in on traditional media, such as newspapers and journals, while Chapter 4 explores Internet-based media, from blogs and websites to Facebook, Instagram, and Twitter. By learning about the various media outlets that are out there, you will be able to make better decisions regarding where you want to focus your promotional efforts.

Whether your book is being produced by a publishing house or is a self-published work, it is vital for you to recognize that you, as the author, are absolutely key to getting attention for your book. Chapter 5 fully explores your role as the author and the chief promoter of your title. It also examines the principal components of the publicity task you have ahead of you and prepares you for the challenges you are likely to face.

An important cautionary note is especially crucial for self-published authors. Too many authors are tempted to begin their book's promotion within hours or days of getting the completed electronic file of their title to the printer. This is invariably a big mistake, since book promotion is best undertaken when a publicity plan is created months in advance of a book's publication. In Chapter 6, you will learn how to design a practical timeline for your project—from the writing of your book, to the all-important pre-marketing steps that must be taken, to your book's release—so that your promotional plan will be well in place and in gear before your book becomes available to the public.

In Chapters 7 and 8, you will learn more about two important promotional tasks—getting advance blurbs and getting reviews. Good blurbs can be an effective promotional tool that can help encourage a journal editor to consider reviewing your book, or potentially turn a bookstore browser into a book buyer. Chapter 7 guides you through the process of obtaining blurbs and using them to gain attention for your book. Following this, Chapter 8 takes a closer look at what is involved in getting your book considered for review in traditional reviewing platforms—such as trade journals, magazines, and newspapers—as well as on free or for-a-fee Internet-based platforms. This chapter leads you every step of the way, from choosing the best media for your book to making contact with the appropriate people.

Your book has been released, and through hard work, you've gathered positive blurbs and perhaps even a few reviews. In Chapter 9, you will learn how to attract further attention to your title by creating a winning media kit and sending it out to both traditional and online media as a means of gaining print, online, network and cable TV, radio, and podcast interviews; feature articles; and more. This chapter also looks at the possibility of hiring a professional publicist who can help lead your promotional venture and guide you toward success.

If you are a first-time author, you may be surprised to learn that your book can open up countless speaking opportunities for you, both free and paid. Authors who speak well can gain attention for themselves and for their titles—which, in turn, can result in book sales and sometimes even speaker fees. Chapter 10 explains how you can obtain speaking engagements and book signings in libraries, in bookstores, and at various conventions and book events. It also offers tips for becoming a compelling and successful speaker.

Chapter 11 looks at two types of events discussed in Chapter 10—public book fairs and industry trade shows—with an eye toward promoting your book by becoming an exhibitor. The fact is that the majority of exhibitors at these events are not there to speak, but to show off their books to bookstore buyers, librarians, publishers, the media, and in some cases, the general reading public. This chapter will guide you from the initial application process to setting up your space to making (and maximizing) those all-important contacts.

Because of my background as a publicist and an author of more than fifty books—both commercially published and self-published through my own publishing company—in every chapter, I am able to offer insights into the publishing world and the promotional process. I also offer proven ways to get your voice heard loud and clear, regardless of the type of book that you are seeking to promote and who published it. You will learn how to create a presence on social media, how to target the publications that are most likely to be interested in you and your book (even if you're an unknown author), how to prepare a professional press kit, and so much more. Even details like the best way to mail out media kits are covered.

Throughout this book, it is emphasized that through your promotional efforts, *you* are the one who is going to make the greatest difference in the success of your book. Whether your work was published by a major company with name recognition or you've seen it from manuscript to published book entirely on your own, book promotion is actually where the playing field can be leveled. If your work is good enough and your pitch is well crafted and appropriately targeted, you *can* get your title reviewed, you *can* get your book featured on traditional media, you *can* create a buzz on social media, and you *can* gain sales.

No one says that book promotion is easy—although there are a lucky few for whom some or even all of the tasks related to book promotion come easier than they do for others. Effective promotion requires time, preparation, persistence, and salesmanship, as well as an understanding of your audience, the marketplace, and the media. But history has demonstrated that in so many cases, authors have been one of the primary reasons their titles have taken off. With *How to Promote Your Book,* you have a far better chance of capturing the attention and sales that your book deserves.

PART ONE

BOOK PROMOTION BASICS

1.

You and the World of Bookselling

Before we begin to explore the world of publicity, it is important to understand how the media and booksellers will see you as an author and what challenges you may face as you work your way through the various marketplaces. As you may already know, it is not an even playing field for a published author. Factors such as whether you are a self-published or a commercially published author will come into play. It's vital to recognize, though, that it has never been easy for any published writer to expand her audience. That's why it's crucial to learn about the obstacles that exist in both the marketplaces and the media and, of course, to know how to avoid or overcome them. In this chapter, we hope to provide you with a clear picture of what you will be facing. The better prepared you are, the less anxiety and confusion you are likely to experience and the greater success you are likely to experience in promoting your book.

THE NEW WORLD OF PUBLISHING AND AUTHORSHIP

As the publishing industry has greatly changed, so have the roles of authors. Today, there are commercially-published authors, hybrid-published authors, academically-published authors, and self-published authors. Because each of these publishing categories is different, the barriers placed in front of various authors may differ greatly. To promote your book successfully, you need to know where you fit in.

Commercially Published Authors

Before the age of self-publishing, which began in the late 1990s with the introduction of POD (print on demand) technology, the vast majority of writers had their works produced through commercial publishing houses if they wanted their titles to be reviewed by the established media and carried by bookstores and libraries. If you were a proven best-selling author—or an author whom the publisher viewed as having great promise—the publishing house would provide you with three weeks to six months of PR, or public relations. The house might promote your book with ads in newspapers and magazines. If you were chosen to get more extensive publicity, the marketing department would assign a book publicist to work with you or hire an outside PR agency to create a regional or national book tour, which would include bookstore and library signings as well as newspaper, radio, and television interviews. While this latter scenario is what many commercially published authors had in mind when they signed a publishing contract, the reality for most authors was very different.

For new authors who were not among the chosen few—authors who didn't have a track record of previously successful books and were not celebrities—the publisher may have promised publicity. But unless PR was specifically spelled out in a contract, the author's initial book sales were usually used to determine just how much or how little the book was going to be publicized. Except for writing a basic press release for each book, as well as, in most cases, creating a press kit that included a press release, author bio, and sample interview questions, publishers left the majority of authors on their own. It was up to them to do as much promotion as they were capable of creating.

Today, little has changed for commercially-published authors. At a certain point, in the absence of impressive early sales numbers, the responsibility of promotion falls squarely on the author's shoulders. And even if the book was published by an established house, getting effective publicity is challenging.

Although this book is focused on the promotion of new books, if you are lucky enough to have your book stay in print with a commercial house, you will want to keep promoting it. Why? Even if you were fortunate enough to initially get your publisher's help with publicity, once your book becomes part of the house's *backlist*—in other words, when it is six months to a year old—the publicity work will fall on you. Knowing about publicity will make a big difference at that time. Be aware that some publishers admit that it is their backlist books that enable them to stay in business when *frontlist* (new) books don't perform as hoped.

Hybrid-Published Authors

With the technological breakthroughs that have produced short runs as well print on demand (POD) single copies, a new generation of publishing companies, known as hybrid publishers, has emerged. After evaluating a manuscript, if the hybrid publisher likes the work, she will take it on with one important twist: In almost all cases, the author underwrites the cost of producing the book, usually by agreeing to purchase a certain number of books at a discount, with the total purchase equaling the publisher's estimated production costs. The royalty percentage offered by a hybrid publisher is normally much higher than that offered by standard commercial publishers, and the cost to the author of purchasing additional books is usually less than the 40- to 50-percent discount off retail list price that is standard in the world of commercial publishers. But the lion's share of the financial risk is squarely on the writer's shoulders.

It should be noted that arrangements can vary from one hybrid publisher to another. One house, for instance, does not require authors to pay for book production, but will take on a title if the author is able to generate a certain number of preorders.

In some cases, the hybrid publisher may offer a publicity package, for which the author also pays. Alternatively, the author can hire her own publicity agent. In many cases, the book is professionally packaged, and in the eyes of the media and the public, the book is coming from a commercial house, which is certainly beneficial for sales. The best of the hybrid publishers have their own sales departments and distribution networks. They may also have sales representatives that contact the various marketplaces to pitch new books, or they may use a distributor that represents their titles along with the titles of other houses. This is something that most self-published authors are unable to do.

Academically-Published Authors

There are a range of academic publishers, from those with major global name recognition, such as Yale University Press, Princeton University

Press, University of Chicago Press, Harvard University Press, and Cambridge University Press; to less well-known but still well-respected houses like Temple University Press, University of Nebraska Press, Duke University Press, and New York University Press.

Most authors who publish with an academic press have the primary goal of meeting the "publish or perish" requirement for being granted tenure at the college or university where they teach. Others are interested in advancing their reputation among their peers and students. Some, however, also want to sell books and potentially see royalties or earnings for their efforts.

Academic publishers generally send out digital review copies, which almost any qualified academic is able to request as part of the adoption process. This can lead to adoptions of the book for required or recommended reading in courses that are a good fit for that topic—potentially throughout the United States or even internationally. Academic publishers may also send out physical copies of the title to reviewers or professionals in your field of expertise. But if you want your book publicized beyond the goal of course adoptions, you may decide to take on the task of promoting it with the media. This will involve the same demands as the promotion of any nonfiction title.

Self-Published Authors

There are essentially two ways of self-publishing a book. The first is to go directly to a printer to have it produced. The second is to use one of the many full-service self-publishing companies to produce a physical book, an e-book, or both.

As a self-published author, it is likely you are doing everything on your own. If you are going directly to a printer, you will be responsible for editing, designing, and typesetting the book you bring to the printer. If you do not have a background in book production, you can hire freelancers to guide you through the various steps required, and you can even hire a project manager.

If, on the other hand, you are using a full-service self-publishing book company, the company can provide you with all the services you need to create a finished book. The company can produce short runs of any book, single copies, e-books, or any combination of these formats. However, unlike situations in which you work with commercial houses, academic presses, or even hybrid companies, you will have to take care of promotion on your own. Yes, you can hire a book publicist to help you with publicity, but you are in fact the book's publisher. You need to manage the myriad of details related to publicity, whether you do it yourself or hire one or more pros to help you. This is not to say that self-publishing companies won't offer a "promotional package" for an extra charge. The problem is that, whether you buy a promotional package or hire a freelance publicist, you won't necessarily get your money's worth—especially if you don't have an understanding of the publicity process and are unable to judge the services that are being provided.

As you will see, self-published authors face several challenges that commercial- and hybrid-published authors do not. This doesn't mean that they cannot conquer these hurdles—if they know what to expect and how they can meet these challenges. In the section that follows, you will learn about the various marketplaces available and how each presents its own challenges to authors.

THE MARKETPLACES

Marketplaces are all the various outlets and venues that permit you to sell your book, whether stores, websites, or places that host speaking engagements. These outlets are where your book should be able to connect with readers. With the right publicity, authors can sell hundreds, thousands, and even millions of books. By knowing where to find these marketplaces and by making sure you have access to them, you will be laying the foundation for an effective promotional plan. There are eight essential marketplaces for books. These include the following:

1. Trade bookstores (brick-and-mortar physical stores)
2. Specialty bookstores
3. Non-bookstores that sell books
4. Libraries
5. Speaking engagements
6. Special sales
7. Direct mail
8. Online marketplaces

Based on your book's subject, one or two of these marketplaces may be more receptive to your work than the others. The idea is to figure out which of them will be the most effective place to promote your work as well as you, and to focus your energy on cultivating those marketplaces.

1. TRADE BOOKSTORES

Independent Bookshops, Chain Bookstores, and College Bookstores

As a commercial- or hybrid-published author, it is the responsibility of your publisher to try to get bookstores to stock your book through its distributor or wholesaler. It is important to understand that, now more than ever, "brick and mortar" bookstores—physical bookstores, in other words—are very particular regarding the titles they carry. While they may specialize in genres, regional books, or specialties that they believe will draw in customers, all their books are normally aimed at a more general readership. This means that the more visibility you can produce for your title, the more likely you are to have readers ask for your title at a bookstore. As a result, your book will be more likely to remain in stock. That element of the bookstore market has remained relatively stable over the years.

For self-published authors, however, bookstore distribution is much more challenging. As a rule, bookstores require their books to come from established publishers, distributors, and wholesalers. This is based purely on economics. If a book from an established publisher does not sell over a period of time—normally, within a year—the store can return the book for full credit. For the most part, though, self-published books are not returnable. Because of this, individual self-published books must operate outside of the normal channels of book distribution.

This means that if a self-published book is not sold through a recognized book distributor, it will not fit the criteria for bookstore purchases as do commercial- and hybrid-published books. Unfortunately, that is a fact of which few self-published authors are aware. On the other hand, bookstores that provide book signings and author lectures are more likely to purchase copies directly from the author for these events. You'll learn more about that in Chapter 10, "Speaking Your Way to More Sales."

2. SPECIALTY BOOKSTORES

Religious Bookstores, Cooking Bookstores, Graphic Novel Stores, Art Bookstores, Architecture Bookstores, and More

This category includes every bookstore that is not a trade bookstore, and as you can see from the examples above, these shops normally focus on one specific topic. As with trade bookstores, many of these retailers work almost exclusively with established publishers and distributors. They, too, normally do not carry titles outside those provided by their book suppliers. However, just like trade bookstores, if they offer book signings and author lectures for their customers, they are more likely to purchase copies directly from a self-published author.

3. NON-BOOKSTORES THAT SELL BOOKS

Big Box Stores, Gift Shops, Cookware Stores, Health Food Stores, Maternity Shops, Museum Stores, Sewing Shops, and Souvenir Stores

According to Dun & Bradstreet, there are 22,500 gift, novelty, and souvenir stores alone in the United States, with a combined annual revenue of $18 billion. And these are just three examples of a huge but diverse marketplace that exists for books that fit these various stores' interests. Considering that there are only an estimated 10,800 bookstores in the United States, you can see that the nontrade store markets are definitely worth targeting for publicity. Approached less often for author events than bookstores, these stores might be eager to host an event where you are allowed to sell your book. (See Chapter 10, "Speaking Your Way to More Sales," for advice on setting up an author event and generating publicity for it, and to learn about your options for handling book sales.)

It is important to learn how each of these stores buys their books. In some cases, they may purchase them through specialized wholesalers, and in other cases, they may order books directly from the publishers. By visiting a store and talking to the manager, you can learn the steps that you or your publisher needs to take to sell in these markets. If it is impractical to visit a store, try to contact the manager by phone. This is not as effective as an in-person visit, but it's still a good option. While sending an email is another possibility, keep in mind that because most people in business receive hundreds of emails on a daily basis, it is unlikely that this would yield the desired response.

Some big box stores—like Costco, based in Issaquah, Washington—have a dedicated book buyer. Having your book selected as an offering in all the Costco warehouses—which total 813 locations worldwide, including 558 throughout the United States and 102 in Canada—might be as challenging as hitting the lottery or getting onto *The New York Times'* Best Sellers list. But if there is a Costco in your area, speak to the manager of the store, since an author event with a table at the front of the store, allowing for a meet-and-greet with a local author as well as sales of your title, might be possible, although these events are rare.

4. LIBRARIES

Public Libraries, School Libraries, College Libraries, and Specialty Libraries

There are more than 110,000 libraries in the United States alone. As with bookstores and specialty bookstores, a library's standard purchasing practice is to buy books from publishers, distributors, and wholesalers. However, every so often, a self-published book gets enough notice to have libraries special order copies. Of course, having a starred review in a major newspaper or magazine will help ensure library purchases. However, most newspaper and magazine reviewers limit themselves to commercially released titles.

There is, however, another way for authors to get their books into libraries that is more readily accessible than a major book review. You can offer to do an author talk or other event at a library. If your request is accepted, the library will usually order one or more copies of books to be placed permanently in its collection because of the upcoming event. And since libraries rarely return books, their policies are a bit more flexible.

If you are a self-published author, it is important to let libraries know that you are offering an author talk and not just a book signing, which is usually reserved for high-profile authors. For example, I recently did a time-management workshop via Zoom for a Connecticut library. This was helpful to me as an author, since the self-published book I discussed is not a new book but a backlist title, and the event allowed me to make people aware of it. The library purchased a few copies of the book because of the event. Of course, if I had been able to conduct an in-person event, I could have offered my book for sale.

Most libraries have a media list that includes local newspapers (online and/or print versions); magazines; websites, including those for the community; and even TV/cable and radio/podcasts that might want to interview you about your upcoming library event. This can turn you and your book into a news event, especially if the event is free and open to the public. In such a case, local media is seen as performing a service for their community by publicizing you and your book.

Finally, when you offer to do an event, you and your book are usually prominently displayed on the library website's home page or elsewhere on the website, usually in the events listings. Often, these events are posted for weeks or even months in advance. Most libraries even allow you to sell the book at retail list price or at a discount, if you choose to offer one. Some may even have the budget to provide a speaker's fee, usually in the range of $100 to $250, although most libraries expect authors to speak free of charge. (See Chapter 10 to learn more about arranging author events at libraries.)

5. SPEAKING ENGAGEMENTS

Bookstores, Book Clubs, Educational Programs at Preschool and K-12 Schools, Colleges and Universities and Professional Schools, Fraternal Organizations, In-Service Programs, Libraries, and Specialty Shops

As you probably surmised from the previous sections on bookstore and library events, the ability to speak well in front of a group can open many doors, even if your book is self-published. For hundreds of years, many well-known authors have toured the country speaking to groups and selling their titles. American author Mark Twain, for instance, sold many of his titles to packed venues. British author Charles Dickens travelled to the United States to talk about his novels. Today, talented speakers who have published a book can make money by both lecturing and selling their books at these events.

Not everyone is a good speaker, but if you put in the effort and practice, you can improve your speaking skills over time. As a speaker, it does not matter how your book was published. All that matters is that many of your listeners will want to leave with an autographed copy in hand as a souvenir of your speaking engagement. If your event takes place via Zoom or another videoconferencing platform, you can create an information sheet that can be sent out after the event. The sheet should include information about you and your book, including where people can purchase copies. You will learn more about speaking engagements in Chapter 10, "Speaking Your Way to More Sales."

6. SPECIAL SALES

Associations, Companies, Government Agencies, School Systems, Societies, and Special Interest Groups

The special sales category refers to any business, organization, or individual that is willing to buy books in quantity to fill a specific need. For example, a local historical society might wish to celebrate the anniversary of their town. If you can provide a book that focuses on the history of their town or a story that centers on their town, they may be interested in purchasing titles and inviting you to lecture at a celebratory event. Another example is a juicing machine manufacturer that wants to accompany its product with a book. Rather than having it written in-house, the company may look for an existing title. If the book looks reasonably good, reads well, and fits the company's needs, and if the pricing works for everyone involved, the business may buy nonreturnable copies, usually at a discount. These opportunities are everywhere. With the right subject matter, all you have to do is recognize opportunities and make the appropriate introductions.

7. DIRECT MAIL

Letters, Postcards, Brochures, and Catalogues

Yes, snail mailings still work. Just check your mailbox. Direct mail can take many forms, from pitch letters enclosed in envelopes to fancy four-color brochures. In addition to selling books, they can promote you as a speaker.

There are five things to consider when creating a mailing campaign. First, the copy needs to appeal to the person receiving it. Second, the copy should always provide information on how to purchase the book and include a link to a website that will tell the reader more about the title. Third, the mailed materials, including the letter, should be visually appealing. You may require the services of a freelance artist to make everything appear as attractive and professional as possible. Fourth, it is crucial to obtain and use the right mailing lists. You can put together your own list gathered from information found on the Internet, or you can buy a list from a reputable mailing list company. Fifth, if you are doing a large mailing, you might need the services of a mail house that specializes in both printing and handling bulk mailings. You can, of course, have some color flyers run off at a local print house and do the mailing yourself, but bulk rate mailings are cheaper, and realistically, it may be impractical for you to address, stamp, and even fold and seal large numbers of pieces. Before you do a bulk mailing, though, consider smaller test mailings. This will tell you whether the mailing is generating adequate response to justify the cost of larger efforts.

8. ONLINE MARKETPLACES

Online Book Retailers, Book Websites, and Blogs

For any and all authors, online book retailers offer a truly level playfield for the sale of books in any format. Of course, everyone knows that Amazon.com is a place where books are sold online, but there are so many other online book retailers that could be selling your print or e-book, including Barnesandnoble.com, Target.com, and Walmart.com, for starters. Additional online book retailers of e-books include Kobo, iBooks, Scribd, Bookshop.org, and others. Most online vendors offer opportunities that you can purchase to market and promote your book. Just be aware that this may be costly, and it may not necessarily result in the number of sales for which you're hoping.

You could also open a store for free or for a monthly subscription fee at one of the online stores such as Shopify, which offers a free fourteen-day trial, then a monthly subscription fee. Other popular online sites where you can either create your own store or add your books to sell include Etsy, eBay, Amazon, Squarespace, and Facebook Marketplace. (See the listings for these selling options on page 254 of the Resources section.)

Yet another option is to sell your book on your own author website or even your publisher's site. (In the second case, the publicity you are doing will drive more traffic, and hopefully more sales, to your publisher's site, which will benefit everyone.) If you do not have an author's website yet, in the Resources section, you will find options for creating one. (See page 259.) Establishing an author page on Facebook.com is another option that some authors choose instead of a dedicated author website. However, there are advantages to having your own author website. For instance, if you have an effective "Contact Us" part of your site, the media will have a simple way of contacting you about possible interviews. The time, effort, and cost of creating such a site and keeping it up-to-date have to be weighed against the site's publicity benefits.

CONCLUSION

Hopefully, the information in this chapter has provided you with a clearer picture of where you stand as the author of your book, and what marketplaces may or may not be available to you. Experienced publishers work in this world every day. But for many authors—especially first-time authors—it is likely to be unfamiliar territory. Without both understanding the barriers that exist and recognizing the many sales opportunities that are waiting for you, it is easy to get lost. As you become increasingly familiar with the marketplaces, though, you will be better able to avoid pitfalls and to find those places that can help you sell more books.

Now that you have a greater understanding of marketplaces, you must determine who your promotion will target. In other words, who are the potential readers of your book? The more you know about your audience, the more focused and effective you can make your marketing plan. Chapter 2 will help you identify the people who are most likely to buy and read your work.

2.

Know Your Audience

Figuring out who would most likely have an interest in a particular book, and how you can reach that person, is one of the secrets to achieving the sales and recognition that will make writing and publishing your book worthwhile. Too often, I have heard writers tell me "My book is for everyone." My response is usually, "What do you mean by 'everyone'? Does that include both children and adults? People who read only romance novels as well as those who prefer thrillers? World War Two enthusiasts as well as dedicated do-it-yourselfers?" The truth is that no book is written for *everyone*.

While you may enjoy writing, if you don't know who you are writing for, you are going to have a difficult time reaching your audience. Once you have a clear understanding of who your potential readers are, you can develop your promotional plan, which you will learn more about in the chapters ahead. Nevertheless, identifying your audience is not always as simple as it sounds. In this chapter, we will look at the various factors that can help you recognize your book's readers. You will also learn what makes audiences different from one another. And you will see that by focusing your publicity so that it reaches and appeals to these readers, you will be better able to design an effective publicity campaign.

WHO IS YOUR AUDIENCE?

Every successful published book has one or several audiences. The first means of categorizing a book in terms of its audience is by considering the target age group. That is the broadest of audiences.

Books for Young People

Books for young people are divided according to age and grade, with text becoming longer and more advanced in vocabulary as you move from titles for younger children to titles for teens. Of course, a child whose reading skills are more advanced than those of his peers sometimes prefers books in categories designed for older children, so although you may target your book for a certain age child, it may appeal to younger or older children, as well. Also, some books cross over different categories. The Harry Potter series, for instance, is famous for appealing to children of many different ages and reading levels, and even to adults!

Below, we'll first look at the children's book audience, which is divided into three general segments. After that, we'll look at books designed for the middle school and young adult audiences.

The Children's Book Audience

As already mentioned, age is most important when you are determining how to promote a children's book. Children's books are divided into several basic categories based on a child's age and reading ability. These include the following:

- *Board books* are picture books designed to be read to babies and toddlers by their parents as well as to be explored and handled by the child. Small in size and made of heavy laminated paper or cardboard, these books are easy for little ones to hold.

- *Picture books* are designed to be read by parents to their preschool children. They are larger in size than board books, but like board books, they tell their stories through a combination of pictures and brief text.

- *Bridge books* are seen as a bridge between picture books, which parents read to children, and early readers, which children read to themselves. Put simply, these books have fewer graphics and more text than picture books. The books vary in difficulty, and some librarians view these books as early readers, described below.

- *Early readers,* sometimes called *easy readers* or *independent readers,* are geared to be read to or by children from ages five to seven. The words used in early readers are very basic, and the sentences are short.

- *Chapter books,* which are to be read by children who are seven to ten years of age, tell their stories primarily through text, although illustrations are included.

Generally, books that are shelved in the above categories in bookstores and libraries are *fiction,* meaning that they include imaginary characters and events. *Nonfiction books,* which are fact-based, are shelved in a separate section, in which the books are arranged according to subject matter rather than age. Thus, you could have a nonfiction book designed for a six-year-old shelved next to a book geared for a ten-year-old. (For more information on fiction and nonfiction, see the discussion that begins on page 24.)

While the ultimate users of these titles are children, it is the parents and librarians who select the titles to be purchased. For early readers and chapter books, it is parents and librarians who buy the books, and teachers who recommend these titles to parents. Especially successful publicity for this category includes the prepublication reviews that appear in journals such as *School Library Journal, Kirkus Reviews,* and *The Horn Book Magazine,* but these reviews are difficult to obtain. A type of effective publicity that is usually easier to secure includes author events at local libraries, with parents and their children in attendance, and author events that take place at schools, with teachers and pupils present. We will learn more about getting publicity for your book in later chapters.

The Middle Grade Audience

The middle grade audience includes children of ages eight to twelve. This is a relatively new category of books. Some even consider it a subcategory of the young adult, or YA, audience, which is described below. The experiences of those in middle school, however, and even the vocabulary and concerns of those just entering puberty are often quite different from the vocabulary and concerns of a YA audience. Just like the YA audience, these books are often chosen by parents, teachers, or librarians, who buy or recommend the books for the children.

In libraries, middle grade fiction and nonfiction books are usually shelved in separate sections. In bookstores, however, they may be shelved together.

The Young Adult (YA) Audience

This audience is composed of teenagers from age twelve and up. The books this audience chooses reflect many areas of interest of adult audiences, but are written to appeal to teen readers. The people who actually buy these books may be parents of teens, teachers and librarians, or the teenagers themselves.

Like middle grade fiction and nonfiction, YA fiction and nonfiction are often shelved separately in libraries but together in bookstores. When determining who might comprise your audience for a YA nonfiction book, you should look at the subject matter of your book, such as how to get along with your classmates, how to make the most of your summers during high school, and so forth.

Graphic Novels

Graphic novels began to appear in the 1970s, and over the years, they have become increasingly mainstream. Written in comic-book style, they are composed of panels made up of sequential images and text. As the word "novel" implies, many graphic novels are stand-alone stories, just like regular novels. Some, however, are published in serial form, like traditional comics, and then bound later as collected editions.

The graphics in these novels allow children to read above their independent reading level, making kids more comfortable with reading so that they can gradually transition to more challenging text. Graphic novels are available for different reading levels, from age five up. Some are original works, and some are adaptations of existing books for young readers. As you may already know, there are graphic novels specifically designed for adults, too.

The Adult Audience

For the most part, books designed for the adult audience are divided into fiction and nonfiction. Within each category there are various genres and subcategories.

The Fiction Audience

Fiction can be defined as literature that is created from the imagination and is not presented as fact. In general, both the people and the events in the stories are not real, although there are exceptions. For instance, a novel may involve the sinking of the *Titanic*, which is a real event, but instead of presenting a factual account of the tragedy, it will usually involve at least some imaginary characters and may also change aspects of the event to serve the plot. Similarly, a work of fiction may include real-life people such as George Washington or Isaac Newton, but again, instead of strictly following the facts, it will weave an imaginary story that includes some fictional characters.

Anyone who has spent time in a bookstore or library knows that there are many types, or genres, of fiction. Some of the most popular genres include:

- Fantasy
- Graphic novels
- Historical fiction
- Horror
- Literary fiction
- Mystery/crime
- Police procedurals
- Psychological fiction
- Romance
- Science fiction
- Suspense/thrillers
- Westerns
- Women's fiction

There can be considerable overlap between these categories. For instance, a book that is categorized as a mystery in one bookstore may be a thriller in another store. Similarly, police procedurals are often found in the mystery/crime section. If you're not sure which readership your book is targeting, look for similar books in your local library or bookstore, and you should be able to home in on your audience.

Why is it so important to know your intended readership in fiction? Readers of a certain genre have certain expectations, and they choose books in that category because they have enjoyed similar stories in the past. As a writer, you can use this to your advantage by modeling your book on the best titles in your genre. As someone who is marketing your own book, it's crucial to make your genre clear to both booksellers and your intended audience. If your book is categorized in the wrong genre, potential readers may never discover it. On the other hand, if you correctly identify your readership, you will not only make your book easier to find but may also be able to recognize special marketing opportunities. You may discover, for instance, that your romance book can be marketed to a romance book club or sold to a company that creates romance book subscription boxes. If you don't know who your readership is, you are likely to miss these kinds of targeted opportunities.

The Nonfiction Audience

Nonfiction writing is based on facts, real events, and real people rather than on stories and characters that have been invented. Very often, these books provide valuable information and guidance in a particular area.

The number of subjects, or genres, included in nonfiction are virtually endless. The following are among some of the most popular genres:

- Art
- Biographies and autobiographies
- Business and economics
- Cookbooks
- Crafts and hobbies
- Health and wellness
- History
- How-to
- Humor
- Parenting
- Pet care
- Philosophy
- Politics and social science
- Psychology
- Religion and spirituality
- Science
- Self-help/motivational
- Sociology
- Sports
- Travel guides

Remember that the above is just a sampling of nonfiction genres. There are many more. Also remember that within each category, there are many subcategories. For instance, under cooking, you are likely to find cookbooks on different cuisines, vegetarian and vegan cookbooks, etc. In the history category, you can find ancient history, books on specific wars, books on the history of different countries, etc. Just as in fiction, if you are not sure where your nonfiction book belongs, you can probably figure it out by determining how similar books are categorized in your local bookstore.

Like the world of fiction, nonfiction provides marketing opportunities for the writer who has correctly identified his genre. If you have written a how-to book on sailing, for instance, you might talk about your subject and present your book to fellow sailors at a local sailing club or at your local library. You might also want to direct review copies of your book to sailing magazines.

The World of Poetry Books

For hundreds of years, poetry was the most popular form of literature. The art of writing in verse could be used in works of both fiction and nonfiction. It could tell stories of adventure and romance, or it could present political or religious beliefs.

Now, poetry is a niche market, and bookstores and libraries usually offer collections of only classic poetry or poems by well-known known modern poets, although there are exceptions. Nevertheless, there are still bookstores that offer a substantial number of poetry books. Poetry lovers rely on these stores, which sometimes provide weekly readings by both local and nationally known poets. Poetry readings (and books) are also sometimes offered at community centers and libraries, and authors can also make themselves known through literary magazines and websites that focus on poetry. If you have published a book of poetry, it is important to learn where your readers can be found and how they can best be reached.

Specialized Adult Audiences

Books for specialized audiences fall within the larger nonfiction category, but instead of being geared for a general audience, they are designed for very specific groups of readers. Generally, they can be organized into the following three categories:

- *Professional books* are designed to develop the skills of people who are working in a specific profession or are training for work in that profession. For instance, a professional book may address educators, nurses, or doctors. For this reason, these books usually use vocabulary and discuss subject matter that would be unfamiliar to a more general audience.

- *Academic books* generally present scholarly research that is of interest to people within a specific field. They are intended for academic study and research, and are normally published by academic and university presses. The vocabulary used in these books tends to be very specialized and sophisticated because the books are designed for people who are already quite knowledgeable about their particular field of study.

- *Textbooks* are written and organized in a manner that makes them useful as a resource for people studying a specific subject, usually in a school setting, such as grade school, college, university, law school, or medical school, for example. The level of vocabulary and other elements of the text should reflect the level of the course. For instance, the vocabulary used in an introductory high school biology text would differ from the vocabulary used in an advanced college biology text. Textbooks may include study guides and workbooks for students, while ancillary materials for instructors may be provided on the publisher's website.

Promoting to a highly specialized audience will obviously require very focused promotional campaigns, but at least you will know exactly who your readers will be. Whether your book is designed for doctors, lawyers, accountants, filmmakers, or research biologists, you may find it easier to figure out what associations that they join, what websites they visit, and what journals and online publications they read. This knowledge will allow you to more easily make your target audience aware of your book.

DOUBLE-CHECKING YOUR BOOK'S AUDIENCE

If, despite your best efforts, you are not sure of your book's category and reading audience, consider writing a one-page synopsis of your book. After you have created a clear, concise overview, you can show it to people you trust and ask them who they think is your book's main audience. An individual's response will be especially helpful if he is a librarian, a bookstore owner, or an aficionado of books in your particular genre.

CONCLUSION

Hopefully, you now have a clear idea of the readers who are likely to be most interested in your book. This is important, because pinpointing your audience is the first step in choosing the media that can best help you reach booksellers, librarians, and your readers.

Now you're ready to look at the various forms of media available to you. Chapter 3 fills you in on traditional media, such as newspapers and journals, while Chapter 4 explores Internet-based media, from websites and blogs to Facebook and Twitter. Even if you decide to delegate book publicity to a pro, knowing what is open to you in the world of media will make you a much wiser client and, ultimately, a much more successful author.

3.

What Is Traditional Media?

For many years, the word *media* referred to newspapers, magazines, journals, television, and radio. These were the means of communication that kept us entertained and informed. Over the years, not only did these media change, but with the advent of the Internet, another type of media was created—social media.

Because traditional media has long been controlled by big business, for an author to get attention on these platforms, she needs to be a celebrity, politician, or best-selling author, or to be represented by a publicist with important professional contacts. After all, as a business, media companies want to feature people who can sell more newspapers or magazines or increase viewership. But while social media may be more friendly to new, lesser-known, or self-published authors, the fact is that you should never ignore traditional media. The best book marketing campaigns, indeed, combine coverage in traditional media with a solid online presence.

While social media, as well as other Internet-based media, will be explored in Chapter 4, this chapter examines the two major platforms of traditional media: *Print media*, which includes newspapers, magazines, journals, and newsletters; and *broadcast media*, which is comprised of television, cable, and radio. In the following pages, you will learn to realistically assess what print and broadcast media offer to the majority of authors, as well as the barriers these platforms have erected. As you will see, the more you know, the better prepared you will be to walk through any media doors that may be open to you.

PRINT MEDIA

Before the advent of the Internet, print and broadcast media were really the only ways for a book to gain national, regional, or even local attention. But, as already mentioned, many barriers existed between an unknown author and media success. Unfortunately, with a number of exceptions, these barriers are still in place. And today, the readerships of print media have already been greatly impacted by the Internet—so much so that many of these traditional media outlets have also created their own online sites, apps, and/or streaming services to remain relevant. But there is still print media that you should consider in your own promotional planning. As you will see, understanding how traditional media is categorized will provide you with a better understanding of what you can do to get attention for yourself and your title.

■ NEWSPAPERS

For well over a century, newspapers have played an important role in bringing attention to new book titles. Almost all national, regional, and international papers have offered book review sections that have the potential to turn a book into a bestseller—or kill it. In addition, newspapers can feature an article on a writer or mention a book title in an article whose topic relates to the book. Each of these provides a permanent record of visibility that can be used in all your future promotional efforts.

The problem is that these three types of newspapers make it difficult for authors published by smaller independent houses to get reviewed, and the likelihood of getting a book reviewed is even slimmer or even nonexistent for self-published authors. Local and specialty newspapers, however, are more open to writing a story or providing a review when the book's topic falls within what they see as their readers' interest. By learning about a newspaper's submission criteria, you will have a better chance of approaching the paper in a productive way.

Local Papers

Local newspapers are essentially focused on their town or city. Some may also cover state and national events, but they usually promote themselves as "hometown" papers. Unfortunately, not enough authors consider contacting their own local newspapers for publicity on themselves and their book. Hopefully, what you are learning in this book will change that. Please keep in mind that local newspapers do not have the same restrictions that national or some regional media have, making this a great place to start your publicity efforts—not just because most local papers have a mandate to highlight local residents and their accomplishments, but also because they are more likely to be receptive to you than other newspapers. Furthermore, many local newspapers are actually part of a larger chain, and they may share the article or review with other affiliated newspapers.

For example, Aiden Global Capital, a hedge fund based in Manhattan, purchased Tribune Publishing in 2021, making it the second largest newspaper publisher in the United States, with more than 200 newspapers. One of the newspapers they acquired in the transaction was the *Hartford Courant*, which is considered the oldest continuously published newspaper in the country. Their other publications include *The Denver Post*, the *Orlando Sentinel*, and St. Paul's *Pioneer Press*. Getting published in one newspaper that is affiliated with other papers may open up the door to having the same article republished in the affiliated newspapers, and may even lead to new articles or reviews.

Regional Papers

Some regions of the country are enormous, such as the New York-Connecticut-New Jersey region—often referred to as the tri-state area—which has a population of well over 20 million people. Newspapers that are distributed to a larger region of the United States will, of course, increase the exposure of any features or reviews written about you and your book. By calling the office of a regional newspaper and asking to speak to an editor, reporter, or book reviewer, you can learn about their guidelines for assigning a story or book review. If it is difficult to get someone on the phone, most newspapers have a website that provides this information as well as a contact email that could enable you to get this information directly or initiate a conversation with someone who can help you.

National Papers

Technically, *USA Today* is a national newspaper in the purist sense of the word. As you may know, it is published both in print and online formats, and its current estimate of daily circulation is around 1 million. *The Wall Street Journal,* with a circulation of more than a million, certainly extends its readership well beyond Wall Street, USA. But certain newspapers that bear the names of the cities in which they are located—like *The New York Times* and *The Washington Post*—are really international papers, as well. Estimated daily circulation is around 5.5 million for *The New York Times,* and *The Washington Post* is estimated to have more than 71 million digital readers. Other papers, like the *Chicago Tribune* or the *Los Angeles Times,* although technically local newspapers, also have national reach and impact. Estimated circulation is 650,000 for the *Los Angeles Times,* and 440,000 for the *Chicago Tribune.*

Although impressive by most standards, the readership numbers for these national papers are down from their heyday, but the papers are still relevant. Getting a story or review in any of these major newspapers, especially those with international reach, can open the door to other forms of media. Just remember that all of these papers have author restrictions and guidelines for submissions that you can learn about on the paper's website or by making a phone call or email enquiry.

Consider Hiring a Publicist to Work With You

Even though you can do all of your own publicity, you should consider hiring a publicist with strong and long-standing connections at major newspapers to do selected pitching for you, or to pitch for only a limited period of time. It might be hard to find someone who's willing to approach only major publications, but if you do locate such a publicist, ask what the fee would be to see if you can afford it. If the publicist is successful with even one of these outlets, it could substantially improve all of your other promotional efforts. (For information on hiring publicists, see page 181.)

Specialty Newspapers

In the past, specialty newspapers flourished in the United States, with each of these papers focusing on a specific topic, from military interests to religious and ethnic affiliations to specific business types. Consider *Stars and Stripes* (a military newspaper first published in 1861), the *Christian Science Monitor* (published since 1908), and *Investor's Business Daily* (published since 1984) as examples. And while their readerships, like those of all newspapers, have declined with the advent of the Internet, these and many other specialized newspapers still address very focused audiences. If you believe that your book's topic is a good match for a specialty paper's readership, you may be in an enviable position. There are, fortunately, many specialty newspapers for certain categories of books and authors.

Keep in mind that the larger a specialty newspaper's circulation, the more restrictions or requirements it may have in choosing a story or review. Call the paper's office or visit its website to learn more about its editorial policies.

International Newspapers

There are many reasons to consider getting featured or reviewed in international English-language newspapers. You might initially wonder: Who in the United States will see the article and get motivated to buy your book? But remember that online retailers have online stores in practically every major book market throughout the world. That means that if you are written up in the *Times of India*—with a circulation of nearly 3 million—it could lead to sales at the Indian subsidiary of Amazon.com, accessible through https://www.amazon.in. It could also lead to newspapers in other countries, including the United States, becoming interested in you and your book through international attention.

The same holds true of other international newspapers, such as the London *Times*, the Canadian *Globe and Mail*, France's *Le Figaro*, Korea's *The Korea Herald*, or Australia's *Sydney Morning Herald*, to name just a few. The other possibility is that an article about you in an international newspaper can come to the attention of a publisher in that country, spurring her to request a copy of your book and consider acquiring and printing it. However, like national newspapers, international papers are likely to be very selective regarding what they review or feature in their publication.

■ MAGAZINES AND JOURNALS

This category, as you will see, includes a wide variety of periodicals, including local, regional, popular, specialty, and international publications. But just like newspapers, the bigger the magazine or journal, the more difficult it is to have a story included about you or to have your book reviewed. On the other hand, local and some regional magazines are much more amenable to highlighting the work of authors who share a common bond with their readers. By learning about a magazine's submission policies, you will have a better idea of whom you should approach and whom you should avoid.

What Is the Difference Between Magazines and Journals?

As you begin to look at the universe of periodicals, it's important to know the difference between magazines and journals. While the word *magazine* can be applied to both types of publications, for our purposes, we will treat them separately. Both are called periodicals because they come out several times a year.

For the most part, *magazines* are publications that are geared for the general public. They may include a variety of different types of articles, such as essays, news stories, interviews, book excerpts, and book reviews. Examples include *The New Yorker* and the *The Atlantic*. Magazines may also focus on a specific area of interest, such as gardening, cooking, celebrities, or retirement. Articles for any of these types of magazines are normally written by professional reporters, writers, and editors. Whatever the topics of these magazines may be, they are designed for general consumption.

Journals, on the other hand, are focused on one specific topic and written for professionals in a particular field of study. Examples include the *American Journal of Nursing, Criminology,* and the *Journal of Teacher Education.* Some articles may be written by in-house staff, but most are written by working professionals in their fields and then edited in-house. While the majority of magazines are made available through retail outlets, journals are usually mailed out to their subscribers or to their organizational or association members.

With periodicals, as with any media, it helps to have a referral. Do you know an editor who might allow you to mention his or her name as your POR, or Point of Reference? Do you have any previous associations with this magazine, such as being profiled or writing an article for it? If you are a loyal reader of the magazine, you can certainly mention that and explain why an article about you or a review of your book would be a good match for the publication.

Local Magazines

Filled with ads for local events, companies, or services, local magazines are an excellent potential source of book publicity for you and your book. These magazines may be specialized, such as parenting magazines. They may also be tied to a town or city, such as Greenwich, Connecticut or Tampa, Florida, and reflect the community in which the magazine is published. Approaching a local magazine may be one of your best opportunities to have a feature article or book review published, especially if you can offer a fresh approach to you, your book, or—if the book is nonfiction—your topic that makes your hometown magazine eager to write about you.

Regional Magazines

Some magazines cover a wider area than just one town or city. Examples are *Texas Monthly*, which covers all of Texas; and *New York* magazine, which covers the tri-state area—the states of New York, New Jersey, and Connecticut—even though it tends to focus on Manhattan. Other regional magazines include *Alaska, Arkansas Living,* and *Blue Ridge Country,* to name just a few.

If the topics covered in your book coincide with the interests of a regional magazine, call the publication to learn about its submissions policy or check the submission guidelines offered on the magazine's website or in the front of the magazine.

Popular Magazines

When we refer to popular magazines, we are talking about periodicals that you see selling on newsstands, in supermarkets, in bookstores, or wherever magazines are sold. And while many popular magazines have experienced somewhat of a decline in their readerships, they have also established a presence on the Internet. Years ago, many popular magazines included fiction, essays, news stories, and book excerpts, and covered a range of topics. (Think of the original *Saturday Evening Post.*) To stay relevant and on the shelves of stores, the majority of popular magazines now focus on specific topics.

From cooking to health and from news to celebrity lifestyles, this new generation of magazines reaches out to a very specific segment of the general population to stay current—and that can be good for any author. Getting a feature, a book review, or even a mention in one of the top national magazines is a huge accomplishment. Even though most of these publications make it extremely difficult for most authors to get attention, it may be worth a try to get yourself or your book featured in *People, Time, Newsweek,* or *Woman's Day,* to name a few popular magazines with circulations in the millions.

Specialty Magazines and Journals

When we refer to specialty magazines and journals, we are referring to periodicals focused on very specific topics that are not usually offered at newsstands or stores. They are normally sold through subscriptions, and their readership numbers have remained relatively steady. In addition, many of these periodicals have established their own online sites. However, unlike national magazines that require a field of interest large enough to support their business, many specialty magazines have to rely on a much smaller readership. That is not to say that there aren't any large specialty publications. *AARP The Magazine,* for example, with a focus on its fifty-plus age group members, has a huge circulation of over 36 million. But many specialty periodicals, such as *Linn's Stamp News* and *Herb Quarterly Magazine,* have a readership of only a few thousand. While that is relatively small, these may be the very hard-core readers who will identify with your book's topic. From hobbyists to scientists, from gamers to doctors, these journals can be a perfect fit for your book's particular audience.

Again, the larger journals have strict submissions rules. However, the smaller and less restrictive journals may be more open to accepting articles, excerpts, or reviews based on the writer's subject matching their own interests.

Association-Related Magazines and Journals

Many associations, clubs, societies, college alumni associations, and labor unions provide periodicals for their members. They may range from scholarly journals, such as the *Journal of the American Medical Association,* or *JAMA,* published by the American Medical Association; to *Columbia* magazine, which is published by the Knights of Columbus for its membership. This may not seem like a big publicity opportunity for book authors. After all, if you write an article for your professional journal, you will be read mostly by fellow association members. But there are at least three reasons why an article written about you or your book may be great publicity:

1. Your association members will see you as "one of them." They may welcome knowing about your new book and spreading the word. Your success is their success, as the saying goes.

2. Your association members may actually buy your book, especially if its subject is related to the association and its interests.

3. Most associations have paid or volunteer staff members whose mission is to publicize the accomplishments of their members. They will likely be more motivated to spread the word than total strangers would be. The psychological benefits of their positive attitude and efforts should not be underestimated. Getting publicity for yourself and your book can seem like an overwhelming task, especially if you are new at it and on your own. Getting mentioned or reviewed in your association's newsletter or magazine could inspire you to keep up with your publicity efforts.

International Magazines

There are a number of international English-language magazines that may be local, regional, national, or specialized. The advantage of getting your book mentioned, featured, or reviewed in an international periodical is that online book retailers can provide an interested reader with a copy of your book—as long as it is available through an established U.S. vendor. And, as noted in the section on international newspapers, there is always the possibility of a foreign publisher expressing interest in producing a translation of that title. Your book may also be featured or reviewed in magazines that are printed in different languages. (*Cosmopolitan* magazine, for instance, is published in thirty-five languages.) Most of the time, the journalists or editors who contact you about your book will write or speak English.

Always keep in mind that when approaching an international English-language magazine, you need to learn about its submission requirements.

■ NEWSLETTERS

Less flashy than magazines, newsletters may still offer strong promotion opportunities for you and your book. These publications may be related to an association, a company, or an alumni group, which all have readers with a shared common interest. If a newsletter's field of interest is a good match for your book's subject, it may be beneficial for you to become a member or subscriber, as this could open the door to any number of promotional opportunities.

Association-Related Newsletters

Newsletters that are published by associations are often mailed out monthly or bi-monthly, either as e-newsletters or as hard copies through regular mail, as part of the association's benefits to its members. Easier to get into, often with shorter lead times—especially if it is an online-only newsletter—some newsletters are sent to hundreds or even thousands of members. If the focus of your book coincides with the aim of the group, the newsletter may have a strong interest in your topic or book.

If you are a member of the association, start cultivating as many connections in the group as possible months before your book's publication. This will help your promotional efforts by demonstrating that you care about the association and its members, and are not merely using it for free publicity. Even if the newsletter states that e-book submissions are welcome, whenever possible, I suggest sending a physical review copy of your book with a personal cover letter to the newsletter editor, whom you should address by name. This usually makes a better and more lasting impression than an electronic submission.

Company-Related Newsletters

Although many company newsletters have migrated to the Internet so that the information is available only on company websites, some companies still send out physical newsletters as well as e-mail newsletters. If you work at the company and you manage to get word of your book included in its newsletter, you will be sharing your latest accomplishment with coworkers and management folks—people who already know who you are and have an interest in you. If your book is related to the company's work, this should be emphasized in your submission.

Even if your publication has nothing to do with the company or your job, you can still submit information about your book with the suggestion that your spare-time pursuit as a novelist—or children's book author, biographer, self-help nonfiction writer, or whatever—might be of interest to fellow employees and supervisors. However, this suggestion needs to be considered very carefully based on the policy of the company and its corporate culture. Some companies may welcome your submission, but with other companies, it could backfire. It can be very tempting to try this, since some companies have literally tens of thousands of employees, but until you are able to become a full-time writer (if this is your goal), you must avoid any actions that could jeopardize your day job.

Specialty Newsletters

Newsletters that cater to specialty topics—such as law, coaching, financial planning, running a business, starting a catering service, etc.—have one thing in common: They constantly need fresh copy to keep their subscribers interested. This is where you can help the publication. You can offer your book for review, or you can offer an article you have written with this newsletter in mind. You might even be able to recycle the same article to different non-competing newsletters, as long as you change the examples that you use and indicate that the piece is based on a previously published article. Of course, you can also offer an excerpt from your book, if that is appropriate. If you write the article, be sure to include the title of your book in your article, if relevant, or at least in the About the Author section.

BROADCAST MEDIA

During the 1930s, 1940s, and early 1950s, people around the world relied on the radio for news, music, and entertainment. Starting in the mid-fifties, television took the lead in providing the same type of information and amusement, but this new medium was enhanced by moving images. Although both radio and television remain major means of communication for the general public, much of their audiences have moved to the Internet. Of course, this does not mean that they are no longer relevant, and in response to the changing times, they have established their own presence on the Internet. But just as in the world of print media, the barriers remain high for the vast majority of authors who try to promote themselves through broadcast media. Being aware of these challenges will help determine how you can use television and radio to greatest effect. And if you decide to gain exposure through traditional broadcast media, either on your own or through a publicist, you will know the roadblocks you face.

■ RADIO

Before there was television, there was radio. It was the place where family members gathered in the evening to hear the latest reports of local, national, and world news or to be entertained by comedy, mystery, or drama shows, as well as major sports events. Today, as is true of other forms of traditional media, radio has lost many of its listeners—especially younger listeners—to Wi-Fi-based media. Still, AM and FM radio remain a good a way to get the word out about books.

Several different time slots continue to hold onto radio listeners. Rush-hour drive times (six to nine in the morning and four to seven in the afternoon and evening) represent the largest audiences, along with various talk show broadcasts offered throughout the days, evenings, and nights. There are also weekend shows that cater to weekend audiences. Many of the talk shows now offer podcasts to appeal to listeners who want the convenience of tuning in through the Internet, via a smartphone or a laptop computer, whenever they have the time and inclination.

Because local and regional stations are now managed by national communication conglomerates, their news programs adhere to strict criteria for interviewing guests. However, talk radio shows that are presented in local areas have less stringent criteria for accepting guests.

National Radio

Among the best-known owners of radio stations are the big five: ABC, CBS, NBC, FOX, and WOR. They operate hundreds or even thousands of national, regional, and local radio stations throughout the country. These stations offer music, news, traffic and weather, and/or talk shows. Normally, these stations cater to regional or local audiences. While music programs are not likely to provide any publicity for authors—unless you are a best-selling recording artist who has written a book—many of the talk shows may be open to book authors.

National and regional talk shows likely have strict guidelines for bringing on guests, but some local shows have less strict criteria even though they are owned by large media companies. As a first step in becoming a potential guest, call the station or visit the station's website to learn whom you should contact regarding a possible interview and to learn about the guidelines that can help you with your pitch.

Local Radio

As mentioned above, when dealing with large corporate-owned radio stations, local radio shows are your best bet. However, there are also a number of local radio stations that manage to reach large cities and towns. For example, at night, 77 WABC in New York City reaches listeners throughout a big part of the eastern United States and even Canada.

What is exciting about local radio is that you can easily research the programs that are available in your area. By turning on your radio at different times of the day, you will learn what the station is presenting. And the fact that you are a local author will give you a distinct edge when you or your publicist contacts the producer or host about becoming a guest.

If you manage to get a spot on a local radio show, see if you can line up a book signing at a local bookstore a day or two later. The host will normally be happy to mention where and when the event will occur. And, of course, bookstore owners are more likely to arrange an event if they know that you will be appearing on a show and plugging the book signing.

Specialty Radio

As is true in other areas of media, radio offers specialty stations that may be of help to you, depending on the focus of your book. Included are religion-based stations, political stations, Latinx stations, family-oriented stations, and more, as well as public radio stations. Each station has its own audience as well as shows designed to appeal to its listeners. And some of these shows have a large listener base. For instance, the politically conservative *Mark Levin Show* has been one of the top-rated talk radio shows since its inception. Syndicated by Westwood One and broadcast daily, it has an estimated weekly audience of 7 million.

In addition, there are a large number of talk shows that focus on one specific topic, including home and car repair, cooking, history, New Age beliefs, relationships, murder mysteries, business, and the list goes on. Many of these shows can be heard on stations throughout the United States, so finding the right shows and presenting yourself as a potential guest can be the start of a very successful promotional campaign. *The Kim Komando Show,* for example, is an extremely popular radio show about technology. A weekly three-hour show that airs throughout the country on 400 radio stations, it can be heard on Saturday mornings as well as on demand, meaning that it is archived for replays. Komando has an estimated 6.5 million listeners.

If you do get an interview on a specialty radio show, try to set up a book signing event, just as you would if you were featured on a local show. Some of the shows are recorded in advance, so you might be able to arrange a videoconference (Zoom) bookstore event to coincide with the broadcasting of your segment or interview.

■ TELEVISION

For many decades, television was dominated by three networks: CBS, NBC, and ABC. Local television stations found their place among the big three. Then, with the conglomeration of local stations, FOX, PBS, and other stations appeared. But when cable television became widely available in the 1980s, the medium exploded. Instead of being limited to thirteen channels, viewers with cable hook-ups could watch literally hundreds of channels. Still considered part of traditional media, cable television has definitely helped to transform the medium.

While the traditional networks still provide programming, now there are networks that cater to a growing number of interests. Shows can focus on religion, news, business, history, hobbies, cooking, home renovation, old television shows, true crime, classic movies, and so much more. Many of these networks also provide online programming, streaming services, and podcasts, which we will discuss in Chapter 4.

The expansion of television has given authors access to many diverse audiences. Once again, it's important to point out that the more established networks still make it difficult for the average author to be seen and heard. However, there are now many more TV platforms that accept a first-time author who may appeal to a distinct audience of viewers.

National TV

For the vast majority of authors, it is extremely difficult to get booked and appear on a national TV show. Not that it doesn't happen. Over the years, I have been fortunate enough to appear on national shows, including one or more appearances on *Today, CBS This Morning,* CBS *Sunday Morning,* ABC *Nightline, Good Morning America, Good Day New York, Oprah,* and *The View.* Early on, I was even a featured guest on *To Tell the Truth,* as well as *The Joe Franklin Show* and the BBC morning show in London. But an author's previous credits and name recognition usually determine whether she gets an opportunity to appear on a national show. Especially today, national TV generally showcases the books of only best-selling authors, reporters from well-known newspapers, expert network contributors, prominent government officials, and celebrities. Of course, you will also find a few scientists and university professors included in a segment to which they can contribute, with their books receiving mention, but these authors really have to be lucky, and the timing must be just right. If you happen to fall within any of these categories, you have a decent shot at becoming an invited guest. However, if you are not, keep in mind that the dream of being on *Good Morning America* or *Fox & Friends* may be just a dream, but it is a worthwhile one for which you can strive.

I do not want to throw a wet blanket over anybody's dream, however, so let's see if there is a feasible path to getting both promotion and recognition for your work, one step at a time. If you obtain enough local and regional publicity, that major TV show appearance just might happen. If you appear in enough social media posts or on enough podcasts, which are discussed in Chapter 4, you might be pleasantly surprised to find national media knocking on your door—or at least sending you an email or text, or calling you on the phone! Yes, dream on, but do all the hard work and the local and regional promotional activities that will make those major opportunities more likely to happen. I remember that when I was featured on several national shows within a few months, a book publicist said to me, "I see you everywhere." I took that as a compliment and as confirmation that all of my promotional efforts were winning me name recognition, visibility, and results.

Regional TV

Regional TV usually falls under the ownership and rules of one of the major networks. These networks divide the country into the East, the Midwest, and the West. Since guest bookings work the same way on regional shows as they do on national shows, regional bookings are difficult to obtain. It may be a tiny bit easier to get on MSNBC than on NBC or on the local affiliate of FOX in Dallas, New York City, or Chicago, than on national *Fox &Friends*, but it still will present you with a challenge. Nevertheless, based on the nature of your book and the character of the show, it never hurts to place a phone call, visit the show's website, or read blogs or articles that authors have published online or in print to discover how guests win appearances.

Local TV

This is where unknown and especially new or first-time authors may have the greatest chance of getting interviewed about themselves or their book. With the expansion of television networks on cable, there may be several shows that could potentially want to interview you. Your job, or that of your publicist, is to find the local shows that are most likely to invite you to make an appearance.

Remember that not all local TV shows or stations are equal. The three or four local stations in Los Angeles, with a potential viewership of many millions, are very different from a local network TV station such as ABC4Utah in Salt Lake City, where the population of the city is approximately 200,000. Still, getting interviewed on a local network TV show is a way to get the ball rolling with your author interviews. As you hone your speaking skills and add these local appearances to your resume, you will increase your chances of getting on more shows. Given the right interviews, a network may consider you as a guest in light of your increasing accomplishments. If you can get a clip of any of the local shows on which you appear, post it on your website and have it available to send around if you are asked for a sample of your media appearances. You should, of course, do this only if you feel that your interview was successful.

Several years ago, I decided to attend a conference in Atlanta, population approximately 510,000. As soon as my plans were firm, I contacted the producer of *Good Day Atlanta*, told her the exact dates that I would be in the city, and pitched my new work relationship book, which I thought might interest her audience. She asked me to send her a copy of the book and to share what I would tell her viewers to make it a worthwhile segment. Within a week, she had booked me on the show.

On the Local News

Most network-affiliated news programs focus only on local news and weather, but a small number of news-based shows bring on guests who have a story to tell that the producers believe will be of interest to their viewers. This is also true of non-network local TV news shows. By watching these programs, you can identify those that feature guests on the broadcast.

In some cases, rather than running a commercial ad, stations feature guests that actually pay to appear on the show. This is done without the audience knowing that the interview is, in fact, a paid promotion. Although this is a more expensive way to get an interview compared with a traditional broadcast media interview, which does not charge a fee, if the interview is recorded and you do a great job, the video can be used to secure other interviews and can be posted on social media. A call to the station can direct you to people who can tell you if these opportunities are available.

As with a local radio show appearance, when doing a local TV show, you should try to line up an in-person book signing or a videoconferencing (Zoom) event at a local bookstore a day or two later. The host is usually the one to mention where and when the event will occur. And, of course, bookstore owners are more likely to set up an event if they know you will be appearing on a local show and plugging the signing.

Ironically, this is a lot harder to do if you are on a network show, since the staff will probably tell you to avoid saying anything that could date your interview. This is done because many network shows repeat their winter and spring shows during the summer rerun time or even during holidays when new shows are not being taped or aired.

Specialty TV

In many cases, specialty TV shows appear on national or local stations. While national shows may be closed to the majority of authors, local specialty shows may offer opportunities to be seen and heard. A specialty show on a local network that has a specific interest in your book's topic may be the perfect place to kick off your promotional campaign. If you have set up a book signing event at a bookstore, library, or even a specialty store—for instance, a book on nutritional supplements or another health-related topic might be appropriate for a health food store—make sure it is mentioned.

CONCLUSION

While traditional media has gone through many changes since the start of the twenty-first century, it continues to be a mainstay of promotion for many higher profile authors and their titles. That doesn't mean that you should not include it in your promotional campaign. However, as you have read in this chapter, if you ignore some of the obstacles associated with media, you will become very frustrated—not to mention wasting a lot of money trying to get around them. On the other hand, if you put together an appropriate promotional campaign, you should be able to open a number of traditional media doors. At the very least, you will have the satisfaction of knowing that you tried and that it is time to move on to other publicity options.

Taking all of the points about traditional media into consideration, it's important to recognize that the Internet has become a true game changer in book promotion. If you know how to take advantage of the opportunities it presents—prospects that you will learn about in the following chapter—you may discover that online sites provide countless opportunities for promotional exposure that can sell a good number of books while also paving the way to traditional media.

4.

What Is Internet-Based Media?

For book authors, this is truly a remarkable time. While once the opportunity for most authors to gain attention was limited to just a few radio or TV talk shows, digital media has leveled the playing field. With the right information in hand, even a small promotional campaign can potentially turn any book into a bigger seller. Obviously, a lot has to do with the topic of the book, its audience, and the market-places that might have an interest in it, but many authors have taken full advantage of this new and always-evolving media. In fact, digital media has propelled some authors onto the screens and pages of traditional media.

In the previous chapter, we discussed what is commonly known as traditional media—newspapers, magazines, TV, and radio—and how it has become increasingly difficult for most authors to get "coverage" on these platforms, especially if the author is self-published. Of course, times have changed, and now, out of necessity, even traditional media outlets have expanded their presence onto any number of digital platforms, although even these platforms are under traditional media's control. This chapter is going to deal with those areas of the Internet that are more accessible, and therefore more useful to *all* authors. No matter who your publisher is—whether it's a large-, medium-, or small-sized commercial or academic house, a hybrid publisher, or you are self-published—there are opportunities on the Internet, all of which offer you the chance to get the kind of publicity that can lead to sales. But you need to first understand these platforms so you will know which ones are right for you.

There is an old adage in marketing that goes something like this: You want to be where the eyeballs are looking and the ears are listening. These days, that place is the Internet. According to the Pew Research Center, eight in ten Americans get their news from digital devices via text, video, or streaming audio. This is a game changer for most authors who are willing to do some work. To help you get your readers' eyes and ears open to your book, we will first look at a brief history of the Internet and then explore various types of Internet-based media that can help you in your promotional efforts.

THE INTERNET

First, let us look at how the Internet started. The origins of this revolutionary technological phenomenon could fill several books, but briefly, it began in early 1983 with a set of cable hook-ups designed to enable instantaneous communication between computers. The success of this digital experiment soon opened up a brave new world for those who needed to communicate quickly with others within their offices, their neighborhoods, or anywhere that cable service would allow. Then, in 1985, the US Federal Communications Commission (FCC) allowed anyone with the proper equipment to issue broadcasts legally through use of a group of frequency bands—much in the same way that TV antennas had received sound and images since the early twentieth century. And with that, the entertainment potential of the Internet first reached beyond the frontlines of computer science and straight into the realm of the general public.

To a great degree, this was the birth of "Wi-Fi," which stands for *Wireless Fidelity*. Wi-Fi technology uses a *wireless router*, which converts Internet data coming in through a cable into a radio signal that is then transmitted to any nearby device that can successfully receive and host a Wi-Fi signal.

Today, that equipment is all around us—from computers and home entertainment flat screens to smartphones. And with the availability of immediate access to this system of communication, new platforms of mass communication have been created. While the traditional media once offered information based on what *they* thought would appeal to their audience, the Internet has flicked open all channels of communication in every conceivable direction. The notion of a gatekeeper has been all but obliterated, at least in comparison with the traditional media model with its producer, booker, or host gatekeepers that exclusively directed the flow of public discourse during the past century.

However, always keep in mind that digital media is a vast universe, and trying to determine which platforms to pursue in order to promote your book remains a constant challenge. To help you swim—or at least tread water—in this river of opportunities, this chapter will provide you with a select introductory list of current popular platforms that an author can use to grab the attention of hundreds, thousands, or even millions of potential readers as well as traditional media.

For the purpose of guiding you through Internet-based media, I have divided this area into two categories. The first is comprised of non-social media, such as podcasts, websites, and the like. The second is comprised of social media platforms, such as Facebook and Twitter. Below, we delve into each of these forms of media and explore how each one can help you let potential readers know about your work.

NON-SOCIAL MEDIA PLATFORMS

Non-social media platforms are somewhat different from social media. Whereas social media content is constantly being tweaked and modified based on a kind of "real time" connection to fellow users, non-social media allows you to provide a more rigidly fixed source of information. Another way of looking at it is that on non-social online media, you, the author of the book, will be the primary contributor of the content. In some cases, the people who access your content may be able to contact you, post comments, or otherwise interact with you, but their participation will be very limited. Because there isn't a constant give-and-take with followers, as there is on social media, once you create a website, podcast, or other type of non-social media, in most cases, you will not have to constantly monitor it and respond to the comments of others.

The most commonly used types of these platforms include podcasts, blogs, e-newsletters, email and email blasts, online videos, and websites. We will explore each of these in turn below.

■ PODCASTS

A podcast is generally an old-fashioned "talk radio" program recorded as digital information—as opposed to sounds captured through radio airwaves—that is made widely available through the Internet. Although podcasts can include video and text in some formats, they are most often *listened to* and can be downloaded at any time to your computer, tablet, smartphone, or any other electronic device. Most podcasts are accessed through what can be called digital media software or an *app*, short for *application*. The most popular of these podcast apps include Apple Podcasts, iTunes (available through Apple Podcasts), Google Podcasts, Spotify, Stitcher, Pandora, Patreon, and TuneIn.

Podcasts come in all shapes and sizes, generally focus on a theme of some sort, last from a few minutes to a few hours, and vary extensively in their popularity. The challenge is to figure out which podcasts are worth pursuing—especially when you consider that according to Podcasthosting.org, there are over 2 million different podcasters available with more than 48 million episodes.

Many podcasts have weekly episodes—or semiweekly episodes, in the case of podcast pioneer and comedian Marc Maron's wildly popular *WTF* program—and they develop and serve an audience of loyal subscribers who tune in on a regular basis. (In the case of controversial podcaster Joe Rogan, his followers receive a new episode two to four times a week.) More important, many podcasts focus on books and are willing to interview authors, provided that the book is a good match with their theme and that it will appeal to their target audience. As an example, there are several popular True Crime podcasts that are open to interviewing authors. Some of the most successful True Crime podcasts have been *Serial, My Favorite Murder, Crime Junkie, Someone Knows Something*, and *Up and Vanished*.

One of the many advantages of being interviewed about your book on a podcast is that most podcasts are archived to make them available to people who could not listen to them live. This will help you in all your future publicity efforts—not just because you can continue to gain listeners even after the live podcast is done, but also because you will have a sample of how you conduct yourself in an interview. Of course, you should remember that in some situations, a podcast archive can actually work *against* you, especially if you were not at your best during the interview. This is why you should ask yourself the following key questions before you agree to be a podcast guest—or, for that matter, before you do *any* interview.

- Judging from the podcasts you've listened to, are you sure that you and this podcast host are a good "fit" and that you'll have good chemistry with the host?

- Are you interested in the overall theme of the podcast, and do you feel you'll respond well to the host's questions?

- Do you usually keep listeners engaged and eager to hear more?

- Is your voice pleasant?

- Do you sound informed about your book and the topic on which the podcast will focus?

- Have you done enough research about the podcast or podcast host to be certain that you want to be forever associated with this podcast?

Remember that you should always be looking for podcasts that interview authors about their books, careers, or areas of expertise—not just podcasts that explore the process of writing and getting published. The latter podcasts usually focus on the host alone, although some might interview other writers so they can share their experiences.

In addition to the previously mentioned podcasts by Marc Maron and Joe Rogan—both of which often feature authors on their programs— there are several other popular "author friendly" podcasts, including, but not limited to, the following:

- *The Authors Show*, which has been interviewing authors about their books since 2005.

- *The Book Show* with host Joe Donahue, a popular author-driven podcast from NPR (National Public Radio).

- *Open Stacks*, which is a podcast from the independently owned Seminary Co-op Bookstore based in Chicago, Illinois.

- *PW LitCast*, the flagship podcast from top book business magazine *Publishers Weekly*.

On page 253 of the Resources section, you will find information on BookBuzzr, which provides a list of the best podcasts for authors. Your job as a book author is to determine which podcasts will be most appropriate for you and your book.

Creating Your Own Podcast

Another step you can take to establish a successful online media presence is to produce your own podcast. For some, this may seem like a daunting task, but if you are ambitious enough to write and publish a book, there's a good chance that you can also produce a podcast. To begin, you will need to buy a good microphone—one that will capture your voice clearly while also filtering out most extraneous background noises. (The last thing you want is to present a program that sounds as if it were recorded inside a tunnel or at the bottom of a well.) The rest will depend on how sophisticated a production you want your podcast to be. Will you include introductory music or incidental sound effects throughout? The good news is that most podcasts are comprised of only one or two people having a conversation. No music or sound effects are necessary. The most important element of a podcast is the *topic* at the heart of your discussion. What you want to do, of course, is focus your podcast in a subject area that is of strong general interest while also giving yourself a continuous way to promote your expertise—and your book.

Your next step will be to decide on your format. Will it just be you talking, or will you be conducting interviews?

After you choose a format, you'll want to decide how often you will release or, to use podcast parlance, *drop* a new episode. Be sure to pick a schedule that you will be able to maintain. Although daily or weekly episodes might seem like the best way to grow your audience, consider whether you will be able to maintain such a demanding schedule given all the other work or personal demands in your life. With these considerations in mind, decide if your podcast will regularly provide new content on a semi-weekly, weekly, bi-weekly, or even a monthly basis—or if you will drop a new episode only when you are in the mood to do so.

Next, you may need to invest in some software to record and edit your content. Finally, in the same way your book needs a cover, your podcast will need some kind of visible art logo along with a specific title that will be attached to each and every one of your podcast's audio files.

These are the basic steps to creating your own podcast. While there are many companies and systems in the market to help you complete these necessary tasks, one in particular that you may want to consider is called Anchor (https://anchor.fm/). Not only is Anchor a free site, but it also lays out each and every step of the podcast-making process in a way that is both user-friendly and highly accessible to anyone who may want to make a go at creating podcasts.

Once you have decided how to create your podcast, you must consider how you will present it to listeners. To maximize its visibility, have it made available through podcast hosts such as Apple Podcasts, iTunes, and Patreon, among others.

Finally, you need to promote your podcast. Just as you may ask friends to buy your book and write reader reviews online at Amazon, you can ask people you know or have as guests on your podcast to tag or mention your podcast on their own websites and/or social media pages. (We'll talk about social media later in the chapter, and will also explore making social media users aware of the non-social platforms you're using to promote your book.) You can also embed a hyperlink to your podcast from within your own website, should you happen to have one.

Last, and never least, there is Google. The most powerful and far-reaching of all online search engines, Google offers a wealth of paid services and online tools that you may want to draw upon in order to better promote your podcast. Google and the rest of the online universe is motivated largely through the use of *keywords*—which can be defined simply as a word or a set of words that online users will "key" into search engines whenever looking for information or—even better, in terms of promotion—when searching for a service or product related to the words. With a core selection of keywords on your end, together with some financial investment and maybe a little bit of luck, a search engine like Google should ideally drive more traffic to your website—and by extension, to your podcast.

■ BLOGS

A *blog* is a regularly updated website or web page that is made available online, and that serves as the Internet's contemporary equivalent of a journal book or diary. The entries that appear in a blog are identified within the blogging community, or the *blogosphere,* as *posts.* A post on a blog is similar to an essay. Remember your elementary, middle school, and high school days? Your teacher might assign you the task of writing an essay, in which you would be expected to express your thoughts on a particular topic. That is essentially what a blog post is, and it has become a very popular way for people to express their opinions or observations on any given subject. It is estimated that there are now more than 600 million blogs worldwide. In the United States alone, there are an estimated 31 million active bloggers who write a new blog post at least once a month.

Blogs can be part of your promotional efforts in two ways: Other bloggers can review or discuss you or your book, or you can establish your own blog as a means of stimulating interest in your title. In Chapter 8, you will learn about book reviewer blogs. (See page 148.) In this chapter, you will learn about creating your own blog.

How can you best use a blog to promote your title? If your book is nonfiction, you likely want to maintain a blog that relates to your book's topic. If your book is a work of fiction, though, it would probably make the most sense to blog about yourself and the process whereby you created your novel, children's book, or short story collection. In this way, your blog can hopefully generate interest in you and your book among potential readers—and perhaps even the media, who might request review copies or seek to interview you for broadcast, print, or Internet media outlets.

A word to the wise: Be *very* careful about the blog posts that you write, and remember the importance of first impressions. Much of the time, your blog will swiftly characterize the quality and relative worth of your writing for those who read it. So spend the time—and money, if necessary—to have your blog posts proofread and corrected by a professional. Although you are not usually paid to write a blog, your writing should never be anything less than your very best.

If you remain interested in making your own blog but feel stymied by a lack of knowledge and a scarce budget, consider the free blogging platforms—Weebly and Substack, among others—through which you can set things up for yourself. Be sure to do your due diligence when it comes to linking up with a blogging platform. You want to spend time working with non-social media platforms, like a blog, only if they will present you and your message in a consistently positive and reputable way.

■ E-NEWSLETTERS

An *e-newsletter* is a newsletter sent out via email. Like the newsletters discussed in Chapter 3 (see the discussion that begins on page 40), it presents content aimed at a specific group of people for the purpose of keeping them informed of and engaged in a specific topic. Over the years, many printed or "hard copy" editions of newsletters have been turned into e-newsletters. This makes a great deal of sense. It's highly cost-effective, it provides an easier way to maintain subscriber lists, and the newsletter never gets lost in transit.

E-newsletters are used by experts, celebrities, businesses, and organizations to keep in touch with their subscribers or followers, and they need to constantly provide fresh content that is of interest to their readers. Consider this: Probably every hobby group, business specialty, alumni group, profession, or group that's passionate about a specific subject creates a number of e-newsletters that go out periodically. By finding and reaching out to the kinds of e-newsletters with whom your own topic and interest will resonate, you as an author may be able to have a story written about you or your book. You may also be able to have an excerpt from your work included. If your book is published by a commercial house, you will, of course, need to obtain permission from the company to allow any portion of your book generally longer than one paragraph to be reprinted in any way. Be aware that if the e-newsletter is open to content that is also available elsewhere, such as the free sample that Amazon offers on its site, most commercial publishers will readily agree to have that same content shared in other formats, including e-newsletters.

The bottom line, though, is that being able to find the right e-newsletters can be a simple and highly effective way to reach the perfect audience for your book.

Based on the topic of your book, you might also think about creating your own e-newsletter. While some e-newsletters are professionally typeset and edited, many appear less than professional to the typical online user, which of course, does not reflect well on the producer of the e-newsletter. Whether you are creating a new e-newsletter or contributing to an existing one, you must make sure that your writing is the best it can be. You and your book will most likely be judged by any writing with which your name is associated. So before you commit to producing and sending out a regular e-newsletter, remember that this will require a good deal of time and effort. There is also the work involved in gathering up, maintaining, and expanding your readership. For some authors, an e-newsletter may be a logical step in drawing more public attention to the subject of their title. This, in fact, may be the story behind many of today's successful and important e-newsletters. For most authors, though, it is easier to work with an existing e-newsletter.

The magic of the Internet age means that there are literally dozens of free website articles available online that can walk you in a step-by-step fashion through the process of putting together your own e-newsletter. One site in particular that can help get you get started is Style Factory (https://www.stylefactoryproductions.com). Still, as you will see in the following discussion of emails and e-blasts, a less time-consuming approach to getting the word out through the Internet might prove just as effective.

■ EMAIL AND E-BLASTS

In today's world, standard communication on the Internet takes two forms—emails and texting. While texting is hugely popular, the best publicity you can provide using this platform is to include a link to a site that offers promotional information. The problem is that a text received from someone you don't know is nearly always going to be deleted by the recipient. On the other hand, we all get emails. Some of them we actually read, while others we quickly scan before removing them from our inbox. Consider a blindly sent email that you received and actually read. What was it that caught your eye? Was it the headline, the image, the subject line, or something else?

You don't have to be a gifted email designer to create an effective email. All you have to do is look at other promotional emails that you have received and liked, and try to model your own promotional copy after those successful examples. If you can't figure out how to put a cover image into the email, ask someone who does. Let them do their homework first, of course. You might also consider using your book's sales sheet as a starting point, and you might even model the layout of your email promotion on that of your sales sheet. (See page 101 of Chapter 6 to learn about sales sheets.) Just be sure to include the book's title, what the book is about, what the price is, and where the book can be purchased. And if you have a good blurb about yourself or your book that you can use in your promotion, always include it as well. (See Chapter 7 to learn about blurbs.)

Once you have put your promotional email together, you can experiment with it. Send it to some friends, and ask them what they think. Don't be afraid to make changes when necessary. One helpful aspect of email promotions is that you can always change elements to make them more effective—particularly if you see that they are not working as hoped. When you are ready and you have put together a list of reviewers, producers, bookers, or other publicity opportunities that could help promote your book, you can begin sending out your email. This can be done either one by one or as an *e-blast*, which is when you blast out a single piece of e-promotion simultaneously to various recipients found within a single strategically organized contact group. (If you prefer to have professional assistance in sending out your e-blasts, see the inset on page 60.)

Send off your e-blast to only a few contacts as a first step. Then see what type of response your email gets over a certain period of time— usually within a twenty-four-hour period. If changes need to be made, make them, and send off a few more. Once you think that your email or e-blast is on the right track, you can start to expand the reach of your promotion by increasing the size of your contact list.

■ ONLINE VIDEOS (YOUTUBE)

So maybe you did not land that *Today Show* interview, or you realized that *The View* books only celebrity guests. Fortunately, in this time of online media, you can go ahead and produce your own video interview or book trailer. Furthermore, you can post it yourself on YouTube, your own website, or someone else's website. You can also post your video on social media, such as Twitter, Facebook, Instagram, or LinkedIn.

YouTube (www.youtube.com), which is owned by Google, is an extremely popular video-sharing platform that has grown into a major source of entertainment and news since it was first introduced in 2005. Individuals known as YouTubers have built major followings by regularly posting video blogs, or *vlogs*, to their own YouTube channels. YouTubers produce content that spans a wide range of topics, from step-by-step makeup tutorials to cooking demonstrations to comedy sketches.

Viewers can subscribe to YouTubers' channels to keep tabs on the video content these vloggers put out. They can also rate, share, and comment on videos. Some authors use YouTube to gain a following through vlogs. If you're a creative, charismatic individual with a quality camera and sharp video-editing skills, you may benefit from starting a YouTube channel. It doesn't necessarily have to be book- or writing-related, although both are viable ideas. If you've written a book on a certain topic, odds are you're already an expert on it. Is the topic interesting enough to attract viewers if you discuss it on camera? If you build an audience on You-Tube, your faithful viewers will likely want to consume any content you put out—and that can include your books.

Professionals That Can Help You Send Out Your E-Blasts

If you decide to promote your book through e-blasts, there are several excellent third-party email management programs that you might want to use, including Mailchimp, Campaigner, and Constant Contact. (See page 249 of the Resources section for more details.) If you have one or more colleagues or friends who have books that would complement but not *compete* with your offerings, you might consider doing an email blast together, thereby equally sharing the cost of the venture. But be very careful when it comes to sending out e-blasts. Since 2003, the FCC's CAN-SPAM Act insists that all recipients of e-blasts either need to have signed up to receive them from marketers or at least have a shared quantifiable interest in what is being sent in the promotional piece. Heavy fines and even jail time hang in the balance if you swerve from due diligence when putting together your lists or associating your-self with others' lists.

There are also companies that specialize in conducting email blast marketing for specific populations, such as book authors. If you are work-ing with a publicist, he may have a working list that he uses for e-blasts as part of his book publicity activities. Effective e-blasts can be a great way to get your name and the name of your book out there, and in many cases, this can result in substantial sales as well as further promotional oppor-tunities. E-blasts create word-of-mouth exposure for your book as well.

Whether you create a separate YouTube channel or just post individual videos to the overall site, YouTube videos are an excellent way to create a buzz for your book. You can do everything from an under-two-minute book trailer to a longer feature-style video related to you and/or your book's topic. Your videos could be made using actors and actresses; could include "man on the street" interviews, like the ones you see on the local news; or can even be animated features. You can do everything yourself, or you can find someone who specializes in book trailers or short videos to do all the production work for you. Let's say that your book is about time management. Go out and interview various individuals about what their biggest time problem is. Or if your book is about your most amazing travel destinations, interview people you meet about the most memorable places they have visited or the places that they wish they could visit.

■ WEBSITES

Websites have now become the most instantly visible face of nearly every business everywhere. If you want to learn something about a company, in most cases, you go to its website and find what you need quickly and with relative ease. For authors, a website can often be an important part of an effective promotional campaign. These sites can advertise, inform, educate, and entertain. Whether the book is fiction or nonfiction, when created correctly, websites can turn a reader into a potential book buyer or influence a producer to invite an author on a show. And websites are available to visitors twenty-four hours a day, seven days a week.

If you're thinking about creating a website, there are a number of essential steps to consider. The first should be naming the website. A website can be named after the author or the author's book title, or each address can be linked together to go to just one website. Next, you must decide on the website's content. While the content is up to you, there are some basics to keep in mind. Consider the consistent inclusion of the following items on your website:

- Your name and the book title.

- The front cover image of your title.

- Blurbs and full reviews.

- Your book's specifications (metadata), such as the format (paper-back or hardcover), size, page count, ISBN, and price. For fiction, include the genre, such as Mystery. For nonfiction, include the subject description, such as History. For children's books, include the target age group.

- Where readers can go to purchase copies, including links to online vendors.

- An overview or brief summary of your book.

- Your author's bio. (Author photos are optional but strongly recommended.)

- A table of contents (TOC) for nonfiction titles.

- Excerpt(s) from your book. (Always include a copyright notice and specific credit line. For instance: "Reprinted by permission from *How to Promote Your Book* by Jan Yager. Square One Publishers, Inc. Copyright © 2023 by Jan Yager.")

In addition to the above information, you can also post your promotional emails, blogs, podcast link, and YouTube video link, as well as the places where you may be signing books or lecturing. Remember, though, that if you post time-sensitive information, such as news of an upcoming book signing, it will quickly date your site if left there after the event is over. You or your webmaster has to be ready, willing, and able to remove information as soon as the associated event has ended. You can post photos related to the past event and archive them in your website for promotional purposes, but make sure that past events are not listed as upcoming events.

Another tool you can make use of is a "popup" window, or a *lead box*, as it is referred to in website development circles. With a lead box on your website's home page, you can provide those who visit your site with a way to enter their name and email address in case they want to learn more about your book, your book's subject, or you. Popup boxes may also be designed to offer a free additional excerpt from your book—one that is not available on other websites—or to offer an author interview. By visiting and using a few best-selling authors' websites, you will probably learn more ways of highlighting the content of your website and reaching your audience.

Of course, creating a website is a challenging task for many people. The good news is that there are a number of services—such as GoDaddy.com—that allow you to register and own your website name and also provide the tools needed to build a website. (See page 259 of the Resources for the names of DIY services.) Another option is to hire a web designer to build your website and make sure that all of its features work. If you wish, you can also hire a webmaster to maintain the website and update it as needed. The web designer and webmaster can be the same person or two different people. The costs of creating a website vary based on just how many bells and whistles you want to include, so don't be afraid to comparison shop. Remember to ask to have your website "secured," as this will tell users that the website is protected and safe to use. A secure website will also prevent Internet services from blocking it.

One final thing to remember about your website: As you use any of the other platforms discussed, always include the name of your website.

CROSSING LINES

While all of the non-social media platforms we have discussed operate in their own unique worlds, be aware that each one can easily cross over into the world of social media platforms. Once you have become familiar with these various platforms, you will see just how easy it is to have an email incorporated into your Facebook account, to post a short video on TikTok or Instagram, or to direct your social media followers to your own website. It simply requires an open and flexible mind, as you will come to see in the next section.

SOCIAL MEDIA PLATFORMS

"In the future, everyone will be world-famous for fifteen minutes." That statement has (rightly or wrongly) been attributed to pop artist Andy Warhol—and with the advent of social media, it seems to be correct.

Today, social media is where you get to communicate with your friends, family, colleagues, and networking connections in a relaxed, socially acceptable environment. The content is always changing, as it is provided not by a single entity, such as a company, but by an online community of countless people who interact with one another. Thus, social media is ripe for anyone trying to promote something, whether a brand of clothing or a book. As of this writing, some of the most influential social media platforms are Facebook, Instagram, Twitter, LinkedIn, and Pinterest, with a growing tide of popularity for additional platforms such as TikTok, WeChat, and Reddit.

In order to promote your book effectively over these platforms, you need a strong social media plan, which must include an ever-growing number of followers. I recently received a review copy of a finance book, and on the back of the book, the author's publisher listed all the connections that author had on Twitter, Instagram, Facebook, and LinkedIn. Those connections represent how many people an author is able to *instantly* share information with without having to go through a third party, such as a book review, or getting interviewed on traditional media like radio or TV. If an author has 500,000 followers on Twitter (discussed on page 67), that means that a positive review, a quote related to his book, or even information that shares the author's life experiences can be posted and seen by a certain proportion of those 500,000 individuals. Of course, having impressive numbers is not all that matters when it comes to maximizing the effectiveness of a social media platform. You need to have readers who actively engage and interact with you. You want to have your tweets retweeted to others, and you want your LinkedIn posts to lead to comments. That is why promotion through social media needs frequent attention on your part.

■ FACEBOOK

Facebook (www.facebook.com) is a highly popular social media platform that connects friends and family members using a simple interface. Of all the platforms listed here, Facebook is definitely the largest, with almost 3 billion active monthly users around the world. It is an excellent marketing tool for companies, brands, public figures, or anybody who wants to spread the word about an interest or an accomplishment—such as the publication of a book.

Today, just about anything and anyone you can think of has a Facebook page, from places to products to celebrities. Facebook users can show their support for their favorite musicians, brand names, political figures, and more by "liking" a page, "liking" or commenting on that page's posts or pictures, or even sharing that page's posts on their own profiles for their hundreds or even thousands of Facebook friends to see.

Setting up a Facebook "page" is different from setting up a Facebook "profile." Facebook *profiles* are personal pages run by everyday individuals who want to connect with friends and family. Facebook *pages* are also run by individuals but often represent bigger entities, such as companies, brands, or even authors. The profiles are private until you add other Facebook users as "friends." But the information on a Facebook page is available to everyone on the website, and people can choose to see the page's posts directly on their timelines by "liking" them. By creating a Facebook page for your book, you will be able to share information on its release date, reviews, and other news with anybody who "likes" the page. You can post status updates, photos, videos, and more. Many authors create Facebook pages under their names—separate from their personal Facebook profiles—in order to brand themselves as professional writers and to share book-related information with their readers. Some authors use their Facebook author site in lieu of a personal author site. If you choose that route, you can share the URL of that site with the media so they can learn more about you when they are deciding whether to book you for a show or request a review copy.

Book authors use Facebook in a variety of ways to publicize their works. The most obvious and common way is to announce that they have written a new book or that it has just been published. They display the cover and offer a short pitch on what it is about, along with a link that can be used to order it on Amazon or another site where it is available for purchase.

Most authors promote their book *after* it is published, but it is usually better to start talking about it on social media at least four to nine months *before* it becomes available to build the momentum necessary to create a market for the book. You might say something like, "Just finished the first draft of my new novel." Two months later, you could say, "Finally got the book to the copyeditor after two years of hard work!" Another post could be, "My publisher shared two possible cover designs. Which one do you prefer?" By encouraging engagement in your Facebook friends, you can create your own band of advocates over the months or even years between the start and completion of your book, and finally, its publication.

Even though a Facebook page focused on your book and/or your career as an author is free, you have to keep updating it to make it work for you. You have to think like an advertiser: Out of sight is definitely out of mind. Mentioning the book only once is rarely enough. You must keep it in front of your network as if this were an ad campaign. To avoid angering or boring your network with repetitive posts, however, each time you post something, be sure to provide *new* information related to the book. This could include an upcoming event to which you want to invite your Facebook friends and fans. If you just received a new blurb or review, you can include that in a new post. If there are news stories that cover the same theme as your book, you could share the stories as well as how they relate to your book.

Facebook can also help you with you book promotion efforts through Facebook Live, a free way to instantly connect with your audience in a live video stream through your smartphone or through the webcam on your computer. If you decide to use this service, you can increase the production quality of your video by making sure that the lighting is good; by using a microphone that you pin on yourself, known as a lavalier mic; or by getting a better-quality external microphone if you're recording from your computer.

You will find more information on Facebook about what Facebook Live is and how you can access it. Be aware that Facebook has strict policies about what you can and cannot do on their live streaming service, so make sure you read their guidelines before using the service. On page 257 of the Resources section, you will find the link to more information about this free option.

The success that you and your book have on Facebook will depend on how much time and energy you are able to invest in the process. A lot will also depend on the number of Facebook "friends" you have as well as who those friends are. I have found that I enjoy the best results when a third party posts something positive about my book. For example, I gave a friend a copy of the illustrated children's book *The Question Is Why*, which was produced by my publishing house. Soon after, the friend posted that it was his three-year-old son's favorite book! I know this led to a sale, because the friend sent me a follow-up post from his buddy, who, based on the post, had bought the book. As this story demonstrates, it may be a good idea to give books to some of your Facebook friends, because they can post about it, singing its praises. This is a great way to start the kind of "word of mouth" exposure that generates interest and, eventually, sales. Book publishing and promotion guru Dan Poynter often said that sending out books for review and giving away books to the right people can be the most cost-effective means of book promotion.

■ TWITTER

Twitter (www.twitter.com) is a social networking service designed for sharing short status updates and messages known as "tweets." Over the past few years, Twitter has evolved into a major social network and news source. It is a quick, easy way for users to share and spread their thoughts and ideas. By creating a Twitter account, you can choose whom you would like to follow, and as a follower, you can see others' tweets directly on your timeline. You can also show your appreciation of someone's tweet by "liking" it or "retweeting" it to share on your personal Twitter page. The more you tweet, the more followers you may gain, and the more people you may reach. By joining Twitter, you can learn more about your audience by engaging with people directly. Twitter is also an effective networking tool—you can follow and communicate with fellow authors or professionals. Your readers will feel a greater connection to you, and you will feel a greater connection to your readers by reading, sharing, and responding to one another's tweets.

■ LINKEDIN

LinkedIn (www.linkedin.com) has carved out a niche for itself as the world's largest professional online networking site. It specializes in helping its users expand their careers and businesses. There are an estimated 830 million members worldwide, and every author should consider having a LinkedIn profile. Creating a profile is free, although LinkedIn does offer job or client searching services and features for which you have to pay.

Once you have created a comprehensive profile, packed with useful background information about yourself and your books—including your author photo—you need to start cultivating your connections. Begin with people you already know and who know you. Then do searches on related connections, such as people who can help in your book promotion efforts.

Over the years, I have found many radio and other publicity opportunities through LinkedIn. Once you are on LinkedIn and you are connected to someone, you can find their contact information, which usually includes a direct e-mail address that otherwise might be difficult to obtain. For example, I wanted to pitch the head of a particular library about an author event, and her contact information was not available on the library's website. Through LinkedIn, I let her know that the two of us already had many shared connections, and she immediately connected to me. Within seconds, I had access to her direct e-mail, and over the next couple of days, I was able to send my pitch directly to her.

If you have a website, you'll want to include it in your LinkedIn information. Although most people include only their e-mail address, website URL, and Twitter "handle" (name), some also include their phone number for quick access. But remember that you have to be linked to someone for your contact information to become visible to them. Otherwise, only your LinkedIn profile and the related URL will be visible.

It is best to use your name for your LinkedIn profile. Once you create your profile on LinkedIn, LinkedIn will create the URL that goes with it.

With LinkedIn, as with all the social media sites, you want to put in as much time and energy as your schedule allows to develop an extensive list of connections or followers. Be aware, though, that once you hit 500 or more connections, it is irrelevant as a way of defining you, since LinkedIn does not list the exact number beyond 500. Twitter, as you may know, lists the exact number of followers, so continuing to grow your Twitter followers has the advantage of showing the world how connected you are.

Once you have built up a strong list of connections to people who can help publicize your book, it can become like a big electronic rolodex of PR possibilities. How well LinkedIn works for you will depend on a number of factors, ranging from your personality to how often you post new content that others find interesting, as well as how much time and energy you are able to regularly put into this platform. I have found that LinkedIn is especially helpful for promoting my books, or even generating sales, when I connect one-on-one with a particular contact. This works better than posting something that may or may not be seen by whomever happens to be on LinkedIn at that particular moment. I take the time to get to know as many of my connections as possible by sending a direct message in LinkedIn and, if I get a response, by following with back-and-forth communication. In my one-on-one posts, I may share information about a new or previously published book if it is related to our discussion. Over the years, I have even asked various LinkedIn connections to consider buying a book, and in some cases, I have offered to send a review copy. When I truly trust someone, I may offer to send an advance reader copy with a request for an advance endorsement.

Each day, LinkedIn posts a list of the birthdays being celebrated among your connections. I try to send birthday greetings only to those with whom I have had a LinkedIn conversation in the past. I rarely send a birthday greeting if I think the recipient is going to think, "Who's that?" In almost all cases, I receive a "thank you" for my message, which further reinforces my connection with that person.

Dealing With Trolls

When it comes to social media, a *troll* is defined as someone who makes a nasty or abusive comment about someone else's social media comment or activity. Remember earlier in the chapter, when I said that a blog post is like an assigned school essay? Well, you can think of a social media troll as the schoolyard bully. The downside of free social media access and engagement is that you never know exactly whom you are reaching in your online media—or how someone out there is going to respond to whatever you put up across your social media channels. The best advice is the simplest, which is to avoid engaging directly with those who troll you, or to utilize any of the tools available within a given social media platform to block or "ban" the troll from further participating in your social media. Depending on the nature of the troll's comments or responses, you may also choose to correct any misstatements or distortions regarding your book or the concepts that are at the heart of your work. Be aware, though, that most trolls are trolling others only to *get attention,* so the best course of action may be to not respond at all. That alone will take away much of the power behind trolling, leaving you free to continue your social media efforts without fear. Do yourself a favor, though, and develop a thick skin. Social media is certainly not for the timid.

■ INSTAGRAM

Instagram (www.instagram.com) is a popular photo- and video-sharing service. People share photos of their friends, family, pets, travels, and just about anything else on their Instagram profiles. Users can follow the accounts whose posts they want to see in their newsfeeds. Many businesses, celebrities, and public figures use Instagram to promote themselves and build their brands.

Instagram is well suited for someone who thinks visually. Depending on how public or private you want to be, you can use Instagram to engage directly with your audience, or simply to advertise your books. Many established authors use Instagram to share personal photos, which their followers appreciate as a small peek into their favorite authors' lives. For many years, Instagram was available only through a smartphone app (which could be downloaded from an online app store), and, as such, it was generally viewed on the go by users at various points throughout the day. Now, it is also accessible by using your laptop to visit Instagram.com. It is no longer necessary to access Instagram through the app.

Consider starting a "Bookstagram" account to connect with dedicated bookworms. Then follow the same advice given for other social media sites—namely, create posts that are appealing, avoid talking only about your book, post regularly, and share interesting news about yourself and your life. Also use giveaways as a way of keeping your long-time followers and attracting new ones. Remember that Instagram is all about the photos and videos that you add to your posts, so make sure the photos are high in quality, memorable, and relevant to the topic about which you are posting.

■ PINTEREST

Pinterest (www.pinterest.com) is a free visual social media site on which you share images of anything you find interesting—thus the name "P-interest." Users—of whom there are over 433 million worldwide—create "pinboards," each of which is a collection of images related to a single topic. Users can see what other people are interested in, as well.

People create pinboards for just about anything—their hobbies, recipe ideas, DIY projects, arts and crafts, and much more. Many businesses also use Pinterest to promote their companies, with pinboards that display their products serving as a sort of "virtual storefront." For each pin you create, you can include a link to another site. This is handy for authors, who can "pin" covers of their books and add a link to Amazon, to another bookseller, or even to reviews of their book.

There is no one right way to market yourself on Pinterest—it is truly something you can make your own. If you upload excerpts from your book and images related to it as pins, users will pin them to their pinboards, starting a chain reaction that can spread information about you and your work across the platform. Depending on how you choose to use Pinterest, your followers can browse your pinboards to learn more about you, your books, your writing process, and so on. They can then pin the images you've posted onto their own pinboards. Some ideas for author-related pinboards include writing tips, lists of books that you recommend or that are on your wish list, and quotations and images from your book.

It will not happen overnight, but if you put some time and energy into creating pins and growing your fan base at Pinterest, you might see an increase in sales as well as inquiries from media about your book or books. No promises, but it is a popular social media platform that you should consider exploring.

Also note that international online booksellers like Kobo.com and book publishers may have Pinterest accounts and promotions for authors and books. If they do, contact the person in charge of social media for that bookseller or publishing company, and see if he will add your book to the Pinterest pins and/or promotions that he is doing.

■ TIKTOK

If you are trying to reach the children's and young adult market—or even adults under fifty years of age—TikTok (www.tiktok.com) may be the social media site for you. Statistics show that nearly half of all users are eighteen to twenty-nine years of age, with 22 percent of viewers being younger, and 22 percent falling into the thirty- to forty-nine-year-old category. Based on these demographics, TikTok seems especially useful for reaching out to Gen Z and Millennials about your children's books, YA novels, or selected fiction and nonfiction titles.

Established in 2016 by a Chinese company, TikTok is one of the fastest growing social media platforms available today. Users post fifteen-second, sixty-second, or three-minute videos shot on their smartphones. In just a few years, this newer social media site has grown to have more than 700 million monthly users.

Teen writer Dominika Pindor has posted TikTok videos that have received as many as 14 million views and thousands of "likes." Her novel *Wings and Shadows* has over 100 ratings, including reader reviews, on Amazon.com. We will discuss the importance of ratings and reviews on Amazon.com in Chapter 8. At this point, just know that this is an impressive number of reviews for any author. Dominika has dozens of TikTok videos, which reinforces that the path to success with all social media platforms usually involves doing multiple posts or videos—not just one now and then. Dominika even has a video in which she highlights the various characters in her next teen novel and tells her followers that she is looking for illustrators for that novel.

The rule at TikTok, which is pretty much the rule for all these social media sites, is that you should avoid being too blatant about promoting yourself and your book, and you should share interesting additional content with your growing fan base. This will keep your followers returning to your site, reading your posts, and forwarding on what you write to their own network of followers.

We've just explored six of the most widely used social media sites for authors, but there are many others you could use to promote you book, such as Snapchat, Reddit, WhatsApp, and WeChat, to name a few. And new ones are starting every day. Since each platform requires time and effort, rather than spreading yourself thin on too many sites, decide which ones are the best fit for you and your book and focus your promotional efforts on those sites.

CONCLUSION

In this chapter, you have learned about various types of Internet-based media platforms that you can utilize to best promote your book. Whether you decide to do all the publicity yourself, do only some of it yourself, or hire a publicist to perform all promotional tasks, knowing what is available to you will put you in a much stronger position to get the most out of your publicity efforts.

Although you now know about some of the many ways in which you can promote your book, before we get into the nitty-gritty of a publicity campaign, it's worthwhile to explore the important role that you, the author, must play in the success of your book. That is the subject of the next chapter.

5.

You As the Author

In the previous chapters, you learned about the basics of the book industry—the marketplaces, book categories, and both traditional and Internet-based media. As you will see in the chapters that follow, there is a lot more to know. This can be a bit overwhelming, but if you intend to have your book read by as many people as possible, the information that follows will put you on the right path. There is, however, one thing that needs to be considered before we begin to guide you in setting up a promotion plan, obtaining reviews, and more. It is the role you have to play as your book's author. Whether your book is being produced by a commercial publisher or is a self-published work, you have to recognize the important part you can play in the success of your title going forward.

Authors can do many things to get attention for their titles both from the media and from readers. This becomes necessary if your publisher fails to create and follow through with a solid promotional campaign, or when you've taken on the job of promoting your book on your own or with the help of a publicist. However, there are a number of questions to consider, with the most critical question being: Are you ready and willing to be the chief promoter of your book?

Yes, you have purchased this book or you have borrowed it from the library, and you feel that you are ready to conquer the world. However, you need to take a long, hard look at the challenging road ahead. I'm not saying this to discourage or frighten you. It is simply the truth that you need to hear. As the author, you can be the most important part of your book's publicity process, regardless of who published your work.

History shows that many authors have been the primary reason their titles have taken off. Some of these authors' successes were due in part to good timing or having media friends in the right place, but those who didn't have the breaks worked hard and smart to make it happen. For example, best-selling author Dr. Wayne Dyer, whose first title was *Your Erroneous Zones*, drove cross-country selling copies of his book out of the trunk of his car. Gregory J.P. Godek, author of *1001 Ways to Be Romantic,* rented a tour bus and drove from state to state, selling copies along the way. More recently, Kalynn Bayron, best-selling author of the YA fantasy novels *Cinderella Is Dead* and *This Poison Heart,* used Instagram to involve potential readers and fans in the publishing process as a way of generating publicity and sales. While you may not be willing to drive cross-country or to sell books out of the trunk of your car, these days, there are numerous ways to make the world aware of your title, such as Instagram, Facebook, LinkedIn, and other social media platforms.

FACING REALITIES

If your book is being published by a commercial house, you may be pleased by the level of promotion and marketing your book will receive, or you may be satisfied for only a few weeks or months, and then find that the company's publicist is moving on to newer books. Or perhaps you will find that your publisher fails to promote your book even when it is first released. These are all common complaints of authors in similar situations.

The fact is that if your book does not garner stellar reviews, including prepublication reviews in key trade publications, or if it does not have impressive presale orders, its promotion may not be one of the company's priorities. This could mean that even if the book initially receives some publicity, the sales force will soon treat it like a backlist title, and it will pretty much have to sell on its own.

If, on the other hand, you have self-published your book, you may soon learn about the major obstacles that traditional media places in your way to prevent your book from receiving the promotion it deserves. (For more information on this, refer back to Chapter 3.) You will also discover the difficulties of getting your self-published title distributed through the traditional book industry channels.

These are just some of the realities facing most authors. However, with all that said, you as the author still have the ability to make a major difference in your book's sales. But you must recognize that you have a relatively big job in front of you that involves eight important components, which include:

1. Preparation.	5. Being persistent.
2. Salesmanship.	6. Being patient.
3. Putting in the necessary time.	7. Making connections.
4. Dollars and sense.	8. Learning from the process.

Not everyone is prepared or willing to take on this task. However, as you will see, each of these components will play an important role in the successful promotion of your work. Let's look at each of these factors.

■ 1. PREPARATION

"By failing to prepare, you are preparing to fail."
—BENJAMIN FRANKLIN

When you read Chapter 6 and you learn about setting up a timeline, you will more fully understand the importance of preparation. While many authors don't seriously think about putting together a promotional campaign until their book is sent to the printer or until it is available for sale, by that time, it is too late to obtain the blurbs and reviews that you need to get the word out about your book. The months before your book's release will provide the time you need to obtain reviews and blurbs, write sales sheets and press releases (if you are going to do that yourself), put together a media kit, create an author website, and otherwise carve out a presence on the Internet. Maximize every minute you have to prepare for your book's promotion before your title is officially ready for distribution and sale.

Keep in mind that virtually everything you are about to do has been done before. Use the Internet to read about what other authors have done to get attention for their work. Visit their websites; listen to their podcasts, if they made any; and read articles that discuss the steps they have taken to promote their titles. This knowledge will prepare you to do the best job you can to reach out to book reviewers, booksellers, and your audience.

■ 2. SALESMANSHIP

*"After you've written a story, the thing to do is
sell it. Sounds simple, and it is, if one will follow
certain basic principles of salesmanship."*

—ERLE STANLEY GARDNER

If you intend to sell books, you will have to be able to sell yourself as both the author and a promoter. Salesmanship requires that you show attention, interest, and conviction. If you appear standoffish or too nervous, you will not be able to open many doors. So even if you've hired a publicist to work with you, drop by and say hello to the bookstore owner who may be able to offer you a book signing, and once you befriend her, make it a practice to visit the store occasionally and renew your friendship. Chat with the local librarians who have shown an interest in your forthcoming book over the time it has taken you to write and publish it. Keep your Facebook or Instagram followers "in the loop" on the progress of your book so they feel invested in its success. These people constitute the base upon which you will build your promotional efforts. You may at first feel uncomfortable talking to people you've never met before, but with practice, much of the apprehension you feel will evaporate.

If necessary, consider hiring a book promotion or book marketing coach for one or more sessions. Coaches are available to work with you by phone, by e-mail, via Zoom or another videoconferencing service, or in person. It may be money well spent if it helps you gain more insight into the various publicity experiences that are in your future. A good coach can get you ready for the interviews you may be fearing and help you gain the confidence you need to more effectively promote your book. The coach you hire might also be able to do media training with you, or you might instead hire a dedicated media trainer for that purpose. You can find these coaches and trainers by asking other authors for referrals, by requesting information from any writers' association you belong to, or by posting a job opening through the Editorial Freelancers Association. (See page 252 of the Resources for further information about the EFA.)

■ 3. PUTTING IN THE NECESSARY TIME

"The bad news is time flies. The good news is you're the pilot."

—Michael Altshuler

While you may be able to create your timeline by working an hour here and thirty minutes there, filling in the particulars and reaching out to your contacts does require work as well as solid blocks of time. If you happen to be independently wealthy or retired, it should not be a problem to devote full days to book promotion—or to hire someone else to handle the publicity work for you. Most of us, however, have personal and professional obligations that limit our free time.

If you have the ability to manage your time properly, you should be able to balance your everyday responsibilities with the promotion of your book. Even with good time management, though, it is more than likely that you will have to make a few sacrifices. You may, for instance, have to wake up earlier every morning to focus on book promotion before heading to your full-time job. Or you may need to work at least an hour every night before retiring to bed or to put in a couple of hours of work over the weekend—moments that you previously spent relaxing and socializing with family and friends. Although this balancing act could be challenging, I strongly advise against prematurely quitting your "day job." However, I suggest you let the people who are important to you know about your publicity efforts so that they understand why you're spending less time with them.

Yes, setting up and preparing for interviews, lectures, and book signings takes time. Creating a popular author's platform using social media takes time. Even waiting for people to return your calls takes time. It's important to recognize this and to be prepared to devote the necessary minutes and hours of work, as dedication is essential to keep moving in the right direction.

■ 4. DOLLARS AND SENSE

"Money is only a tool. It will take you wherever you wish, but it will not replace you as the driver."

—Ayn Rand

It is amazing that some authors will pay money to get a cover designed or to have a copyeditor review and improve their book, but they will refuse to spend money for fifty or more copies of their completed book to be used as ARCs or review copies. Unfortunately, too many authors concentrate all of their efforts on turning their manuscript into a finished

Crowdfunding—
A New Way to Fund Your Book

Today, crowdfunding is a way of enabling authors to underwrite the cost of their book. It is the practice of funding a project by getting relatively small contributions from a large number of people via the Internet. While there are several types of crowdfunding, the type that is most relevant to an author trying to fund her book is reward-based.

In reward-based crowdfunding, people give an online contribution in exchange for a reward. The rewards differ depending on the size of the contribution, but often include a product. Since you are producing and promoting a book, the product would most likely be a copy of your book or perhaps an invitation to a book-related event, such as a book launch, but other rewards, such as imprinted mugs, are also possible.

To raise money through crowdfunding, you should first research the rules of the different platforms—for instance, how long you can run your campaign, the audience your campaign will be aimed at, etc.—and then select the one that seems right for you. You must then fill in the online forms and provide the documentation requested by that platform so that it can make sure that you're legitimate. Once the platform accepts you, you can make your pitch to potential donors by describing your project, why you want funds, and how much you hope to raise. Since it's a reward-based platform, you will need to state what the backers will get. This pitch may require occasional updates so that the campaign continues to remain attractive to the backers.

Besides creating a compelling campaign page on whatever crowdfunding site you choose, you will also need to advertise it on as many social media platforms as you can. Post a link to your campaign on your personal media pages, and encourage friends and family to do the same. The most successful crowdfunding campaigns span across several social media platforms, landing on as many different profiles as possible.

product without looking at the bigger picture—a picture that may include a publicist, giveaway copies, mailings, ads, travel, and other publicity-related costs. As an author, it is vital to have a reasonable idea of how much money you are willing and able to spend *before* you move ahead with your book production and promotion plans. (You will read

When the crowdfunding campaign is over, with some platforms, you will get your money only if you managed to reach the target amount that you set at the start of the campaign, while with other platforms, you will get your money even if you failed to reach your goal. The platform will then arrange the payment of funds to you minus their commission fees. Crowdfunding has several advantages, such as being a debt-free way to raise money. However, in order for the platforms to make money, they charge fees such as a percentage of the amount you raised plus transaction fees, so don't expect to receive all the money that was donated.

Probably the best-known rewards-based crowdfunding platforms are GoFundMe, Kickstarter, and Indiegogo. Another option is Unbound, a London-based crowdfunding publisher that is specifically focused on obtaining funding for its authors' book projects. You pitch your idea to the company's editors and crowdfund to raise money for the project. Then Unbound's team of editors, designers, and publicists produces and promotes your book.

It's important to check each platform's website, as each has its own rules and regulations. Be aware that you will have to pay taxes on the money you receive, so when you set up the budget for your crowdfunding campaign, you should set aside those tax-related funds. Providing perks can take time and money, especially if you are sending books or customized mugs or t-shirts. If you decide that you will ship your rewards internationally, that will be even more costly, so consider shipping only within the United States or requiring the funder to pay the added cost of international shipping. Remember to include the costs of producing and shipping these rewards in the budget for your crowdfunding campaign so that you don't end up spending more money than you actually raise. Turn to page 248 of Resources to find contact information for various crowdfunding sites.

more about this in Chapter 6. See also the timeline table on page 261, which indicates what various tasks might cost.)

I have three pieces of advice that I would like to pass on to you regarding budgeting. First, plan to spend as much money on publicity as you can afford to spend. Second, if your book is selling, do not be afraid to reinvest in your project. And third, if you have exhausted your budget, think carefully about what you want to do next. For instance, if you paid your way to one or two cities for author events, you might want to focus your energy on publicity efforts that require time but no money, such as social media or email blasts that you send off yourself.

Now let us say you do not have enough money to cover your overall production and promotion costs. The good news is that crowdfunding sites on the Internet may be able to provide you with funding for your book. All you have to do is make sure your project can attract an audience to pay for your book in advance. (See the inset on page 78.)

In this new world of book publishing, you are likely to run into so-called professionals who will make crazy promises of success. "We can turn your book into a bestseller!" or "We can get you a hundred radio interviews across the country." While these guarantees may be tempting, you need to make sure that you are not going to be ripped off. Yes, someone may be able to get you dozens of radio interviews, but at the end of the interviews, if you wind up selling only twenty copies of your title, will it be worth the effort? As Ayn Rand said, you are the driver, so be a smart one.

■ 5. BEING PERSISTENT

> *"A professional writer is an amateur who didn't quit."*
>
> —RICHARD BACH

Persistence is one of the most significant traits that a book author can have. It was persistence that enabled you to go from that first word on page one to a finished manuscript. Whether it took you six months, a year, two years, or ten years, you did not give up. You kept working on your book, rewriting it, and fine-tuning it until it was done. Now, whether you are beginning the production process or ready to start publicizing your work, you are justifiably proud of your achievement.

Book promotion will require the same persistence—the same commitment of time and energy—that you needed to complete your manuscript, but it will draw on different skills and tactics. When you were writing your book, you probably tried to avoid repeating the same idea or the same group of words more than once. However, when you are going on podcast after podcast, as long as each of the podcasts has a different audience, you will probably make the same key points over and over again, because you will realize that those ideas and points work well with an audience. Similarly, every time you are interviewed, you may want to use a term or phrase that you know resonates with your audience.

Initially, book promotion might be fun. But it may soon turn into very hard work, and that at that point, you need to embrace the effort and remain persistent. Those authors who do so are likely to experience more publicity exposure and related sales. If a freelance reporter contacts you because she has read about your book, and she is on deadline for a story, even if you are tired and somewhat frustrated, if at all possible, you need to do that interview.

You may think that getting five or ten radio or podcast interviews set up back to back is every author's dream. The truth is that whether you set these interviews up yourself, have a publicist do it for you, or hire a radio media tour company to secure the interviews, it will be demanding work. You will need all the stamina you can muster to make sure that each interview sounds fresh and interesting.

Remember that there was a reason you started writing your book. If you begin to feel exhausted and lose sight of your original motivation, get back in touch with your vision, and keep finding ways to share it with others. In the remaining chapters of the book, you will learn about more ways to generate book publicity. No matter which publicity routes you choose, persistence will be the key!

■ 6. BEING PATIENT

> *"Patience is not passive, on the contrary,*
> *it is concentrated strength."*
> —Bruce Lee

For some of you, this will be a first-time experience. Others may have already written and promoted books once, twice, or even many times in the past. But regardless of your previous experience, promoting a book can be a frustrating process. You must be prepared to have doors close on you, to have phone messages go unanswered, and to deal with unexpected disappointments. As you move forward, you will learn what works and what does not, but it will likely not be easy. So, in addition to being persistent, you must be patient. Good things can happen, but they won't necessarily occur as soon as you would like them to. You will be able to get through many hard times by cultivating patience.

■ 7. MAKING CONNECTIONS

"I know that the harder you work, the more you learn,
the more connections you make. You've just got to be
prepared to keep putting yourself out there."

—AISLING BEA

Book publicist Irwin Zucker, founder of Book Publicists of Southern California, always counseled authors to "make friends with the media." That advice can take you far in your book promotion efforts. Show an interest in the media people who show an interest in you. When I started out as a published author, I took the time to send thank-you notes to producers or hosts who interviewed me. In those days, I mailed out old-fashioned greeting card thank-you notes. Today, it is so much easier, because you can send a quick thank-you via e-mail—although, of course, you can still send a card. I was amazed by how many media people told me that I was the very first author to send them a thank-you note, and they appreciated it.

In the business world, there is an expression that repeat business is the best business. Recognize that cultivating connections is vital to building your author platform, and that when you do so, you are also developing fans, readers, and interviewers or journalists who will hopefully return to you again and again. Recently, a writer for *The Washington Post* contacted me through my website. She reminded me that she had interviewed me several years before for a magazine article. Fortunately, I had entered her in my database, so I could find information about that previous interview, including the publication, the date, and the topic. She was now writing a new article on a related topic, and she asked if I was available to do a new interview for the Wellness section of the newspaper. By building a successful relationship with her—and adding this new information about her to my smartphone so I would be reminded of our relationship when she called again—I had increased the likelihood that she would seek me out in the future and that I would get further mention in one of her articles.

If you connect with the media through Linkedin, follow up with news about yourself and your book through a message on LinkedIn, by email, or by phone. As I wrote in Chapter 4, posting a message that is seen by hundreds or thousands of LinkedIn connections will not have the same impact as making a one-on-one contact. Yes, it is much more time consuming to follow up with each individual, but the results will be worth the effort.

■ 8. LEARNING FROM THE PROCESS

"Nothing is a waste of time if you use the experience wisely."

—AUGUSTE RODIN

Lining up book signings and speaking engagements may be a new experience for you. Being interviewed by a host who appears to know nothing about your book may also be a new experience, although I can assure you that it is quite common. As you move forward, you are sure to learn many new things both about book promotion and about yourself. For instance, you may discover that you can give terrific interviews over the phone or via email to journalists and feature writers, or you may find that this is not one of your natural strengths.

Rather than getting discouraged by disappointing experiences, use the feedback you receive to fine-tune your publicity efforts. For example, if the first pitch to a radio host is ignored, maybe you need to review your pitch and rewrite it to be more effective. If the next couple of pitches receive a more positive response, you will know that you learned something from that first experience. The more you do, the better you will become. Every effort—including the unpleasant ones—is an opportunity to learn more and hone your skills.

After you have carried out a number of promotional tasks, from doing book signings to posting on LinkedIn, evaluate which ones are working best. Concentrate your efforts on those that are making a positive difference, and drop those tasks that you find are a waste of time.

The time management field refers to the Pareto principle, or the 80/20 rule. Simply put, approximately 20 percent of your efforts produce 80 percent of the results. So be ready to learn from the promotional process, identify the efforts that have produced the best results, and channel your time and energy into proven practices.

CONCLUSION

Writing a book is really a two-step process—first you write it, then you promote it. Although most authors labor for months or years on writing their book and then devote only a week or two to publicizing it, the two processes are equally important. Throughout this chapter, you have learned that you as the author are key to getting attention for your book. Hopefully, you will now be open to putting the necessary energy, time, and money into the promotion process.

If your book will be published by a commercial house, and it does a wonderful job of promoting your book, you will be one of the lucky few. But if your publisher never works to market your book, if her efforts stop after only a few weeks, or if you are self-published, *you* will be the key to your book's success. It will all be on your shoulders. To look at it in a more positive way, with the tools you are learning through this book, you will be able to make a huge difference in the success of your work. Whether your goal is to educate people about an issue that you care about, to expose a grave injustice that others are ignoring, to share an amazing story that you created in your imagination, or to entertain children through poetry or prose that have delighted your own kids over the years, it is only through your efforts that your book will win the attention it deserves.

Now that you recognize the vital role you will play in your book's success, it's time to start making it happen. In Part 2, "What to Do Before Your Book Is Published," you will begin laying the groundwork for an effective publicity campaign.

PART TWO

WHAT TO DO BEFORE YOUR BOOK IS PUBLISHED

6.

Setting Up Timelines

Advance planning is a vital key to a successful book promotion campaign. If you are published by a commercial house, the publisher will pick a publication date for your book, possibly in consultation with you. Hopefully, between the time your book is put into production and the date of its publication—anywhere from eight to eighteen months—plans for the book's promotion will be put in place. This will normally include sending out advance reading copies (referred to as ARCs) four to six months ahead of the publication date and creating a press kit.

Unfortunately, too many self-published authors are tempted to begin their book's promotion literally within hours or days of getting the completed electronic file to the printer. This, of course, is a big mistake since book promotion is best undertaken when a publicity plan is in place well in advance—usually from six to nine months in advance. The question then is: Exactly what do you have to do to get started? The answer is: To begin, you need to put together a timeline.

In this chapter, I will explain how to create a practical timeline for your project—from the writing of your book, to the all-important pre-marketing steps that must be taken, to your book's release. To understand this better, we will first look at how publishers schedule the work necessary to produce and market a title, and how you—whether you have been commercially published or you are self-published—can maximize your ability to get attention for both yourself and your book.

It is important to point out that one standardized timeline is not likely to fit every title perfectly. The fact is that books can focus on any number of subjects, appeal to different audiences, and sell to a wide range of marketplaces. Moreover, if you will be doing the promotional work yourself, you need to consider how much time you will have available for each step of your book's production and marketing. This chapter will guide you in creating the best timeline for your book.

COMMMERCIAL PUBLISHING COMPANY SCHEDULES

Standard publishing contracts provide a date by which a manuscript is going to be completed by the author and ready for editing by the company. The lead time for a book to be readied for publication can range from eight to eighteen months, based upon the complexity of the manuscript.

Once an acquisitions editor signs an agreement with an author for a book project, the editor and/or production manager puts together a *production schedule*. Be aware that, depending on the size of the company, the schedules governing the production and marketing of the book can work in different ways. In a large publishing house, the production team's schedule includes stages of production, such as editing, typesetting, proofing, and printing. Based on this production schedule, the sales and marketing department come up with their own schedule for promoting a book. In a smaller company, however, instead of two departments coming up with two schedules, only one person may coordinate the production and promotion schedules.

The Release Date

The *release date* of the book—the date on which physical copies of the book are shipped from distribution centers to stores and become available to readers—is based not only on when the book is actually in print, but also on the most appropriate sales season. In the book industry, there are three fixed seasons in which sales and marketing departments plan the release of their new titles—the fall season, the spring season, and the summer season. (At one time, publishers tried to create a winter season, but it never seemed to catch on with the bookstores, so it was dropped.)

Different factors can come into play in the selection of a release date. Let's say, for instance, that based on the production schedule, a book about Martin Luther King, Jr. will be in print in time for the spring season. But is spring the best time to release that book? The fact that

Martin Luther King, Jr. Day occurs in the middle of January would be an important factor in the choice of an appropriate season. In other words, the book should be released in the fall so there is time to get the book out to bookstores before mid-January. A book on gardening, however, would be a natural for a spring release.

The Three Seasons of Book Publishing

Fall season: September through December

Spring season: January through May

Summer season: May through August

Sales and Marketing Department Planning

Once the release date is set, the sales and marketing departments make their plans accordingly. Budgets are estimated, advance release information begins to be put together, and weekly editorial meetings keep track of how quickly or slowly the work on the book is progressing. If all goes according to the schedule, when a book is ready to be released, the advance promotion of the forthcoming list has gone out, reviews for the book have been received, bookstores have pre-orders for the title, and the publicity department has developed a tentative promotion plan. Since there are bound to be difficulties in even the best thought-out schedules, changes may be made as necessary.

For the most part, this system has worked for many years. Of course, with the advent of print on demand (POD), short runs, audio- and e-books, speedier means of communication, new marketing techniques, and faster printing technology, the pace has quickened somewhat. Nevertheless, the production schedule remains a mainstay of the industry and is used whether the book is published by a major publisher, an independent house, an academic press, or any other professional organization or business.

Once your book has been published, it will be a lot harder to generate the excitement that you could have created if early on, you had sent out advance promotion, secured reviews, and taken other steps that normally occur before a book's release. So the question is: Can you use

Estimating and Documenting Costs

As you put your timeline together, it is crucial to think of it not only in terms of the time you have to work on the book, but also in terms of the money that you have to spend on the project. Consider the costs involved in editing; typesetting; proofreading; securing illustrations; indexing, if necessary; and printing. While it may be more complicated to estimate the costs of promotion, which should be ongoing, do your best to calculate the expense of producing ARCs; of mailing free copies to reviewers, if you choose to do that rather than sending out PDFs; and of other promotional efforts that you'll learn about throughout this book. Feel free to comparison shop for the best services at the best prices. Then compare the money you have on hand—your budget—with the money that you will be required to pay for the services you need. If it appears that you can't afford the costs involved in promoting your book, reconsider the timing of your project. Perhaps you will have to set your manuscript aside, even for only a short time, as you look into other sources of funding. On the other hand, if your budget seems workable but a little tight, you might consider ways in which you can trim costs.

As you pursue your book project, keep a running tally of the costs of editing, typesetting, obtaining illustrations, printing, and promotion. Most important, keep all your receipts! Be aware that *anything* related to the production and promotion of your book is likely to be tax deductible, although you should, of course, seek expert guidance from an accountant. Tax-deductible expenses include not only obvious things such as typesetting, printing, and placing ads, but also telephone bills for promotional calls, visits to museums to find information for your book, parking and toll charges incurred while visiting that museum or attending a book signing, business meals related to your promotional efforts, and much more. When in doubt, keep the receipt and make a note regarding how that cost was related to your book project. Your accountant will want you to add the receipts together so that at tax time, she can use them to offset some of your taxable income and potentially save you some money.

the same timeline that is created in most production schedules to direct you as you produce, market, sell, and promote your own book? The pages that follow will guide you through the steps of the production process and help you understand how you can design a plan that works for you and your title.

YOUR BOOK PROJECT TIMELINE

As you have already learned, publishing houses create timelines that they follow in the publication and promotion of every title they produce. The timeline that follows, however, was designed for authors who want or need to plan their own course of action in advance—from writing to production to marketing and publicity. While the majority of this timeline is designed for the self-published author, there will be several steps that commercially published authors can incorporate into their own timelines. Remember that the steps that follow are meant to be customized to your own project, your own time restrictions, your own budget, and the level of commitment you are willing to make to your book. Please see page 261 for a sample filled-in timeline table, which includes helpful suggestions as well as information about the potential costs of various tasks.

STEP 1. A TIME TO WRITE
[6 MONTHS TO A DATE THAT WORKS FOR YOU]

For some of you, the manuscript has been written, but for others, the writing is about to begin or the manuscript is in progress. If you are still in the early stages of writing a book, decide on a fixed period of time during which you will complete the manuscript. Some writers are able to finish a book within six months, while others might take a year or two to complete the work. Be realistic and base your goal on the time you have available. Post that date in a spot that you will see every day to remind yourself that you have a book to write. If you finish early, great.

As you prepare your working draft, see if you can have someone whose judgment you trust read your manuscript and provide you with comments and suggestions. Sometimes getting another viewpoint can help you make your copy better. If you decide you want professional help, consider working with a developmental editor, who can help improve content and structure. (To find a developmental editor, ask author friends for referrals, if they used one, or contact the Editorial Freelancers Association listed on page 252 of the Resources section.) Still, don't be afraid to trust your own instincts as the writer.

STEP 2. FINALIZING YOUR MANUSCRIPT
[2 TO 8 MONTHS]

There are four components to consider when finishing a manuscript. The first is copyediting; the second is getting any illustrations, photographs, and/or necessary permissions finalized; the third, if you are self-publishing, is possibly getting Cataloging-in-Publication Data, or CIP data, which should normally appear on the copyright page of your book before your manuscript is completed; and the fourth is proofreading.

COPYEDITING

A good copyeditor identifies and corrects errors in grammar, spelling, syntax, and punctuation; technical inconsistencies in capitalization, numerals, and the like; errors in continuity; factually incorrect statements; and inconsistency within a fiction or nonfiction book. When looking for a good copyeditor, always make sure that your candidate has a solid resume as well as past clients whom you can contact by phone or email to confirm the quality of the copyeditor's work, if you choose to do so. Alternatively, you can ask for a complimentary sample edit of one or two pages. You can also seek a referral from another book author or get in touch with the Editorial Freelancers Association, which can help you find a qualified professional. (See page 252 of the Resources section for contact information.)

FINALIZING GRAPHICS
AND GETTING REPRINT PERMISSION

If your book requires any illustrations, photographs, or other copyrighted material, such as excerpts from books, begin to obtain the permissions from the copyright holders or agencies that control the rights.

Public domain material that is no longer under copyright protection is free for you to use. However, keep in mind that the quality of the image must be good enough to allow for a clear reproduction in your book. If you are in doubt about the quality of a photo or other graphic, check with your printer.

There are several well-known photograph services, such as Shutterstock, Getty Images, and 123RF, which have literally tens of thousands of photographs and some illustrations that you can purchase for use in your book. Prices and terms vary, and each one offers purchases on a subscription or one-purchase basis. (To find a list of photo resources, read the introduction to the Resources, which begins on page 233.) Depending on the nature of your book, you may have to get the graphics you need from a museum, library, or other organization. In some cases, you may even need to have a freelance artist create the illustrations for you.

Consider gathering any illustrations, photographs, and/or necessary permissions during Step 1, as this will save you time later on. It can take weeks or even months to secure reprint permission, so it's best to start the process as soon as possible. If your book includes a great many graphics and other copyrighted material, when you are budgeting for your book's production, consider allocating funds for a permissions editor. Based on the guidelines you provide, this individual can secure illustrations or photographs as well as the rights to use them in your book. Once again, you can likely find a permissions editor through the Editorial Freelancers Association. Payment may be calculated on either an hourly basis or as a flat fee per project.

OBTAINING CIP DATA

Cataloging-in-Publication data, usually called CIP data, is the bibliographic record created by the Library of Congress for a book prior to its publication. This data is printed on the copyright page of all commercial books. If your book is being produced by a commercial, hybrid, or academic publisher, the publishing house should secure the CIP data for you. If your book is being self-published, you will have to take care of this task yourself. (See the inset on page 94 for details on CIP data.)

What Is CIP Data and Do I Need It?

For every book that is professionally produced, the Library of Congress issues CIP data—Cataloging-in-Production data—to classify the book and make it ready for inclusion in any library system. This block of data, which is normally printed on the copyright page of the book, is comprised of cataloging information—the title and author of the book; the ISBN number, which is assigned by the publisher (see more about this in the inset on page 99); subject headings; and full Library of Congress and Dewey decimal classification numbers. The publisher's name and some facts about what's included in the book, such as bibliographical references and index, are also part of the CIP data.

It is to your advantage to have CIP data in your book, as it marks your book as being professionally produced and also makes it attractive to librarians by furnishing cataloging information. As mentioned earlier in the chapter, if your book is being published by a commercial, hybrid, or academic press, it will obtain the CIP data for you. Unfortunately, self-published books are not eligible for this free government service. In that case, you can pay private providers to produce PCIP information for you. This is identical to CIP data, but is provided by a professional librarian on a fee basis at the request of a publisher. (See page 247 of the Resources section for a list of providers.)

If you cannot get CIP Data and do not want to pay for PCIP information, you can apply for an LCCN, which stands for Library of Congress Control Number. While not as extensive as CIP data, it is an identification number that can be used by librarians to locate a specific book in the national databases, and it is available to self-published authors. Like CIP data, it should be printed on the copyright page.

To get an LCCN, you must set up an account with the PCN program by going to http://www.loc.gov/publish/pcn. Note that e-books and audiobooks are not eligible for an LCCN assignment. The government usually issues the LCCN number within a few days of your online request.

PROOFREADING

Although people new to publishing may think that copyediting and proofreading are the same thing, they are not. Proofreading is the process of reviewing the final draft of the manuscript—*after* it has been copyedited—to ensure that there are no remaining errors. A proofreader will look for and correct spelling errors, punctuation errors, typos, missing words, and other problems that may have been missed in previous stages of editing. This is an important step, since it can get expensive to fix these problems after the manuscript has been typeset.

STEP 3. THE TYPESETTING PROCESS
[1 TO 3 MONTHS]

Your manuscript has been finished and is ready for typesetting. You have four components to consider at this time. The first is the physical format for which the typeset pages will be designed. The second is the font (typeface) style and page layout the typesetter will be using for your book. Third, if your book is nonfiction, you will probably need to have an index created. Finally, once the manuscript has been typeset, you will need to have it proofread, or proofed.

THE BOOK'S PHYSICAL FORMAT

If your book is being produced by a commercial or academic publisher, the publisher will usually determine the format of your book. Your contract may even state that the publisher has full design control. But whether you or someone else is choosing the book's design, it is useful to understand the process, especially if you will be asked to provide your input on these matters.

Selecting the physical format of the book is important. The format refers to the trim size, discussed in the next paragraph, and the cover, which can be either paperback or hardback. If you are determining the format, it can be relatively easy to choose it based upon other titles similar to yours. Find a book you like—paperback or hardcover—and give it to your typesetter to use for sizing the copy on the pages.

As mentioned above, the format of the book includes its *trim size*, which is the height and width of the finished book. Common trim sizes include 6 by 9 inches, 5.5 by 8.5 inches, and 8.5 by 11 inches, as well as a large 9-by-12-inch format referred to as a coffee table book. Make sure that the trim size you choose reflects the size of other books in its genre. For instance, 6 by 9 inches is common for many nonfiction books. If you want to get your book into bookstores, it should not be oddly sized, as this will make it clear that the book is self-published.

Whatever physical format you wind up choosing, before getting your book typeset, make sure that your printer has the capability of producing such a book economically. Not every printing press can handle every possible book size in a way that will keep costs down.

THE TYPEFACE STYLE AND PAGE LAYOUT

Above, you chose a book size that you thought would work best for your title. You may also want to choose the font styles (typeface) and page layout that were used in the chosen book. There are, of course, hundreds of typefaces you can choose from when typesetting your book, but there is a reason why certain font styles and sizes are used in many books—they are easy to read. Originality may be good for some things, but using traditional book layouts and typefaces seems to work best.

THE INDEX

Normally, an index is a requirement for nearly all nonfiction works if you want your book to be reviewed by journals, newspapers, and magazines. The inclusion of an index will also increase the book's appeal to librarians. Of course, an index also makes a nonfiction book far more reader-friendly.

Indexing cannot be done until the interior of your book has been typeset, the page numbers finalized, and the copy made available to you as proofs. It can be performed by you or your copyeditor. As an alternative, you can hire a professional indexer. (For contact information for the Editorial Freelancers Association and the American Society for Indexing, see page 252 of the Resources section.)

THE FINAL PROOFING

If you have followed the suggestions presented earlier in this chapter, your manuscript was proofread before it was typeset. Why, then, would you need to have it proofed again? Problems can occur during the type-setting process. Part of a line of type can disappear, unwanted spaces can be inserted, or graphics can end up in the wrong place. All of this should be caught during the final proofing. If your book is nonfiction, you may have included references to specific discussions in the text. (For instance, "See the discussion on page 39.") Of course, you cannot fill in these page references until the book has been typeset. Finally, don't you want to have a final check for typos and other problems before you send your book out for blurbs (see below) and to be read by reviewers? Whether you or a hired professional performs this final proofreading, it is a vital step.

STEP 4. GETTING BLURBS [1 TO 2 MONTHS]

A *blurb*—also referred to as a *testimonial* or an *advance endorsement*—refers to a one-, two-, or three-line quote that praises your book. You've undoubtedly seen blurbs printed on the back covers of books you have purchased. Blurbs can be extracted from a longer published book review, or can be obtained from any high-profile people you know who would be willing to offer positive comments. Using these blurbs properly can help sell books.

You should start reaching out to appropriate people for blurbs before the cover and interior of your book have been finished. For complete information on obtaining and using blurbs, see Chapter 7.

STEP 5. COVER DESIGN [1 TO 3 MONTHS]

If your book is being published by a commercial or academic house, the publisher will usually create the cover design and then ask you to review it and either approve the design or suggest changes. But if you are self-publishing, you will have to take care of this aspect of production.

As you already know, the design of your book cover and the copy printed on it can make or break a book. If designed incorrectly, the cover will make it painfully obvious to bookstore buyers and book reviewers that the book has been self-published. And if the copy on the cover does not clearly explain what the book is about, it will make it that much harder to get publicity. If you have spent months or years making your manuscript as good as it can be, now is not the time to skimp on time and effort. While you may not be able to tell a book by its cover, many people will not even pick it up if the cover is unattractive or amateurish in any way.

In Step 3, you or your publisher decided whether your book would be paperback or hardback and chose its size. By examining the front covers of best-selling titles that fit the format you have selected, you can see how these covers have been laid out. You can design your covers with the help of your typesetter or a hired artist. If he is experienced, he will guide you in producing effective and professional-looking graphics and type.

While the front cover may be the first part of the book to catch a potential reader's eye, the back cover deserves just as much of your attention. Here are the components that the back cover of any book should feature:

- A 13-digit ISBN, or International Standard Book Number. This is the standard way books are identified by a library, bookstore, book wholesaler, or distributor. (See the inset on page 99 for information on getting an ISBN number.)

- A BISAC subject listing. BISAC is short for Book Industry Standards and Communications, and BISAC subject headings are industry-approved lists of book descriptors. While it may sound technical, BISAC headings simply refer to a word or several words printed in small type that identify the subject matter of a nonfiction book. "Reference/ Writing" is one example, but there are many more. This is a quick way for bookstores to know where to place a book on their shelves. Libraries, of course, use the CIP data or LCCN, discussed on page 94, to decide the book's placement. (Visit the BISG website at bisg.org to determine your book's BISAC headings.)

- The book's price followed by "U.S." Yes, I know, who would forget to put a price on the back cover? But it happens far more often than you would imagine. For hardbacks with dustjackets, the price is placed on the front or back flap. Although some self-publishers prefer not to include a price, be aware that many wholesalers or distributors, and the bookstores they service, will accept only books that include a specific price on the back cover. Therefore, I strongly suggest printing the price on the cover.

- You might consider providing credit lines for the cover designer and the front cover photographer on the back cover, if you are using a photo. Alternatively, these credit lines can be placed on the copyright page of your book.

What Is an ISBN?

Whether you are applying for CIP data or putting together the back cover of your book, you will need an International Standard Book Number, or ISBN. An ISBN is a thirteen-digit number that acts as a unique identifier of a book for booksellers, libraries, book wholesalers, and book distributors. You will therefore require one if you wish to sell your book to these entities. International Standard Book Numbers are specific to their countries of issuance, and in the United States, they are exclusively provided by a company called R.R. Bowker LLC.

If your book is being published by a commercial or academic publishing house, the company you're working with will provide an ISBN for your book. If not, you can acquire an ISBN by visiting the Bowker identifier services website at www.myidentifiers.com and consulting the drop-down menu marked "ISBN," which should present you with options for purchasing one or more ISBNs. You can save money by buying ten ISBNs instead of just one, and you can save even more by purchasing one hundred numbers at a time. Just make sure that you will have enough projects to make use of all the ISBNs you buy.

Be aware that use of an ISBN is limited to the exact edition of the book for which it has been acquired. For example, a hardback version requires a different ISBN than its paperback counterpart, and an e-book gets its own ISBN. Once you have assigned an ISBN number to a book and put it into the system, you cannot reuse that ISBN number even if you decide not to go ahead with the book's publication.

Once your preliminary cover design has been put together, show it to people whose judgment you trust. These may be the same people who reviewed your book's working draft. By making the front and back covers as attractive, eye-catching, and informative as possible, you can help increase your book's sales and broaden its exposure.

STEP 6. PUTTING TOGETHER YOUR PROMOTION PLAN
[1 TO 4 MONTHS]

Before, during, or after you turn your book over to the typesetter and finalize at least the front cover of the book, take the opportunity to put together your overall promotion plan. If you are being published by a commercial or academic house that has an active publicity department, their staff should be putting together the publicity plan for your book. But even if someone else is creating a plan for you, it's a good idea to understand what goes into it. And, as mentioned earlier in the book, some commercial publishers fail to create and follow through with a solid promotional campaign, or stop promoting a book after a certain period of time. If you run into this problem, you will want to know how to gain publicity for your titles.

A promotion plan should include several important and necessary items that you will need to have on hand to begin letting the market-places and your potential audience know about your title, including:

- A formal release date for your title.

- A sales sheet.

- Advance reading copies (ARCs) of your book.

- A media kit.

- A list of the media that you believe will get the best visibility for you and your book.

THE RELEASE DATE

On page 88, I discussed factors that publishing companies keep in mind when they establish a release date, such as the sales season that would be most appropriate for a particular title. You must also keep in mind the timing of the release date relative to your submission of ARCs for reviews, as well as the time needed to establish a media presence. For example, most major reviewing journals require at least a four-month lead time, and some require as much as a six-month lead time, before a book's official release date. Although there is no guarantee that the eight major prepublication review outlets— *Booklist, Choice, Foreword Reviews, The Horn Book Magazine, Kirkus Reviews, Library Journal, PW (Publishers Weekly)*, and *School Library Journal*—will review your book, if you fail to submit a review copy within the specified time, you will eliminate the possibility of your book even being considered.

As a matter of practicality, I would have the ARCs of your book printed four to six months in advance of your official release date. (For more about ARCs, see page 115 of Chapter 7.) If your book is ready for the printer, you might print the actual book. You will then be able to give out the copies to reviewers and the media. However, for general sales purposes, you should keep to your official release date.

THE SALES SHEET

A sales sheet—sometimes called a sell sheet or tips sheet—is a one-sheet summary of your book's basic information. (See the sample sales sheets on pages 102 and 103.) It is important to put your sales sheet together as soon as you can, because it pulls together critical data that you will need to draw on in the months ahead, first, as you seek to secure blurbs and reviews, and later, when you set up speaking engagements. Every sales sheet should include the following material:

- An image of the book's cover.

- A two- or three-paragraph overview of the book.

- An "About the Author" paragraph.

- The book's all-important metadata, which is comprised of the book's title and subtitle, the author's name, the format (trim size and statement of its being paperback or hardback), the page count, the ISBN (see page 99), the retail list price (of all editions), and BISAC subject headings. (See the inset on page 104 to learn more about metadata. For information on BISAC subjects, see page 98.)

- A contact name, phone number, and email address for the person handling publicity.

Sales sheets can vary slightly in format as long as the basic information is presented in a clear and easy-to-understand manner, and the

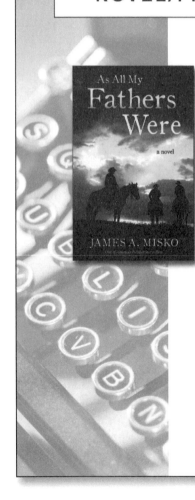

Contact Info: Anthony Pomes, VP – Marketing/PR/Rights
Square One Publishers (www.squareonepublishers.com)
Email: apomes@squareonepublishers.com
Phone: 516.535.2010 x 105 /

FEBRUARY 2017

$19.95 US / $29.95 CAN

416 pages

6 x 9-inch paperback

ISBN 978-096408264-9

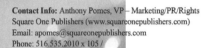

NOVEL/FICTION

AS ALL MY FATHERS WERE

James A. Misko

Brothers Richard and Seth Barrett are devoted to running the family ranch on Nebraska's Platte River, and they plan to do so for the rest of their lives. But their mother's will requires them to travel by horse and canoe along the river to understand why their maternal grandfather homesteaded the ranch three generations earlier. From her grave, their mother also commands them to observe the harm that industrial farming has done to the land, air, and water.

The Barrett brothers' journey is not to be a smooth one. A ninety-year-old bachelor farmer with a game plan of his own threatens to disrupt and delay the will's mandatory expedition. Using a gullible hometown sheriff and a corrupt local politician, he seeks to thwart their plans and seize the property. In this turbulent novel, the Platte River—a mile wide and an inch deep—becomes its own character and lives up to its legend of being too thick to drink and too thin to plow.

ABOUT THE AUTHOR

James A. Misko was born in Nebraska, then moved to Oregon and Alaska, completing what for him was a natural bridge to the frontier. He has worked as an oil field roughneck, a logger, truck driver, saw mill hand, teacher, journalist, real estate broker, and writer. With numerous published articles and five novels to his credit, he continues to work at being the best author of fiction he can be. Jim and his wife Patti live in Anchorage, Alaska during the summer, and Palm Springs, California in the winter.

WINNER OF

The IBPA Benjamin Franklin Award in Popular Fiction

The 2016 Feathered Quill Book Award
for the Best Adult Fiction

The NABE Pinnacle Book Achievement
Award for Fiction

The Nebraska Book of the Year Award

sheet is attractive. Because it is prepared in advance of a book's publication, a number of specifications may change—such as the page count and the price. It's very important to keep your sales sheet up to date. It can be handed out at lectures and book fairs, and used as a persuasive tool whenever an opportunity arises.

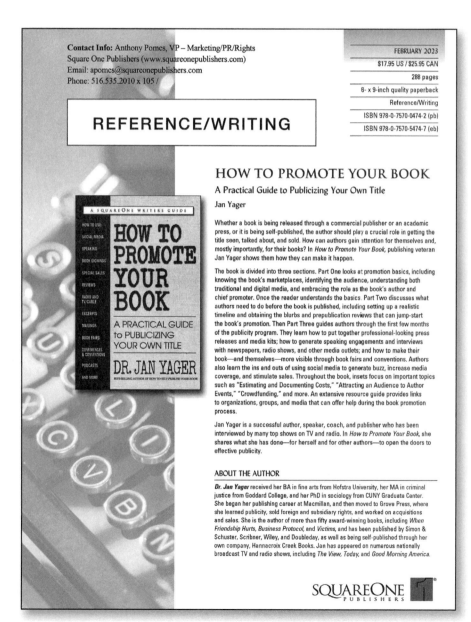

Contact Info: Anthony Pomes, VP – Marketing/PR/Rights
Square One Publishers (www.squareonepublishers.com)
Email: apomes@squareonepublishers.com
Phone: 516.535.2010 x 105 /

FEBRUARY 2023

$17.95 US / $25.95 CAN

288 pages

6- x 9-inch quality paperback

Reference/Writing

ISBN 978-0-7570-0474-2 (pb)

ISBN 978-0-7570-5474-7 (eb)

REFERENCE/WRITING

HOW TO PROMOTE YOUR BOOK
A Practical Guide to Publicizing Your Own Title

Jan Yager

Whether a book is being released through a commercial publisher or an academic press, or it is being self-published, the author should play a crucial role in getting the title seen, talked about, and sold. How can authors gain attention for themselves and, mostly importantly, for their books? In *How to Promote Your Book,* publishing veteran Jan Yager shows them how they can make it happen.

The book is divided into three sections. Part One looks at promotion basics, including knowing the book's marketplaces, identifying the audience, understanding both traditional and digital media, and embracing the role as the book's author and chief promoter. Once the reader understands the basics. Part Two discusses what authors need to do before the book is published, including setting up a realistic timeline and obtaining the blurbs and prepublication reviews that can jump-start the book's promotion. Then Part Three guides authors through the first few months of the publicity program. They learn how to put together professional-looking press releases and media kits; how to generate speaking engagements and interviews with newspapers, radio shows, and other media outlets; and how to make their book—and themselves—more visible through book fairs and conventions. Authors also learn the ins and outs of using social media to generate buzz, increase media coverage, and stimulate sales. Throughout the book, insets focus on important topics such as "Estimating and Documenting Costs," "Attracting an Audience to Author Events," "Crowdfunding," and more. An extensive resource guide provides links to organizations, groups, and media that can offer help during the book promotion process.

Jan Yager is a successful author, speaker, coach, and publisher who has been interviewed by many top shows on TV and radio. In *How to Promote Your Book,* she shares what she has done—for herself and for other authors—to open the doors to effective publicity.

ABOUT THE AUTHOR

Dr. Jan Yager received her BA in fine arts from Hofstra University, her MA in criminal justice from Goddard College, and her PhD in sociology from CUNY Graduate Center. She began her publishing career at Macmillan, and then moved to Grove Press, where she learned publicity, sold foreign and subsidiary rights, and worked on acquisitions and sales. She is the author of more than fifty award-winning books, including *When Friendship Hurts, Business Protocol,* and *Victims,* and has been published by Simon & Schuster, Scribner, Wiley, and Doubleday, as well as being self-published through her own company, Hannacroix Creek Books. Jan has appeared on numerous nationally broadcast TV and radio shows, including *The View, Today,* and *Good Morning America.*

A SQUAREONE WRITERS GUIDE

HOW TO USE:
SOCIAL MEDIA
SPEAKING
BOOK SIGNINGS
SPECIAL SALES
REVIEWS
RADIO AND TV/CABLE
EXCERPTS
MAILINGS
BOOK FAIRS
CONFERENCES & CONVENTIONS
PODCASTS
AND MORE

HOW TO PROMOTE YOUR BOOK
A PRACTICAL GUIDE to PUBLICIZING YOUR OWN TITLE
DR. JAN YAGER
BEST-SELLING AUTHOR OF HOW TO SELF-PUBLISH YOUR BOOK

SQUAREONE
PUBLISHERS

The Importance of Metadata

In the discussion of sales sheets on page 101, you learned that all sales sheets should contain your book's metadata. Since metadata is a crucial element of your book's marketing and sales strategy, it deserves further examination.

Formerly referred to as *specifications* (or *specs*), *metadata* is the data that describes your book, including the title and subtitle, the author's name, the trim size, the page count, the price, the ISBN, the category, and other relevant information. Why is it so important to supply this information when getting the word out about your book? Readers who search for books online unintentionally access book metadata, making your book easier to discover. By including good metadata, you will put your book on a potential reader's radar.

For a real-life example of how metadata is used online, look up a book that is similar to yours in genre and topic on Amazon.com. If you scroll down the page provided on that book, you will eventually find a section called "Product Details," which provides metadata such as the book's ISBN, format and page count, and the like. Within these details, you'll see "Best Sellers Rank," which shows how the book is ranked in sales within different categories. If you discover that a book which is similar to yours is selling well in several categories—for example, a work of fiction might be selling in "Women's & Literary Fiction," "Family Life Fiction," and "Mother's and Children's Fiction"—make sure to include these categories when providing your metadata. Don't stretch too far away from the topic and genre of your book, but use as many of the BISAC codes (see page 98) as are appropriate. Take every opportunity you can to provide metadata that will promote and guide potential readers to your work.

ADVANCE READING COPIES (ARCs)

ARCs (advance reading copies), which are bound typeset pages of a forthcoming book that are sometimes referred to as *bound galleys*, play an important part in getting blurbs and reviews and in generating media opportunities. You'll want to put these together as soon as your book has been typeset and proofed so that you can begin requesting blurbs and prepublication reviews. To learn more about creating ARCs, turn to page 115 of Chapter 7.

THE MEDIA KIT

A media kit, which is also called a press kit, is a package of key information about your forthcoming book and about you, the author of that book. It is called a media kit because it provides people with everything they need to know if they want to feature you or your title on their website; in their magazine, newspaper, or other publication; on their television or radio show; or on another media outlet.

Generally, a media kit consists of the following components:

- A press release.

- An author bio, including at least one author photograph.

- A list of potential questions for interviewers.

- A page of blurbs and/or excerpts from prepublication reviews.

- For fiction, an excerpt from your book.

- For nonfiction, any facts or statistics that highlight your book's importance.

You should begin working on your media kit before your book's release date so that the kit will be ready to go as soon as your book is available and you can begin publicizing it. Turn to Chapter 9 for detailed information on how you can create an effective media kit that will help you win media attention and spur sales.

MAKING A LIST OF APPROPRIATE MEDIA AND OTHER OUTLETS

Learning about and establishing a presence on both traditional and digital media will take some time. Based on what you've read in Chapters 3 and 4, put together a list of appropriate radio shows, TV shows, and podcasts, concentrating your efforts on shows that would be most likely to invite you as a guest. Then, as described in those chapters, visit each show's website to learn whom you should contact regarding a possible interview and to find the guidelines that can help you with your pitch. Also learn as much as you can about websites that you think could feature your book, and see if they offer selling tools that can provide you with a wider viewership. (You'll learn more about choosing appropriate media on page 177 of Chapter 9. If you are considering hiring an experienced publicist to handle your book promotion, see page 181 of Chapter 9 for information and guidance.)

Finally, call a few local bookstores and libraries to see if you can arrange some speaking engagements and book signings timed around your book's release. Make sure you have someone take photos and videos of each of your appearances, and call some local newspapers to see if they can send a reporter to cover the events. The worst that can happen is that they will say no.

Give yourself enough time to design a promotional plan that works within your budget and the time you have available. You will discover that there is a good deal of promotional work that you can and should get done before your book's release date. This work should help prepare you for the next step of your timeline.

STEP 7. YOUR RELEASE DATE HAS ARRIVED
[TIME TO BE DETERMINED]

It's the date of your book's official release. What if nothing happens—no phone calls from media outlets, no book signings, no interviews? While this is certainly a possibility, if you have planned correctly, the day your book is released will be one that you will always remember with great pride, because it will be the start of the next exciting phase of your promotional campaign. Perhaps you've lined up several book signings at bookstores, you have an appointment for an interview with a local newspaper, and you are throwing a party at a restaurant and have invited friends and some members of the media to attend. At the party, you speak about your book and you sign copies for all those who have come. Or perhaps you've created a publication-day party on Zoom attended by friends, family, early readers of your book, and even some media people who are interested in you and your title.

There are many scenarios that could occur based on all the effort you've put into your timeline, but that official release is really only a date you have chosen so you could create an effective promotional campaign for your book. Planning is the key to any author's promotional plans, and at this point, you should have a clear idea of what you need to do and how you will accomplish it.

CONCLUSION

In this chapter, you learned about the realistic timelines that you need to consider. One of the most important concepts that the chapter discussed is this: Just because you can go from a typeset manuscript to printed copies within a few days, or even within a few hours, it does not mean that doing so would be in your best interest. Book promotion takes time, and you need to learn and follow the book industry's protocols for pitching a book and setting up a promotional campaign. For example, those publications that state they require ARCs to be sent four to six months or more before publication, and no later, mean just that. They will not review a book that has officially been released.

As the timelines in this chapter reveal, there is a good deal that your publisher, your publicist, or you need to take care of in terms of promoting your book. It might seem as if you'll be twiddling your thumbs during the months between the completion of your book and its release date, but far from it! If you perform all the many promotion-related tasks that require your attention during this period, you will be very busy, and the time will fly by. In the next two chapters, you will learn more about two important promotional tasks discussed earlier in this chapter: getting advance blurbs and getting reviews.

7.

Getting Advance Blurbs or Endorsements

Whether this is your first book or your tenth, it's important to get advance positive blurbs (quotes) and endorsements that can help you announce to the world that you are a credible author and that your book is worth reading. The fact is that getting blurbs will start the promotional ball rolling. When authors are commercially published, it is often their publisher who obtains the advance blurbs for the author's titles, but that is not always the case. Some publishers rely on their authors to obtain blurbs. If you are self-published, of course, this responsibility will fall entirely on your shoulders. When blurbs are good quality and provided by the right people and publications, they not only put a positive spin on a book, but can also open doors to book reviews, book signings, interviews, speaking engagements, and other opportunities.

In the previous chapter—which set out a timeline for the completion of your manuscript, your book's production, and pre-marketing tasks—we began to explore why getting blurbs is an important part of marketing. In this chapter, you will learn about the two major types of blurbs, why and how you should get them, and how they can best be used to promote your book.

WHAT IS A BLURB AND WHY IS IT IMPORTANT?

A *blurb*—also referred to as a *testimonial* or an *advance endorsement*—is a one-, two-, or three-line quote extolling the merits of a book or the talents of the book's author. There are two types of blurbs. The first type you will be gathering are *unpublished endorsements*. As the name implies, these come not from published reviews but from individuals, including authors of similar books or, if your book is a work of nonfiction, from experts in the subject of your book. The second type of blurbs are called *published endorsements*. This refers to any positive reviews that are produced by an established periodical, organization, or association.

Blurbs can be effective promotional tools before your book's publication, when the book becomes available to readers, and even years after it is published. When strong unpublished endorsements are sent to a periodical along with advance reading copies (ARCs), the blurbs show that someone—maybe just one, but perhaps a half dozen people who are hopefully notable—think that your book is worthwhile. This may impress editors so much that they mark your book for review. Published endorsements show that a trusted source—such as *Library Journal* or perhaps a magazine or newspaper—has deemed your book to be outstanding, and that it is worth reading, stocking in a bookstore, or adding to a library's collection. In other words, blurbs can be a powerful way to make people pay more attention to you and your book.

If you are a self-published author, and especially a first-time author, it may be difficult or even impossible to obtain a review in industry-based journals. (You'll learn more about this in Chapter 8.) It is far more feasible for you to get an unpublished endorsement from an individual. Don't let this discourage you, though! When people see a blurb from a well-regarded author printed on your book's cover, it may very well persuade them to buy the book. And as already mentioned, if you are able to get strong unpublished blurbs, they may help you catch the eye of editors of journals or other publications.

WHEN SHOULD YOU BEGIN TO GATHER BLURBS?

As explained in Chapter 6, you should start reaching out to appropriate people for unpublished blurbs before the cover and interior of your book have been finished. This will allow you to gather quotations before the book is released so that you can potentially use the blurbs on your book cover, in the interior of your book, and in media kits. (On page 119 of this chapter, you'll find a more comprehensive list of effective uses for blurbs.)

Published endorsements—which can be culled from reviews in trade journals, but can also come from other publications—are based on ARC (advance reading copy) submissions sent to periodicals. Most major reviewing journals require at least a four-month lead time before a book's official release date, and some request even longer lead times. This protocol exists because most journals are published for the benefit of bookstores and libraries, who need time to order books so they can make them available for sale or loan as soon as the books are released. For this reason, journals normally want to publish their reviews months before a book's actual publication.

The process of obtaining reviews from the main trade journals and other publications is treated in detail in Chapter 8. The discussion below, therefore, focuses on getting unpublished endorsements and blurbs.

WHOM SHOULD YOU ASK FOR UNPUBLISHED ENDORSEMENTS?

The most effective unpublished endorsements should come from people whose books are similar to yours in genre or subject matter. They should not come from people who have no relationship to the type of book you have written unless the blurb writer is so famous that she has thousands or even millions of followers. It pays to remember, however, that getting a review from a person with this many followers is a long shot.

Let's say that you have written a novel, and that your friend, a lawyer, loves your book and is willing to write a glowing recommendation for it. Would this look good on your promotional material or book cover? In most cases, the answer would be "no." While some people might not notice the inappropriate blurb, those who did would think, "Why is a lawyer I've never heard of praising this book?" And then they'd realize that she's probably your friend. Worse yet, anyone in the book business would immediately know that this type of endorsement is common in self-published books. In what case would you say "yes" to the lawyer's blurb? If your book is a crime novel, and the lawyer is a defense attorney, her blurb could be helpful. Use your judgment to decide whose endorsements would influence a potential reader or the media in a positive way.

So who should supply you with a good early blurb? It depends on the nature of your book.

If Your Book Is Fiction

If you have written a work of fiction, blurbs should ideally come from authors whose books are similar to yours in genre. For example, the best blurbs for a thriller should come from the authors of thrillers, the best blurbs for romance novels should come from romance book authors, etc.

Having a best-selling author endorse your title would be wonderful, so if you are lucky enough to have a connection with a highly successful writer of fiction—for instance, if you are members of the same association—don't be afraid to reach out to her. If you don't have that type of connection, though, getting the endorsement of any published author might do the trick. Just make sure to place the best-known book title of that author under or next to her name so that the reader realizes that this person is a published writer.

Over the years, I have reached out to best-selling authors through writers associations that I belonged to, and some authors have been open to reading and endorsing the manuscript that they received. Of course, I have also received quite a few responses to the effect that the author was sorry, but she was not doing any more endorsements at that time, or she was just finishing up her own novel and she never reads someone else's writing when she's working on her own book. But when the answer was "yes" and the endorsements were positive, the results were well worth the effort, as those quotes definitely helped to launch several titles. (For advice on how to reach out to authors and other people for blurbs, see the discussion on page 113.)

If Your Book Is Nonfiction

Like the best blurbs for fiction books, the ideal endorsements for non-fiction books come from nonfiction authors whose books are related to yours. So if you've written a book on economics, for example, an ideal "blurber" could be the author of a respected book on economics or, for that matter, simply a well-known economist. Preferably, the quote should come from someone who has a strong association with both the material in your book *and* your potential readers. In other words, it's better to get a quote from a person who is unknown outside your niche but is well known by your particular audience than it is to get a quote from someone who is well known by the general public but has no connection to your book or its topic.

Of course, it is not always easy to get a recognized expert in your subject to provide you with a quote, but there is a good alternative. If the endorser's name does not stand out, be sure to include her credentials after her name—such as PhD, MD, MBA, or MSW—to make it clear that she is a professional in that field of study. As a writer who is knowledgeable in your area, you should know exactly which qualifications would be impressive, as well as which organization that the endorser belongs to would impress a potential reader.

Especially if this is your first nonfiction book, the more unpublished endorsements you can get from related authorities, the better. When I was finishing my book *Friendshifts: The Power of Friendship and How It Shapes Our Lives*, I looked over a copy of Stephen Covey's bestseller *The 7 Habits of Highly Effective People*. On the book's half-title page— the sheet that precedes the title page—I counted more than a dozen endorsements, so I set a similar goal for myself. Through persistence, I reached my goal, and those blurbs probably helped my book become a success!

REACHING OUT TO PEOPLE FOR BLURBS

While some writers know a number of people whom they can contact to get appropriate blurbs, some do not. If you are not acquainted with anyone suitable, try to network with your friends to see if they have any contacts. If you belong to a writers group, see if any of the group's members would be appropriate. And don't limit yourself to one or two people. Because everyone is so busy these days, unless you know that the people you are contacting are a "sure thing," ask as many as ten or twenty people for blurbs. While you might wind up with ten blurbs, you don't have to use all of them. Use only the ones that you think will work best for your book and your promotional material.

Once you have come up with the names of people who might provide an effective quote, you face the task of reaching out to them and making your request. For some authors, this can be embarrassing and difficult. However, if you are determined to promote your book, requesting a quote is really just part of the territory. You are going to wind up asking a lot of people for many such things, such as book signings and interviews, so now is a good time to start honing your skills as a salesman, a role that was discussed in Chapter 5. If you personally know someone or you know of someone—such as another author or an expert in your field—who could provide an appropriate blurb, one of your best options is to make your pitch over the phone. But if you cannot find the author's phone number, or if your phone call goes to voice mail and you choose not to leave a message since it is doubtful that it will be returned, your second-best option is to query the person in an email and follow it with an old-fashioned letter and an advance reading copy (ARC) of your book. If the person prefers a PDF, send that instead. (To learn about ARCs and PDFs, see the discussion on page 115.)

Before contacting someone by phone—or in person, if that is possible—rehearse what you are going to say. If you approach a well-known author, for instance, begin your pitch by mentioning one or more of her books that you have read and admired. Succinctly explain why you hope she will read your manuscript and, if she likes it, provide you with an endorsement. Prepare yourself to hear that person say, "No, sorry, I'm just too busy," without taking it as a rejection. Also consider what you will say if someone says "yes." Be aware that she may ask you how soon you'll need the quote. Avoid saying, "Whenever you can get it to me" or "ASAP." Most people prefer a specific date. Your potential endorser can then tell you if the deadline is reasonable for her. If it is not, and if you are able to provide more time, offer a later deadline.

During my years of requesting blurbs for my books, I have rethought the idea of a blurb as a favor for only the book author who is making the request. Seen in a different light, it is also a potentially positive source of exposure for the person who is writing the blurb. When another author or expert is associated with a quality book, she is benefitting from getting her name out there. You should never imply that the prospective endorser is lucky to get the free publicity provided by a blurb that features her name, because that would seem self-serving and smug. But if you look at the process from this perspective, you might feel less intimidated, as you will no longer think of yourself as someone who is begging for assistance. Instead, you will view it as an exchange of favors.

In most cases, you will probably be contacting people by email. On pages 116, 117, and 118, you will find three letters that I have used when contacting prospective writers of blurbs for my books. Sample 1 is a template for writing to a total stranger to determine if she would be willing to read your book and provide a blurb. Sample 2 is a template for writing to someone you've made contact with through social media to see if she would provide a blurb. Sample 3 is template for responding to someone who has already provided a review of your book via email. In such a case, it is a good idea to obtain written permission to use the author's words and name in a promotional piece.

If you don't know the person whom you want to contact, how can you find or request her email address so that you can submit your initial blurb request? If you already have a connection to that individual on LinkedIn, even though you are not colleagues, you will probably be able to find a personal or business email in the Contact section of her profile. If she is not yet a LinkedIn connection, see if you arrange it by asking for a connection. If you prefer to find the person's contact information outside of LinkedIn, visit her business or personal website, if she has one. In most cases, the website will provide a means of getting in touch, whether it is a direct email address or a Contact Us form. You might also try the person's Facebook or Twitter accounts. If she has published a book, you may find an email address (or a related website) included in the About the Author page of the book. Finally, if you belong to the same association and it offers a directory of members, that might give you the information you need.

HOW SHOULD YOU SEND YOUR BOOK TO PROSPECTIVE ENDORSERS?

Commercial publishing companies send out *advance reading copies,* or *ARCs*—bound typeset pages of a forthcoming book—to obtain endorsements and reviews. This can be expensive for a self-published author, but it's also the safest route. When you use ARCs, your book is less likely to end up on the Internet, where everyone can read it free of cost. You can have printed-out pages bound fairly inexpensively by Kinko's, Staples, Amazon, and Lightning Source. The phrase "ADVANCE READING COPY" should appear on the front or back cover and/or on the title page of the ARC. These words can be printed on labels, such as Avery labels, and run off on a printer.

A more cost-effective route is to send out password-protected PDFs to the people who will potentially provide blurbs. (You can password-protect a PDF using a program like Adobe Acrobat.) This means that you provide the password in your accompanying emailed letter so

SAMPLE 1—REQUESTING A BLURB FROM A STRANGER

Dear [Name of Recipient]:

I have admired your novels, including _____,
for several years, reading _____ as well as
_____. Although we have never met, we are
both members of the _____ Association.

    [Name of Recipient], I know you are very busy, and I know
that you also must get many requests like this one, but if you
could please give my new novel, _____,
a reading, I would be so very grateful. If you like it and are able
to share a short blurb about it, I will, of course, mention the
title of your book after your name.

    A brief summary of the plot is as follows:

_____

_____.

    For more about my background, please visit my website:

_____

    My publisher is planning to do a big push on my novel to
bookstores, libraries, and media, so your quote and title will
be exposed to a many potential new readers and fans. *[Note:
If you are going to be self-published, replace "my publisher is
planning to do" with "my marketing plans include."]*

    Thanks again for your consideration. I will be forever
grateful if you are able to read my novel and provide a blurb.

Sincerely yours,

[Your Name]

SAMPLE 2—REQUESTING A BLURB FROM SOMEONE YOU KNOW THROUGH SOCIAL MEDIA

Dear [Name of Recipient]:

I'm pleased to follow up on our pleasant recent exchanges on LinkedIn. As you may remember, I've been working on a book about _____ for the last few years. I'm happy to let you know that I finally have a working finished draft!

I'd like to send a copy to you, and if you like what you read, to ask you to provide a blurb or advance endorsement I might use on the back cover, in the front matter, or in the marketing materials. I would, of course, include the title of your own book, _____, after your name, or include whatever credit you think is appropriate.

If you are open to this, please let me know if you prefer to receive the manuscript as a PDF file attached in a follow-up email or if you want me to print out the manuscript and mail the printed copy to you.

I look forward to hearing from you at your earliest convenience, and I thank you in advance for your consideration.

Best wishes,

[Your Name]

SAMPLE 3—GETTING PERMISSION TO USE A BLURB EXCERPTED FROM AN EMAIL

Dear [Name of Recipient]:

I'd welcome pulling this quote out of your wonderful email below, with your permission of course.

> *[Note: Insert here the quote from the original email that you would like to use, followed by the person's credentials and/or identifying publication.]*

Of course, you should feel free to expand on this quote, to rewrite it, or to turn down this request. Whatever you decide to do, I'm still very grateful for the comments you provided in your original email.

Best wishes,

[Your Name]

Another Source of Blurbs

In addition to requesting quotations from other authors and experts and selecting them from published material, if you've written previous books, you can use old blurbs or published reviews from previous books as testimonials. Search your old reviews—including those on Amazon and other retail websites—for an extra blurb or two. It's true that the quotation won't specifically refer to your latest book, but if it praises you, your writing, or your expertise, it can make an effective blurb—until you have something to share about your new book. Be sure to indicate which book is being referred to.

that anyone else who comes across the PDF can't open it. If you absolutely trust the people who are receiving the PDFs, you don't have to supply password protection, but in your email, be sure to request that the recipient not send the PDF to other people.

HOW CAN YOU USE YOUR BLURBS?

You can use blurbs in many ways to garner publicity for your book, and, of course, to sell more copies. Here are some effective uses:

- Place blurbs on the back cover of your book or on one or both sides of the half-title page, which is the sheet that comes before the title page.

- Print an especially strong quote—one from a popular author, a well-known expert, or a prominent journal—on the top of the front cover.

- If your book is a hardcover with a dust jacket, place a quote on the inside front or back of the book jacket.

- Incorporate blurbs in your sales sheets and media kits.

- Include blurbs on your own website where you're promoting your newest book.

- Feature blurbs at the top of your book description on retail sites such as Amazon.

- Include a blurb for your newest book on your Facebook cover page, your Twitter header photo, and elsewhere in social media.

- Print a short but compelling blurb on bookmarks, mugs, t-shirts, and other imprinted items that you use as crowdfunding rewards or promotional giveaways.

Whether you are printing a blurb on the cover of your book, on a sales sheet, or elsewhere, make sure that the quotation stands out and is legible. Don't use a font so ornate that the reviewer, bookseller, or potential buyer won't be able to quickly read and appreciate the wonderful comment that someone made about you or your book. If you look at blurbs on the covers and half-title pages of some best-selling books, you'll see how these quotations can be made both attractive and readable. An examination of professionally produced books may also show you that you can pull out the most powerful phrase from an endorsement and use that phrase as your blurb rather than using an entire sentence.

One last thought on using blurbs. You may get only unpublished endorsements during the time you're typesetting your book and preparing your cover—which, as you know, is a good place to feature blurbs. But if you do get a great published endorsement through an advance review, you may want to hold up printing so you can add it to the front or back cover. If there really isn't time to add a particularly strong blurb during this first printing, consider including it in the next printing. If your book is being produced as a POD (print on demand) title, add the blurb when you are able to make updates.

CONCLUSION

As you've learned in this chapter, good blurbs can be effective promotional tools that can help persuade a journal editor to review your book, turn a bookstore or website browser into a book buyer, or win the attention of the media. The trick is to start gathering blurbs as soon as you can in the production process and to get them from the right people. Unfortunately, many authors realize too late that it would have been a good idea to solicit quotes ahead of their book's release date. That doesn't have to be you. By recognizing just how important these blurbs can be, you can use the same promotional tactic that all the major publishing houses employ. We have all heard that a picture is worth a thousand words, but I have found that a few well-chosen words from authors and experts can sell more books than any picture ever could.

Now you may be wondering how you can get the reviews from which you will be able to select published endorsements. Before you begin sending off ARCs, printed books, and PDFs, you need to know that a good many barriers exist between an author and a published review. The next chapter takes a closer look at what is involved in getting your book considered for review in traditional reviewing platforms—such as trade journals, magazines, and newspapers—as well as free or fee-based Internet-based platforms.

8.

Getting Reviews

I n Chapter 7, you learned how to secure and use blurbs to help make your book stand out. Part of that strategy involved gathering selected excerpts from book reviews. But as you discovered in previous chapters, it is challenging to obtain published reviews from the larger traditional media outlets when your book has been produced by a small press or has been self-published. Even if you have been published by a major commercial house and its publicity department submitted your book for review, your title could have been overlooked because of the sheer volume of books submitted each month. On the other hand, gathering positive book reviews from the comparatively new (and always evolving) social media landscape, as well from smaller local and specialty publications, presents far fewer barriers.

This chapter looks at the many different types of media that can potentially review your book, from prepublication trade journals to magazines and newspapers to Internet sites and more. Before covering these different media in depth, however, it's important to address some of the tougher realities that are at play when an author sends out a book for review.

WHO GETS REVIEWED—AND WHO DOESN'T

The task of getting a book past an editorial assistant's desk and into the hands of an actual book reviewer is less challenging for a commercial publishing house than it is for self-published authors. When dealing with most trade prepublication journals, a publishing house's publicity person knows who should receive an ARC (advance reading copy), when it should be sent (generally, at least four months prior to publication), and what materials should accompany it. This does *not* mean that the book will definitely be reviewed, but it does mean that the book will at least be considered by the right group of people. There are time-honored procedures within the world of book publishing, and these protocols are a major stumbling block to those who don't know about them.

Be aware that even those who have long worked within the book industry face a decidedly uphill battle when they try to get books reviewed by key publications, including trade journals such as *Publishers Weekly*, commonly referred to as *PW*. If, however, the author of the new book is already a proven best-selling writer, a celebrity, or a well-known newsmaker, this added level of status and popularity can frequently place the title on the "fast track" for review. This does not mean that a good book by an unknown writer published by an established publisher will not be reviewed. It does happen, as publishing history has quite often shown. But certain attitudes and practices in the publishing and reviewing world have changed very little over the past one hundred and fifty years.

Now the question becomes: Can books that are produced by hybrid publishers or self-publishers get reviewed? The answer is a bit more complicated than one might think. In the past, self-published books were almost *never* reviewed by the mainstream media. However, things have steadily begun to change—to a point. If a book is self-published and looks like a commercially published title, and the book's topic is compelling or falls in line with what the reviewer is looking for, these titles can (and *do)* get reviewed. If a book *looks* self-published—and, unfortunately, many do—the ARC is quickly tossed into the rejection pile. While this allows some self-published books to get reviewed, just keep in mind that it is still a long shot.

Fortunately, with the surge of self-published books in the past few years, a new way of getting reviews has emerged. Some book-reviewing journals now offer "paid" reviews. As you can imagine, this new service was initially frowned upon and even ridiculed by many in the industry, who regarded it as nothing more or less than an unprincipled cash grab. As time passed, however, this paid review scenario has become increasingly commonplace from season to season. While paying for a review does not guarantee a positive appraisal, and it certainly doesn't have the clout and status associated with reviews that appear in prestigious journals, it often does allow self-published authors to receive reviews for use in their book's promotion. (We will take a closer look at paid review services later in this chapter.)

Due to the growing popularity of e-books, there is now another way for self-published books to win reviews. Updated constantly, Amazon's list of Kindle e-book bestsellers shows the best-selling e-books available at that time. In many cases, the authors or their publicists have done a really good job of promoting their titles to get these sales. If an e-book lands on these lists, it is more likely to win coverage by an established book reviewer who might have otherwise ignored the title. Clearly, these lists are game changers for self-publishers—both in securing book review coverage and in increasing a book's relative visibility.

With all of this in mind, it's time to consider your best options for getting your work actually seen, considered, and, hopefully, reviewed.

THE REVIEWERS

There are two types of reviewers of which you should be aware. The first are highly qualified book reviewers who normally get paid to read and evaluate titles. These reviewers may be librarians, journalists, educators, or professionals in their own respective fields, and their reviews are published in traditional reviewing publications.

The second type of reviewer is a nonprofessional. These are people who have read a book and then posted their comments online. They do not get paid. As you will see, both professional and nonprofessional reviews are found on the many Internet-based reviewing platforms. They are both important and should be used appropriately.

Good reviews written by professionals should be made part of your media campaign and can be used on many online platforms to enhance the credibility of a title. How about good reviews from nonprofessionals? Consider a book on Amazon that has received ten five-star ratings from readers. This rating will definitely attract the attention of other readers who are browsing the site. But would you use this nonprofessional review in your promotional copy? Probably not. On the other hand, driving people to your book's Amazon site to read these reviews and post further reviews would be a good idea and can lead to sales. (See page 151 for information on encouraging readers to post reviews on online retail sites.)

How Should You Send Out
Copies of Your Book for Review?

Before you begin choosing the publications and other media outlets to which you will send your book for review, let's explore the various forms in which advance book copies can be sent or otherwise made available to the media.

For many years, prepublication trade journals, such as *PW* and *Kirkus Reviews*, usually wanted to receive ARCs, or advance reading copies, which were bound printed pages of the typeset book. As discussed earlier in the book (see page 115), you can have these pages bound fairly inexpensively by businesses such as Staples. If you intend to print twenty or more copies, you might instead want to use a POD (print on demand) printer, as this will reduce the price per copy.

Nowadays, many prepublication journals—as well as many magazines, newspapers, and other media—will accept digital copies of a book, and some even prefer this form. As explained in previous chapters (see page 115), a PDF read-only document is usually acceptable. By using a program such as Adobe Acrobat, a PDF can be password-protected so that only the recipient of your email can read the document. This will prevent your digital book from potentially being made available free of charge to everyone with Internet access.

Which version—paper or digital—is preferable? Well, if the submission guidelines of a publication or other media outlet stipulate that it only wants "bound galleys" (ARCs) or it only wants a digital version of the book, you should provide what the guidelines request. When given a choice, however, my personal preference is to use paper ARCs. Sure, they're more expensive to send out, but I feel that even when digital versions are accepted, they may just sit unread in someone's in-box.

Yet another option for getting copies of your book "out there" is available via the Internet. The paid services NetGalley and Edelweiss enable you to post a DRC, or digital review copy, of your book on their sites. Then, interested reviewers can request review copies directly from these companies. You will learn more about these services on page 126.

Finally, some media will accept final printed copies of your book. It should go without saying that you should always carefully read the media outlet's submission guidelines—usually available on their website—to determine which form of the book they want to receive as well as what other materials and information should accompany the book. (To learn more about ancillary materials, see the discussion below.)

WHAT SHOULD YOU SEND REVIEWERS ALONG WITH YOUR BOOK?

The inset on page 124 explains the various forms in which advance book copies can be made available to potential reviewers. Once you are ready to mail or email out the review copies of your book, you'll also want to put together appropriate material to send along with your title. Generally, your book should be accompanied by a well-written cover letter that is customized to fit the recipient and his particular media outlet.

A good cover letter to a potential book reviewer should include the following:

- In the first paragraph, state that you are providing an "uncorrected advance reading copy," or whatever version of the book you're sending. In this same paragraph, provide the book's title and subtitle, the author's name, and the expected date of publication. When adding the book's release date, remember the lead time, if any, required by that particular type of media.

- Below the first paragraph, provide a block of text that presents the book's all-important metadata, including the ISBN (or ISBNs, if you have more than one version of your book, such as paperback and e-book), retail price (or prices), trim size, subject category or categories, and page count.

- In the second paragraph (and possibly continuing for two or more paragraphs), provide a full description of your book. This description can be copied from your sales sheet, the book's back cover, or, if your book is a hardback, the inside flaps.

- In the final paragraph, request that the editor/reviewer contact you or your publisher if the review has been assigned and is set to be published. Be sure to include your full contact information—your name, email, and phone number.

Making Your Book Available to Potential Reviewers Through NetGalley and Edelweiss

In the inset on page 124, we discuss sending out review copies of your book via email and regular mail. But there are other ways to make your book available to potential reviewers, including reviewers who you might not even know exist.

The digital platforms NetGalley (owned by Media Do International) and Edelweiss (owned by Above the Treeline) are designed to help both commercial publishers and self-publishers gain visibility for their titles with print and online reviewers, librarians, booksellers, educators, bloggers, and the media. Publishers or self-published authors pay a fee to make DRCs (digital review copies) of their books available on the NetGalley or Edelweiss website. (Note that members of the Independent Book Publishers Association, or IBPA, pay a reduced subscription rate.) In addition to providing a DRC, you as the author enter bibliographic data about your book so that other site users can find the title. When potential reviewers and others ask for access to the DRC, depending on the service, either the reviewer will automatically receive the DRC or you will be given the chance to accept or deny his request. Both systems may flag potential reviewers as being questionable. Reviewers and others who request DRCs do not have to pay a fee.

The two services mirror each other in many respects, but there are some differences between them. Although both NetGalley and Edelweiss make digital copies and audiobooks available for review, only Edelweiss makes it possible for users to print out paper ARCs. For some self-publishers, this is an important option. In addition, while Edelweiss gives you the option of accepting or rejecting the request for a review copy, some of NetGalley's service packages do not provide you with this option, so you should select your service package carefully. In the end, either service can potentially help you to obtain a number of book reviews—above and beyond those you might obtain by just following the usual submission protocols.

A sample cover letter designed for a prepublication journal is provided on page 128. But be aware that in some cases, you should customize the letter according to the type of media you're approaching. For instance, if you are writing to a local newspaper, in the first paragraph of your letter, carefully spell out the "local" connection that exists between the recipient's publication and your book (or you as the author). If you are addressing an alumni newsletter, point out that you are an alumnus. In other words, when possible, use that first paragraph to explain why your book is such a good fit for that particular publication or show.

In Chapter 7, you learned that blurbs can help persuade people in the media that your book is worth reviewing. While this is true, be aware that blurbs should be used only when appropriate and only selectively. If your nonfiction book has received praise from an expert in your field, if your work of fiction has been endorsed by a best-selling author in your genre, or if you have received a great blurb from an individual who is universally known and respected, include that blurb in the first paragraph of your letter. To make sure that the recipient of the package will notice the blurb, set it in a bold font, and even use a yellow highlighting marker to make it stand out. If you have received several outstanding blurbs, you can print them on a separate page entitled "Advance Prepublication Blurbs" and place the sheet behind the cover letter in your package. (Be sure to mention the sheet of blurbs in your cover letter.) But avoid sending reviews written by professional reviewers to other professional reviewers, as it may seem as if you're telling the recipient what to write. And if none of your blurbs meets the standards just described, simply don't use any.

At this point, you may be wondering if you should include a sales sheet in your package. After all, a sales sheet presents all the important information about your book. But when sending out books for review, it is advisable to send out a letter rather than a sales sheet, as a letter allows you to address the recipient by name and potentially customize your approach.

WHERE TO REACH OUT FOR REVIEWS

As you will soon discover, there are literally thousands of places where books can be sent for potential review. While it would not make sense to

SQUAREONE
PUBLISHERS

June 25, 2021

Kirkus Reviews
Attn: Nonfiction Reviews
49 West 23rd St., Ninth Floor
New York, NY 10010

Dear Eric:

Enclosed you will find an *uncorrected advance reading copy* of our forthcoming Health title, *Max Your Immunity: How to Maximize Your Immune System When You Need It Most* by Pamela Wartian Smith, MD, MPH. This book has a publication date of **October 2021**, and we are pleased to let you know that **Dr. Smith will appear on PBS-TV nationwide** this Fall to discuss and promote this book.

Book specs: ISBN: 978-0-7570-0512-1 (E-book ISBN: 978-0-7570-5512-6) • $16.95 US ($23.95 CAN) / 6 x 9-inch quality paperback • Health / Nutrition * 280 pgs.

The word *immunity* has unfortunately become an all-too-common term in our vocabulary, and for good reason. When the pandemic hit, many of the major drug companies created vaccines that offered us "immunity" against this specific virus. Yet, few of us understand that almost all these vaccines work based upon their activating our own built-in systems of defense. It is our very own immunity to these viruses that can make the difference between illness and health. To help clarify what each of us can do to protect ourselves and our loved ones, Pamela Wartian Smith, MD has written **Max Your Immunity**. Here is a complete guide to understanding and maximizing your natural defenses against various infectious diseases.

Max Your Immunity is divided into three parts. Part One explains how our innate and adaptive immunity systems work. Our innate immunity system is based on our built-in barriers designed to fi ght or separate us from infectious agents. Our adaptive immunity, also called acquired immunity, is composed of lymphocyte cells that are triggered when a specific pathogen enters the body. These cells learn to identify the invading pathogens and hunt them down. In this section, each component in both systems is clearly identified and explained. Part Two provides ten important things that you can do to increase and strengthen all of these components. And Part Three provides specific nutritional plans to increase your body's immunity to help defend off the most common health disorders.

By simply having a clear understanding of how our internal defenses work and what we can do to increase our immunity; we can play an important role in maintaining good health. *Max Your Immunity* can help show you what you need to know to protect yourself and your family.

Please let me know when a review of this new book may run in *Kirkus Reviews.* You can reach me by phone, fax, or by email.

Thank you, Eric.

Sincerely,

Anthony Pomes
Vice President, Marketing/PR/Rights

Enc.

spend the time and money necessary to reach out to every one of them, there are still a number of important review sources to consider. Most of them fall into one of three general categories: traditional reviewing platforms, Internet-based reviewing platforms, and reviews for pay platforms. When used appropriately, they can provide visibility and creditability for your title, while also generating sales. The trick, of course, is to get these media to review your book. Let's look at how that can be done for each of these platforms.

TRADITIONAL REVIEWING PLATFORMS

Most of us have been exposed to any number of traditional book reviewing platforms. These include newspapers and other periodicals, television, and radio—all based in traditional media. As a general rule, however, there is an established order in which you should seek reviews. First, you should submit your book for prepublication review in book trade journals. After that, you can send your book to post-publication reviewing platforms, which include almost every traditional media outlet that offers book reviews. So you don't wind up going down a rabbit hole, these reviewers should be carefully selected based on the audience you hope to reach. It should also be noted that with the expansion of the Internet's reach, all periodicals and television and radio shows that review titles are now also available online.

■ PREPUBLICATION BOOK TRADE REVIEWS

The eight periodicals discussed below are the key prepublication trade journals in which all commercial book publishers hope to have their books reviewed—based on the book's audience. Many years ago, the reviews that appeared in these journals ranged from starred reviews to toxic killers. This is less true today, because some journals have chosen to print mostly positive reviews and leave out negative ones. This trend is especially true of journals whose readers include a good number of librarians, as the publications' editors have found that librarians want them to highlight good-quality books that would make valuable additions to their collections.

Each of these journals has a rigid submission process that all publishers must follow. Their submission requirements are available on their websites, which are provided in the discussions below. Depending on their guidelines, your title may have to be sent as an ARC, PDF, e-book, or final printed book. (See the inset on page 124, which focuses on the forms in which your typeset book can be provided to reviewers.) In some cases, only one paper ARC—or *bound galleys*, as they're often called—or one book is requested, but in some cases, you are asked to send two. It is important to submit the format requested. As a general rule, you must send in your book at least four months before its official release date, although as you will see when you read each publication's guidelines, some journals request a longer lead time. Since these policies can change, it's important to check each publication's current guidelines before making a submission.

As I've said many times, if a book is not submitted from a commercial publisher or it appears to be self-published, the chance of its getting reviewed in these eight key publications is very slim. However, if your book looks professionally produced and is in line with the target publication's focus, you stand a chance. If it doesn't happen, keep in mind that this chapter discusses many other outlets that might be more receptive to your book.

Booklist

Established in 1905, *Booklist* is an official journal of the American Library Association (ALA), the key trade association for librarians, with an estimated 55,000 members. It is published twenty-two times a year, reviews over 7,500 titles annually, and has a circulation of 11,000 subscribers, with a pass-along of approximately 77,000 other readers.

Booklist offers critical reviews of audiovisual materials and books on all topics and genres (including reference books) designed for readers of all ages. It is a respected resource for school librarians, educators, public librarians, and booksellers, helping them decide which materials are best suited for their students and patrons. In addition to its print version, *Booklist* can be found online at www.booklistonline.com.

Booklist accepts ARCs and PDFs at least four months (fifteen weeks) in advance of the book's publication date, along with a cover letter containing specified data. One ARC is requested for adult books, and two ARCs for children's and YA books. The *Booklist* website states that their editors "carefully consider self-published titles that meet our reviewing criteria." However, the website also encourages authors to consider the services of their partner *BlueInk Review,* a pay reviewing service discussed on page 153.

You can find *Booklist's* detailed submission instructions, along with a list of editors and the categories they cover, at: https://www.ala.org/aboutala/offices/booklist/insidebooklist/book listproc/proceduressubmitting

If you send paper rather than digital copies to *Booklist,* the following address should be used. Be sure to include the appropriate editor's name in your address.

Att: [Editor's name]
Booklist
American Library Association
225 N Michigan Ave, Suite 130
Chicago, IL 60601

Choice

Choice is part of the Association of College and Research Libraries, a division of the American Library Association. It reviews nonfiction books that are likely to be of interest to colleges—including community colleges and graduate programs—and thus covers college course topics ranging from anthropology to zoology, and everything in between. Geared for academic librarians, public librarians, and college educators, *Choice* has a circulation of 85,000 subscribers, not including pass-along readers. It is available both in print and online, and comes out monthly.

Choice's submission process is a bit different from that of other reviewing journals. It will not review titles in uncorrected proofs or PDF form. Instead, it requires a final printed book, which should be submitted as soon as it becomes available. Submission instructions can be found at the following web address: https://www.ala.org/acrl/choice/publisherinfo. For a list of editors to whom you can send submissions, once on the website, click on the "CHOICE staff" link.

Send your submissions to the following address:

Att: [Editor's name]
Choice
575 Main Street, Suite 300
Middletown, CT 06457-3445

Foreword Reviews

Founded by Victoria Sutherland in 1998, *Foreword Reviews* has become a strong option for independent presses—including university presses and self-publishers—who want to get their titles reviewed. Published bi-monthly, this journal has a loyal audience of over 20,000 readers. It is distributed free to buyers in the trade, including librarians, booksellers, and rights agents, and is available in both print and digital formats.

If *Foreword* does not review your book, you may want to consider sending a submission to *Clarion Reviews, Foreword's* fee-for-review service. *Clarion* is discussed on page 154.

A review copy of your title must be received by *Foreword* a minimum of four months ahead of the book's publication. Digital submissions are preferred, although printed review copies are accepted. The publication's submission guidelines can be found at: https://publishers. forewordreviews.com/reviews/

Hard copies of ARCs can be mailed to:

Attn: Book Review Editor
Foreword Reviews
413 E 8th Street
Traverse City, MI 49686

The Horn Book Magazine

Founded in Boston in 1924 by Bertha Mahony Miller, *The Horn Book Magazine* is the oldest bimonthly magazine dedicated to reviewing children's and young adult books published in the United States. An authoritative resource for librarians and educators alike, the magazine reviews books very selectively, presenting appraisals of approximately one hundred hardcover trade books in each issue and generally considering books notable for high standards in plot, theme, characterization, and style. Board books and original paperbacks are occasionally reviewed. The magazine also features articles and editorials that explore all aspects of children's literature. In 2020, *Horn Book* introduced a fully searchable database of reviews called the Guide/Reviews Database.

Be aware that *The Horn Book Magazine* does not review self-published books, and that all submissions must come from a commercial publisher. Therefore, your children's or YA book will be eligible only if it has been published by a commercial house and the publisher submits the book for review. Publishers should send appropriate titles at least three months before the publication date. All submissions must be accompanied by complete publication information, including price, publication date, and ISBN.

The Horn Book Magazine requests that all titles be submitted in digital form—preferably as PDFs—to sflax@hbook.com.

If your publisher decides to submit physical material to *Horn Book*, two physical advance reader copies of the book should be sent to:

Book Reviews
The Horn Book, Inc.
300 The Fenway
Main College Building, Suite A375
Boston, MA 02115

Kirkus Reviews

Based in New York City, *Kirkus Reviews* was established in 1933 by Virginia Kirkus. It has a circulation of approximately 15,000 subscribers, including librarians and booksellers, and is published twice a month. The magazine reviews books submitted by major publishers and independent publishers, including all new adult hardcover or original trade paperback fiction, general-audience nonfiction, and children's and teen books. It is available in print and online.

Like several other review journals, *Kirkus* offers a counterpart, *Kirkus Indie,* that reviews self-published books on a fee basis. *Kirkus Indie* reviews are posted on KirkusReviews.com, and in some cases, they are also printed in the magazine. (See page 154 for more information on this service.)

Kirkus requests that titles be submitted as PDFs. The submissions must be received at least four to five months before the title's publication date, and it should be addressed to the appropriate editor. Submission guidelines, including the email addresses of editor/reviewers, can be found on: https://www.kirkusreviews.com/about/publisher-submission-guidelines/

If you do decide to submit physical material to *Kirkus's* editorial office, send it to the following address:

Editorial Office
Kirkus Media, LLC
65 West 36th Street, Suite 700
New York, NY 10018

Library Journal

Founded in 1876 by Melvill Dewey, who invented the Dewey Decimal System, *Library Journal* has a circulation of approximately 100,000, including librarians, booksellers, authors, and the media. Highlighting books that librarians may wish to add to their collections, it is a key prepublication trade journal for librarians in public, school, and special interest libraries.

Library Journal reviews books submitted by major publishers and by independent publishers. Accepted categories include new general trade books, original paperbacks, e-originals, graphic novels, reference books, and professional development titles for librarians and educators prior to their first U.S. publication.

Library Journal will accept PDFs or ARCs. Only one copy is necessary when sending physical copies. Submissions should be received six months prior to publication, but when that is not an option, they should be sent as early as possible. Even finished books can be sent in some situations. The publisher's review guidelines can be found at: https://www.libraryjournal.com/page/Review-Submissions. Digital submissions should be sent to: ljsubmissions@mediasourceinc.com

When sending physical copies to *Library Journal*, address them to:

Library Journal: Book Room
123 William Street, Suite 802
New York, NY 10038

PW (Publishers Weekly)

Established in 1872, *Publishers Weekly*, now called *PW*, is still very much the voice of the book publishing community. It has a circulation of over 60,000 readers, which include librarians, booksellers, authors, literary agents, the media, and, of course, publishing industry professionals. *PW*, which is available in print and online, reviews books submitted by major publishers and independent publishing houses. One of the publication's most famous features is its lists of best-selling books in various categories, including self-published titles.

PW also publishes *BookLife*, which reviews self-published book on a fee basis. *BookLife* appears twice each month within *PW's* weekly editions. Turn to page 153 to learn more about this service.

PW requests that all titles be submitted via the GalleyTracker platform found on its website and include a digital galley, such as a PDF. If physical galleys (ARCs) are available, you should also submit two ARCs for your title. Send submissions at least three months—preferably four—prior to the first day of the month of the book's publication. For full submission guidelines, visit the website at: https://www.publishersweekly.com/pw/corp/submissionguidelines.html

Physical copies of your book should be sent to the following address:

Publishers Weekly
Nonfiction Reviews [or "Poetry Reviews" or other relevant category]
49 West 23rd Street, Ninth Floor
New York, NY 10010

School Library Journal

School Library Journal (*SLJ*) is affiliated with *Library Journal*, but is a completely separate publication. This monthly journal has a circulation of over 23,000 subscribers with an estimated pass-along total of 92,000 readers. Its reviews and articles are designed for school librarians, media specialists, and public librarians who work with young people—from preschool through high school.

SLJ reviews new general trade books for children and teens (including Spanish-language materials), classroom and library books from institutional publishers, graphic novels, reference books, and professional development titles for librarians and educators before their first publication in the United States. Books must have a national distributor and be of national interest.

Currently, *SLJ* is accepting only PDFs or shareable digital copies. For updates and further information about submissions, visit the *SLJ's* website at: https://www.slj.com/page/review-submissions.

If you do decide to send physical material to *School Library Journal*, use the following address:

SLJ Book Review
School Library Journal
123 William Street, Suite 802
New York, NY 10038

■ POST-PUBLICATION REVIEWS

Once you have evaluated the suitability of your book for the eight pre-publication reviewing journals, and you have made your submissions, you truly have a world of traditional post-publication reviewers to consider. The media in this category include magazines, newspapers, newsletters, radio, and television. Be aware that although many of these news sources do write stories on authors and present author interviews, in this chapter, we are specifically looking at book reviews that could provide a publication's or show's audience—and your potential readers—with a critique or mention of your title.

As you consider potential reviewers, you will want to keep several important points in mind:

- Remember that you are submitting your book for review to gain exposure for yourself and your title. Good reviews can open a number of traditional and online media opportunities for you in the future.

- If you get good reviews, you will be able to gather blurbs to use in your media kit and, potentially, to include in a future printing of your book.

- Always keep the potential reviewer's audience in mind. You can give away a great many books to reviewers, but if their reviews are not going to be seen by the people who are likely to read your book, they will probably not help you sell your book.

- Last, but not least, always be aware of the reach and power of each review. Some reviews reach the library market, some reach bookstores and libraries, and some include the general reading public. A positive review can quickly stimulate orders, so make sure that readers will know where to buy your book in advance of receiving reviews.

If you have been lucky enough to receive a positive prepublication review, be sure to include part of it in your sales sheet and your media kit, as well as in any cover letter you send requesting reviews from magazines, newspapers, and other media. (To learn about sales sheets, see Chapter 6. To learn about media kits, see Chapter 9. See the discussion on page 125 for information on the cover letter that should accompany review copies.) With that in mind, we will now take a closer look at the world of post-publication reviews. Because there are so many post-publication options out there, it is impossible to provide contact information for every magazine, journal, newspaper, and other media outlet below, as we did in the section on prepublication trade journals. To learn how to locate contact information for the media outlets you select, see the inset on page 144.

Magazines and Journals

The world of magazines and journals has gone through a great many changes over the last decade or two. For well over a century, their subscribers represented a good portion of the reading public. As a commercial publisher, if you were lucky enough to get a positive review in one of these periodicals, you were likely to sell a decent number of books. However, since the advent of the Internet, and especially social media, these periodicals have shared much of their readership with other sources of diversion. While their overall subscriber base has declined, many popular magazines still maintain a million readers or more. Because so much of the reading public has shifted its attention to online sources, a number of magazines and journals are now available both in print and online. In fact, many publications have entirely given up print editions and now appear only online.

As you learned in Chapter 3 (see the inset on page 36), there is a difference between magazines and journals. Briefly, magazines are geared for the general public, while journals are focused on one specific topic and often written for professionals in a particular field of study. The question, then, is how you can get reviewed by one of these periodicals.

While many magazines and journals provide book reviews, nationally distributed magazines and journals rarely, if ever, review, self-published titles. Normally, they work only with established publishing houses. Should a self-published book be reviewed in such a widely read publication, it is like winning the lottery. While you can certainly submit your book for review to large magazines and journals, you will have a better chance of garnering reviews from the types of publications discussed below.

Magazines

Chapter 3 discussed the different types of magazines available. (See pages 36 to 40.) As you learned, the bigger the magazine, the more difficult it is to win attention for a little-known author—especially a self-published author—and his book. This means that you will have to choose the publications you approach wisely.

As you know, many cities and towns throughout the country have local magazines, whose articles normally focus on the places and people within their area. Some of these publications are given away free at stores and malls, while others are available by subscription. Most important, because the people in the magazine's geographic region are at the heart of the publication, the editor may be willing to provide you with the opportunity you need to get your book reviewed.

Call the editor of a local magazine to learn if he would run a review of your book. If you are a local self-published author, that may be enough to pique the editor's interest. If the magazine does not run reviews, consider buying space to have a review appear in the magazine. While this won't be the same as having your book reviewed in *The Atlantic*, it may attract the attention of local readers and perhaps result in quotes that you can use when promoting your book. If you have arranged book signings at a local bookstore or library, be sure to have the editor include a mention of the signing in the review.

With that said, no review you use in this manner should be written by you. If you have reached out to others earlier on, as suggested in Chapter 7, you should have one or two advance blurbs or endorsements that carry the name of an expert in your field or a well-known writer in your genre. Pick out the best one for use in your local magazine.

One last point should be made about submitting your book to magazines for review. Print magazines may require a four- to six-month lead time for a book to be considered for review. Online magazines may need a shorter lead time.

Specialty Journals

First discussed in Chapter 3, specialty journals are focused on specific interests, and therefore have a small but often dedicated readership.

Normally, they are sold through subscription rather than at newsstands or in stores.

Like larger publications, specialty journals may be receptive only to books produced by major publishers. However, if the topic of your self-published book is in line with such a publication, it may be a good fit for your book—especially if you, the author, have the professional credentials the publication is looking for. Never be afraid to reach out to the magazine or journal's editorial office to learn its reviewing guidelines.

Exceptions to the Unwritten Rule

In this chapter, we often say that magazines and journals are usually not open to reviewing the books of self-published authors, but there are exceptions to this rule.

For instance, a book with a focused audience that aligns with that of a specialized magazine or journal has a better chance of being reviewed, as does a book that has the earmarks of a commercially published title, such as a great cover that features a terrific blurb. If the author is an "influencer" or has a very large following on social media, that also might help clear a path for reviews. And, of course, having a direct contact on an editorial board has been known to open a few closed doors. It could be an uphill battle, but it's often worth fighting.

Other Specialty Publications

The next possible source of book reviews includes specialty publications such as newsletters and small magazines that are good targets either for your book or for you as an author.

Las Vegas-based author and marketing expert Brian Rouff sold thousands of copies of his first self-published novel, *Dice Angel,* in part because he landed reviews in Las Vegas-related publications, including a newsletter that went out to 100,000-plus subscribers. As another example of targeted review submissions, I sent a review copy of my co-authored thriller *Just Your Everyday People*—whose heroine is an oral hygienist—to an association for oral hygienists. The editor loved the novel and wrote a glowing review in the group's monthly publication.

Within this category of specialty publications are all the alumni magazines, print or online, from all the schools that you have attended, including:

- Preschool
- Elementary school
- Middle school
- High school

- College or university
- Graduate school
- Trade school

Many schools include information about their alumni in their school publication, and some even produce a separate alumni magazine or newsletter. It's very possible that a publication such as this might want to review a book by a former student that would appeal to other alumni and possibly even to students, parents, and teachers.

Newspapers

Newspapers, first discussed in Chapter 3 (see pages 32 to 35), are the next major category of publications that should get your attention. Although you may cherish the idea of getting your book reviewed by a major publication such as *The New York Times,* if you were published by a small press or if you are a self-published author, that is probably not a realistic goal. Your best bets are local and regional papers—such as the one in the town in which you now live, the one in your home town, or even the one in your state—and, if appropriate, a specialty paper whose focus is a good match for your book's topic.

Check the target newspaper's website—or make a call to the paper—to find the name and contact information of the writer who is most likely to review your book. (For more information about getting the names and contact information of suitable writers and editors, see the inset on page 144.) A hardcover book of fiction stands the greatest chance of being reviewed in a newspaper's books section—even more so if its author is a member of the community served by the newspaper. A nonfiction paperback, however, stands a better chance of getting coverage in a section that either addresses the same general subject matter of your book or is in some way related to it. For example, a book on how to treat high blood pressure without the use of conventional drugs might be of interest to a newspaper's health reporter. Similarly, a book on how to minimize the symptoms of ADHD through diet might grab the attention of a columnist who deals with parenting issues.

In the battle to get newspaper coverage for your self-published book, you may find that one of your best friends will be the online versions

Working With a Commercial or Academic Publishing House

Too often, when commercial presses fail to assign a dedicated publicist to send out review copies of a new title, the author fails to do anything on his own because he incorrectly assumes that if the work is not performed by the publisher, it cannot be done at all. This isn't true. Many times, you can share the promotion of your book with your publisher, and you will both benefit.

If your book was published by a commercial house or academic press, but your publisher does not seem to have the personnel or time necessary to submit your book for review to magazines and journals, you might consider forming a type of partnership with your publishing house. Suggest that you do the research and provide your publisher with a list of potential reviewers (editors and journalists), and that the company follow up by sending out the actual print or electronic submissions. When the submissions come from your publisher and not directly from you, it will make it clear that your title isn't self-published. This may increase the likelihood that the submission will be seriously considered by your target publications.

If you have hired your own publicist, he will hopefully submit your book to magazines and journals on your behalf. Nevertheless, you should ask which publications are receiving the submissions, when the submissions are being sent out, and what the responses are. Be aware that many publicists will not share their lists with their clients since they consider the lists to be proprietary information. But if your publicist does provide you with that information—even with the caveat that you will not contact those individuals on your own—you will learn more about the process. And if you ever publish another book, you will have a head start on your next title's publicity campaign.

of newspapers. More often than not, coverage that cannot be granted in a newspaper's print edition may instead be provided in its digital version. Rather than thinking of online-only coverage as a consolation prize, realize that you might actually be able to do more to promote your book by having an easily accessible write-up on a respected newspaper's website.

The lead time for newspapers is shorter than that for magazines. For print, the lead time may be one to two weeks prior to publication; for online publications, the lead time may be even shorter. Nevertheless, you will want to give the newspaper as much time as possible to read and write about your book.

Television and Radio

In Chapter 3, we first discussed television and radio in terms of their potential value to the author who is hoping to obtain media attention for his book. (See pages 42 to 48.) Of course, it would wonderful if a talk show host offered glowing remarks about your book during an interview, but remember that in this chapter, we are focused on obtaining *reviews* of your book.

With that said, be aware that today, few TV and radio shows offer book reviews to their audience. Occasionally, a host may decide to discuss a bestseller that he read and is keen to recommend, or a network may plug a book produced by a publishing company with which it has a financial relationship, such as the affiliation that CBS had with Simon & Schuster or that FOX has with HarperCollins. But note that in both of these cases, we are talking about books produced by major publishing houses.

Is it possible for a self-published book to win a review on TV or radio? Sometimes, it is. If your book has generated a number of positive advance reviews, if your book has created a buzz on social media, or if you have enjoyed a healthy number of sales, you can try submitting your book to a show whose point of view is good match for your title. For instance, if you have written a book on how to live a life of passion and purpose, you might approach the John Tesh radio show *Intelligence for Your Life,* which is heard on over 300 radio stations. And, of course, you can send submissions to local television and radio shows, which are often receptive to local authors.

How to Locate and Record
Contact Information for Media

Years ago, the contact information for book reviewers, editors, producers, and other key people in media were available in reference books that were printed annually. But in this digital age, these handy reference books have disappeared. So how can you find the names and contact information for individuals who might review your book?

If you are lucky enough to be working with a publishing house or you have hired a book publicist, your PR person should have a list of media people with whom he works. He may even be able to customize his list to fit your particular book, since that is a big part of his job.

If you are working on your own and you have a good-sized budget, you can subscribe to the Cision Connect database for several thousand dollars a year. This electronic database provides extensive contact information for every newspaper and magazine editor, TV producer or host, and radio interview and producer. Thousands upon thousands of contacts are available on Cision.

If Cision isn't an option and you're not working with a publicist, you can probably find the names and contact information for the people you wish to reach on the websites of your target publications and shows. This definitely involves some work, but it will be well worth the effort if you end up with some great media attention. If you can't find the contact information of the appropriate people, call the office of the publication or show, and try to obtain the information over the phone. Lastly, if you have print versions of the publications in which you're interested on hand—either because you subscribe to them or because your local library subscribes to them—you can probably find the desired information on the mastheads, which are usually located in the first few pages of the publications.

Who are the appropriate people to contact for each form of media? When approaching publications such as print magazines, newspapers, and journals, the best job titles to zero in on are "Book Reviewer," "Book Editor," or "Book Columnist." When seeking an online review, look for the "Online Editor," which you'll sometimes find listed alongside the print media contact. When searching for contacts at a television or radio show, find the "Producer" or "Booker" (as in "Guest Booker"). Normally, the show's host is too busy hosting the show to get directly involved in guest selection, although at shows with smaller staffs, the host may also be the booker and the book reviewer.

As you collect names and contact information, be well-organized from the start by creating an Excel spreadsheet in which you record all the pertinent data. Your spreadsheet should include the following:

1. Name of contact person

2. Title of contact person

3. Name of newspaper or other media outlet

4. Physical mailing address

5. Email address

6. Website

7. Cell phone (if available)

8. Main phone

9. When book is submitted and how

10. Response

11. Follow-up

In the follow-up column, you can record what you do to follow up after receiving a response to your submission. If your contact person does *not* respond but you think that this media outlet is a great fit for your book, you might even want to try again after waiting two to three weeks. In such a case, you should ideally include a new piece of information—perhaps highlighting a news event that ties in with your book—to capture the recipient's attention.

A good spreadsheet will enable you to efficiently send out review requests and track any responses you receive. And if you write additional books in the future, you will have a head start in promoting your new titles!

INTERNET-BASED REVIEWING PLATFORMS

While many of the prepublication and post-publication periodicals are also available online, there are just as many sites for book reviews that exist online *only*. Moreover, there are sites that, although not designed expressly for the posting of book reviews, may be used for this purpose. Below, we will discuss some of these platforms, including Amazon, Barnes & Noble, Goodreads, TikTok, YouTube, reviewer blog sites, and the sites of social media influencers.

AMAZON

Since Amazon began selling books from its website in 1995, it has become the leader in book retailers. It's not surprising, then, that getting a portfolio of positive Amazon reviews can make your book stand out in the market and boost your sales.

There are many different opinions regarding how many Amazon reader reviews it takes to attract the attention of the media. Some say as few as twenty-five or fifty can get the media to take note, while others say that you need a hundred reviews or more. Of course, there are many considerations, such as whether the reviews are marked "Verified Purchase," indicating that the reviewer actually bought the book on Amazon. This is important because it implies that the reviewer is an unbiased reader rather than the author's pal. Unfortunately, this is something you can't control, because anyone can post a review on Amazon regardless of where he made his purchase. Remember that even if your positive reviews don't attract the attention of the media, you can be fairly sure that they will help persuade casual browsers to buy your book—and, hopefully, to post more good reviews.

Every author dreams of an overall five-star Amazon ranking, which is based on the rankings of all the different reviewers. Of course, the occasional negative review can bring your ranking down. Although you do have the option of disputing any review you don't like, your response can backfire by making you appear to be a bad sport with a sour grapes attitude. An alternative is to ignore the review and try to inspire additional positive reviews. (To learn about generating good reviews, see the discussion on page 151.)

BARNES & NOBLE

Although Amazon continues to dominate online book selling, it is not without competition. Like the Amazon website, the Barnes & Noble website allows people to post reviews of books and rank each book by awarding stars, which can be a big plus for you as an author. If you promote your title as advised in this book, you will hopefully enjoy good Barnes & Noble reviews that stimulate sales and media attention.

GOODREADS

Launched in 2006 and acquired by Amazon in 2013, this popular site remains a dependable place for millions of readers to find and share good books, and for publishers and authors—including self-published authors—to promote their books and interact with their readers.

Many readers post their reviews on Goodreads as a means of guiding other book lovers to the best titles. Like the Amazon and Barnes & Noble reviews, Goodreads reader comments begin with star rankings. Just as important, any author can join the Goodreads Author Program free of charge. Basically, you complete and submit an application, and then wait for approval. This will allow you to promote your book, run giveaways, connect readers to your blog, take questions from readers, and more. Each Goodreads giveaway involves a standard cost per book. Nevertheless, both traditional and self-publishers have incorporated Goodreads' "pre"-publication book giveaways as a key part of each new title's promotional campaign.

TIKTOK

First discussed in Chapter 4 (see page 71), the social media platform TikTok is a great way to reach kids, young adults, and even older adults under the age of fifty. Chapter 4 encouraged you to promote your book by making your own TikTok videos, but be aware that some TikTokers review other people's books. This makes TikTok another way to reach out for reviews.

To get your book reviewed in a TikTok video, first do some searches on hashtags such as #BookTok, #BookReview, and #TikTokBookClub.

(TikTok uses hashtags to label content. If you tap on a hashtag of inter-est, you'll be taken to a search page with other content that is labeled with that hashtag.) You can also search genre-specific hashtags. Then connect with appropriate book reviewers and ask if they'd like to read your book and post a video review. If they express an interest, you can send them a digital or paper book—whatever they request. And remem-ber that every book review you get on TikTok exposes your title to *all* of that TikToker's followers.

YOUTUBE

In Chapter 4, you learned how you can promote your book by posting videos on YouTube. But YouTube has also become a popular place for readers to post book reviews. In fact, the BookTube community, which emerged around 2010, has, to date, reached hundreds of thousands of viewers worldwide.

Although the majority of *BookTubers*—people who make videos about books and post them on YouTube—focus on young adult liter-ature, many are interested in other genres. Every BookTuber has his own niche, such as science fiction or fantasy, and you want to find the person or people who are interested in your particular genre. Some BookTubers have posted videos on their channel that actually explain the best way to send them a book review request. If you can't find such a video about a BookTuber of interest, check out his blog or website, drop him a tweet on Twitter, or send out a private email to ask if he'd like to read your book and possibly review it. If he agrees, you can send him a copy, being sure to attach a personalized letter that talks about you and your title. Since some BookTubers have thousands of subscrib-ers, getting your book in the right hands can do a great deal to attract the attention of people who are hungry for good books in your genre.

BOOK REVIEWER BLOGS

As you learned in Chapter 4, blogging has become a popular way for people to express their opinions on a range of subjects—including books. While you can create your own blog in which you talk about your book's subject or about yourself as a writer for the purpose of generating reader interest, you can also get your book reviewed in other people's blogs. As you might guess, this is far easier than getting your book reviewed by traditional media. Many bloggers review books, and they tend to be open to a wide range of titles and authors—not just books written by best-selling authors and produced by commercial publishing companies.

Using your preferred Internet search engine, you can track down a number of blog sites or web pages and explore the contents of each site to learn which ones might be interested in your title. Don't waste your time and a free copy of your book by sending an ARC to a blogger who has no interest in reviewing it. If a blog is only about romance novels, do not send your sci-fi novel or your nonfiction book about self-esteem.

Once you have selected one or more promising blogs, follow the provided instructions to contact the blogger about potentially sending a review copy of your book. Depending on what the blogger requests, you might send a physical ARC, a PDF, or even a finished book. If you do send a PDF, identify it as a read-only copy, and ask the blogger by email to not send your PDF to anyone else. You can also encrypt your PDF and supply a password so that only the recipient of the PDF can read it. (For more about this, see page 124.)

Most blogs review for free, but some charge a small fee. In such a case, you have to decide if you want to pursue getting a review on that blog. Be sure to check the reach of the blog; whether or not previous blog reviews have been well-written; whether the reviews have usually been positive or negative; how long your review will stay on the blog; and if it will be easy to find by title, genre, date, or some other searchable means after it has been reviewed. In fact, you'll want to look into this before sending a book to *any* blog that posts reviews.

If the blogger likes your book and writes a positive review, he may also offer you the opportunity to participate in an online event, such as a Q & A with the blogger or an event in which free copies of your book are given to a certain number of readers or to those who have submitted a question for the Q & A. If a blogger doesn't propose an event such as this but has posted a positive review, consider offering yourself as a guest blogger.

Be aware that if you don't want to do all the research involved in selecting appropriate bloggers, there is an alternative. You can find a book publicist who specializes in submissions to bloggers.

SOCIAL MEDIA INFLUENCERS

Social influencing is nothing new. For centuries, people have looked to their friends and family—as well as to celebrities and even royalty—to decide what they are going to buy. But just as the Internet has altered so much in our society, it has dramatically affected the world of influencing. Now there are people who have built reputations on their knowledge and expertise in a specific subject, and they use social media as a megaphone to cultivate large numbers of followers and share their recommendations with them. Instagram is often viewed as the platform of choice, but social media influencers also use Twitter, Pinterest, Tik-Tok, and other platforms. So-called mega-influencers have more than a million followers, but even micro-influencers may have the attention a thousand or more people.

What does this have to do with getting your book reviewed? Many social media influencers—like the Bookstagrammers on Instagram—review and recommend books. If you are interested in getting influencers to review your book, first use your favorite search engine to research influencers and find those who focus on your subject or genre. When you've zeroed in on several appropriate influencers, support them in any way possible—for instance, by commenting on their blogs in a positive way. Then, when you feel that you've established a connection—and this can take a while—find out how they prefer to be contacted. Most influencers have contact information associated with their account or have an associated website that includes an email address or a "Contact Us" link.

Contact each influencer directly, telling him plainly that you would like him to review your book. Keep your request brief and to the point, allowing him to offer a quick "yes" or "no." Include a very brief summary of your book and a letter telling him why he should care about it. Keep the summary short, effective, and appealing. It's a good idea to offer a link to an online document so that, if desired, the influencer can learn more about you and your title.

If you receive a response of any type, show appreciation for the influencer's time. And if he says "no" to your request, don't try to convince him to say "yes." You may want to contact him again in the future, and you don't want to burn any bridges.

Before we leave the subject of influencers, a few words should be said about fees. Not all influencers require fees. If an influencer loves your book, he may be happy to review it free of cost. Be aware, though, that many influencers, and especially those with large followings, will expect compensation for promoting your book. Understandably, micro-influencers are going to charge less than mega-influencers, who sometimes charge tens of thousands of dollars because they have so many people following them. Prices also depend on the platform used and on how many times you want your book mentioned. Before contacting an individual who could potentially promote your title, do some research on him. If he is a mega-influencer and you have a big budget, hiring him may prove worthwhile. If you have a modest budget, you will want to look for micro-influencers whose followers are enthusiastic about books and may be eager to find a title like yours.

WHAT YOU CAN DO TO ENCOURAGE GOOD ONLINE READER REVIEWS

In previous discussions, you learned about Amazon, Barnes & Noble, Goodreads, and other online sites where readers can post reviews of your book. When an author is lucky enough to get numerous positive reader reviews, these endorsements can do a great deal to drive sales. For an example of a book that has won a large number of reader reviews, visit online bookseller retail sites and track down some bestsellers, like John Green's *The Fault in Our Stars*. This book, which was eventually made into a feature film, has more than 57,000 reviews. You read that number right. How about the children's board book *I Love You to the Moon and Back,* written by Amelia Hepworth and illustrated by Tim Warnes? It has more than 45,000 reviews and ratings. When a potential reader visits these websites in search of a book, it is highly likely that the mountain of praise from readers will help persuade him to order a book or two.

The question is: How can you get these good reader reviews? Although I mentioned luck above, believe me when I say that more than luck is involved—especially if you are a little-known or unknown author. Fortunately, you have a few options.

If someone contacts you and says, "I just want you to know how much I enjoyed your novel," you can encourage him to share his feedback online. In your response, you should, of course, first thank your reader for sharing his positive reaction, but you can then follow this with a line such as, "Would you be kind enough to share your feedback in a reader review on Amazon or any other retail book site?" In my experience, the reader will often write back to say that he would be pleased to do so, and he may even thank you for the suggestion. Be aware that it is best if someone posts his evaluation of your book on the site where he actually purchased the book, because a rating from a verified purchaser carries more weight.

You can, of course, also ask acquaintances—or friends, colleagues, or family members—if they will read your book and write a reader review. But avoid saying that they can only post a *positive* review. Instead, keep it neutral: "If you want to share your opinion of the book, that would be appreciated." Of course, you hope it will be positive—and you hope that those you send your book to will love it—but you want to generate readers' reviews that seem unbiased. A review that is forced is unlikely to seem genuine and to have a positive effect on potential readers. Also, most people don't like to be manipulated.

If someone you know requests that you send him a complimentary copy of your new book, you can do that—or, if you have the option, you can have your publisher or publicist do it for you. This may rule out his review getting posted on certain sites, but that might not matter if you know that the person is influential and will share his feedback with his own circle of friends and acquaintances, perhaps on social media.

Hopefully, you are already using social media—LinkedIn, Twitter, Facebook, and other platforms—to communicate with the people you know and with potential readers. (To learn about using social media to promote your book, see pages 63 to 72 in Chapter 4.) When you announce the publication of your book on these sites, tell your readers that you hope they will post a review of your book after they have read it. This may seem obvious, but many readers will not think about posting a review without a little urging from you. If they love your book, they will probably be happy to tell others about it on retail websites and, perhaps, on their own social media pages.

REVIEWS FOR PAY PLATFORMS

As mentioned earlier in the chapter, paid review services used to be much more controversial in the book business than they are now. These days, the consensus is that a paid prepublication review—especially one from a notable source such as *Foreword's Clarion Reviews* or *Kirkus Indie*—is an option that should be considered, especially if the chances of getting a free prepublication trade review are remote. Obtaining a positive, well-written paid review that you can include in your media kit is better than having no review at all! Because they do not promise a favorable review, most paid review services do offer the client the chance to "kill" a poor review rather than having it posted. Check with each service regarding the cost, conditions, and posting outlets for their reviews. All paid services allow you to reprint the review and post it wherever you choose, but some will post to certain sites, such as Amazon, on your behalf.

BlueInk Review

Founded by a literary agent and a book review editor in 2010, this fee-based service offers several review options: Standard Review, which is completed in seven to nine weeks; the Fast Track, which is completed in four to six weeks; and the 2-Review Package, which includes a *BlueInk Review* and a *Foreword Clarion Review*.

Once a review has been completed, *BlueInk* emails a copy to you, and you have fourteen days to decide if you want the review published. If you do, the review will appear on the *BlueInk* website and will be distributed to the company's partners, which include Ingram, among others.

To learn the prices of the different *BlueInk* packages and to discover more about *Blueink Reviews*, visit the company's website: https://www.blueinkreview.com/

BookLife Reviews

A service launched by *Publishers Weekly* in 2014, *BookLife Reviews* are written by *PW* reviewers and paid for by authors. When you submit your book and purchase a review, a 300-word review is guaranteed and will be sent to you six weeks after the purchase date. The review will be released for print publication in the next *BookLife* supplement of *Publishers Weekly*.

For more information on *BookLife Reviews*, including fees and step-by-step instructions for purchasing a review, visit the *BookLife* website at:. https://booklife.com/about-us/booklife-reviews.html

Clarion Reviews

The sister company of *Foreword Reviews, Clarion Reviews* is designed primarily for independent publishers who missed submission deadlines or who need a review from a trusted source. When your review has been completed, you can have it posted on the *Foreword Clarion* website and distributed to licensing partners at wholesale databases, including Ingram's iPage, Baker & Taylor, and BowkersBooksInPrint. You also have the option of "killing" the review.

Clarion accepts all books in all formats from all publishers, regardless of publication date. To learn more about *Clarion* and to start the submissions process, visit the following website: https://publishers.forewordreviews.com/reviews/#service-foreword-review

IndieReader

In 2009, Amy Edelman, an author who had written both self-published and commercially published books, created *IndieReader* with the goal of leveling the playing field for self-, hybrid, and small-press published authors. Costs of reviews vary according to the turn-around time. The regular service provides a review in seven to nine weeks, but if you want to receive a review in four to six weeks, you can pay a premium for rush service.

To learn more about *Indie Reader's* costs and services, visit the company's website at: www.indiereader.com

Kirkus Indie

Kirkus Indie, established in 2005, is the paid review service of *Kirkus Reviews.* Its reviews are written by qualified professionals, such as librarians and journalists. Fees are based on turn-around times, with the standard service providing a review within seven to nine weeks of the date your submission is received, and the express service providing a review within four to six weeks.

When you receive your review, you can choose to have it published on KirkusReviews.com or, if the review is negative, you can opt out of the program. If you do make the review public, *Kirkus* editors will consider it for publication in the *Kirkus Reviews* magazine. (In other words, not all *Kirkus Indie* reviews appear in the magazine.) *Kirkus* will also share the review with BarnesandNoble.com, Ingram, and other partners.

For information on fees and other details of the *Kirkus Indie* program, visit the following website: https://www.kirkusreviews.com/indie-reviews/

Online Book Club

Created in 2008, this service will review your book and post the review on its website, where it can be seen by *Online Book Club's* members. For more information, visit: https://onlinebookclub.org/reviews/

Self-Publishing Review

Established in 2008, *Self-Publishing Review* offers various book review and related book marketing services. Four book review options are available—Editorial, Jump Start, Classic Review, and Lead Story—each of which has its own fee, word count, turn-around time, and associated benefits. At the highest level, your review will be shared on several social media sites, including Facebook, Pinterest, Instagram, and Tumblr.

For more information, visit the *Self-Publishing Review* website at: https://www.selfpublishingreview.com/

CONCLUSION

Reviews are a key promotional tool for getting the word out about your book. Whether you send your book out for review, or this task is performed by your publisher's PR department or by a publicist that you have hired, someone has to do the heavy lifting of getting out those review copies along with persuasive cover letters that pitch your title. It is hard work, but the results usually justify the effort. You may get one prepublication review that you can add to your book cover, or you may receive reviews on or after publication from a variety of print and online sources.

As you obtain new or more impressive reviews, remember to put them to work for you. Add them to your media kit, post them on online retail sites like Amazon, feature them on your own website, and provide links on your social media accounts. Every time another review appears, it can be used to focus further attention on you and your book and to drive sales.

PART THREE

WHAT TO DO AFTER YOUR BOOK IS PUBLISHED

9.

Launching Your Publicity Plans

n the previous chapters, I laid out the fundamental information
you need to promote your book and yourself. In Chapter 3, you
learned about traditional media, and in Chapter 4, you learned
about Internet-based media. Chapter 6 helped you create a timeline to
follow and a sales sheet that pulled together all the critical information
(including metadata) on your title, and Chapters 7 and 8 guided you
in obtaining positive blurbs and reviews. In this chapter, you will learn
how to attract further attention to your work by creating a winning
media kit and sending it out to both traditional and online media as a
means of gaining print, online, TV, and radio interviews; feature articles; and more.

I have been very fortunate in my career as an author to have
appeared on a number of major—i.e., nationally aired—network television shows, including *Today, The View, Good Morning America, Sunday
Morning, Nightline*, and *The Early Show*. But that was a number of years
ago, when there were more opportunities for self-published authors and
noncelebrity authors of midlist titles (books expected to have average
sales) to get this type of exposure. As the Internet began to vie with
established communication channels of mainstream media, it became
far more difficult for lesser-known authors to secure guest appearances
on these types of shows. Although you may be facing a challenging
publicity environment, by crafting a persuasive pitch, creating an effective press kit, and targeting the right media, you can still do a great deal
to make potential readers aware of your book.

CREATING A PITCH

Whenever an occasion arises in which you need to describe your book to someone else in order to get some type of promotion, the description you offer is called a *pitch*. When you are gearing up to go out and pitch your book in order to get publicity, there is one important thing that you must do first: Figure out where your book would work best as part of a media news story.

If your book is a work of fiction, your search for publicity is going to be much tougher than it would be if you were a nonfiction book author. The lion's share of national media focus given to fiction these days is reserved for those writers who have recognizable names. Year after year, the morning news shows air short segments with well-known authors like John Grisham, Nelson DeMille, James Patterson, Jodi Picoult, and Nora Roberts. It's tough, although not impossible, to break through as an unknown. If, however, your book is a nonfiction title, your chances of successfully pitching your work for publicity and presenting yourself as an expert on your book's subject increase dramatically.

As you prepare to pitch your book for media coverage or yourself for show appearances, it's important to memorize what you would consider the key data from your book's sales sheet. Most of the time, you will be given only a few minutes—via email, on the phone, or face to face—to pitch your book. Competition for media coverage is fierce, and you will need to be ready to provide compelling reasons why an editor or segment producer should cover you and your book as a story of interest and value. It is very easy to become flustered while pitching your book, but pitching is a necessary part of getting publicity, and a task for which you should be prepared.

Having participated in various writers' workshops over the past several years, I have watched dozens of motivated and seemingly confident authors become nearly speechless when asked to pitch their books or themselves in only a few minutes' time. Many authors have been there, including me—but in order to survive and thrive within the publicity process, you are going to have to learn a few tricks.

I would suggest that you always be prepared to deliver your pitch by having five to eight concise yet dynamic topics to discuss in relation to your book and yourself. These topics are called talking points, and they are the foundation upon which all pitches should be built. As you come up with talking points, many of which you can draw from your book's sales sheet, it is best to write them down and speak them out loud. Doing so will help you determine if your topics are clear and understandable. Something that is brilliant on paper can become awkward and confusing when spoken, so you should do all you can do to trim the fat away from your core points. Practicing your talking points out loud will also bolster your confidence and ease any anxiety you might have in connection with public speaking. (To learn more about public speaking, see Chapter 10.)

The talking points presented on page 162 are for a novel. As you will see, they are meant to bring focus and direction to a pitch, and to help potential interviewers find topics to discuss with the book's author.

By way of comparison, the talking points on page 163 are for a non-fiction book and provide a secure underpinning to any discussion of it with the media.

As you further refine and target your book's pitch, try to be aware of what is going on in the news each day. More often than not, a pitch becomes more attractive to the media when it is shown to be relevant to another story that has just hit the news cycle.

The press release on page 165—which, like the talking points on page 163, is for the book *Unsafe at Any Meal*—was generated one day after a new scientific study offered additional support to the claims made by the author of a new book. As you can see, the lead-in to the pitch of the book is a nationally released story containing specific health statistics that would be of interest to almost anyone. (Note that you will learn more about press releases on page 164.)

CREATING A PRESS KIT

Your press kit, also called a media kit, is often the way a member of the media first meets you—and it can make an impact on the media even more readily than your book can. As such, you must write your press kit with the same amount of care and precision that you employed in writing your book. A solidly presented press kit can help open the door to publicity just as effectively as a bad and sloppily constructed press kit can close it. In addition to your full contact information, which should

The Path of the Wind: **A Novel**

James A. Misko

TALKING POINTS:

1) *The Path of the Wind* is the story of Miles Foster, a young newlywed whose "can-do" spirit and educational ideals are put to the test when he is assigned to teach at an underfunded school in a remote central Oregon town.

2) Although it is a work of fiction, *The Path of the Wind* is based on the author's own brief stint as a teacher in the rural Pacific Northwest.

3) Set during the late 1950s, Misko's newest novel—which is his fifth—seeks to return readers to a time in America when life was simpler, dreams were bigger, and public discourse was not bound so tightly by the confines of political correctness.

4) Misko hopes that *The Path of the Wind* might bring about a renewed appreciation of teachers in this country—especially at a time when the majority of teachers remain grossly underpaid and often unappreciated for their care and commitment to the education and overall lives of their students.

5) Misko considers his creation of a key female character in *The Path of the Wind*—Eleanor Foster, the wife of Miles Foster—a pivotal moment in his continuing evolution as a novelist; so much so, in fact, that his next novel, *Tomorrow Is My Day*, will be his first novel in which the main protagonist is a woman.

Unsafe at Any Meal

What the FDA Does Not Want You to Know About the Foods You Eat

Dr. Renee Joy Dufault

TALKING POINTS:

1) *Unsafe at Any Meal* tells the true story of how Dr. Renee Dufault, former food investigator for the Food and Drug Administration (FDA), first detected alarming levels of heavy metal contaminants (mercury, in particular) in the plumbing systems of many US-based food manufacturing plants—and upon further examination, also found those same toxins in a number of popular processed foods commonly sold in supermarkets.

2) When she revealed these disturbing findings to her superiors at the FDA, Dr. Dufault was told in no uncertain terms to stop her investigation. Caught in a crisis of conscience, Dufault chose to take an early retirement from the FDA and soon thereafter founded the Food Ingredient and Health Research Institute (FIHRI)—a nonprofit organization devoted to food ingredient safety, education, and continued research.

3) With her ongoing studies and publication of her book, Dr. Dufault is trying to make the general public aware of the fact that exposure to toxic substances in processed foods continues to serve as a gateway to a variety of serious health issues, including cancer, type 2 diabetes, metabolic dysfunction, organ damage, decline in sperm count levels, cardiovascular disease, and a far higher prevalence of autism and ADHD among young children in the United States and Canada.

4) In October 2017, The Clean Label Project announced that alarming levels of "arsenic, lead, and other heavy metals" were found in eighty percent (80%) of infant formulas sold on the market. Dr. Dufault's own research, however, turned up this data in 2005, twelve years earlier. She has been trying to inform the public of these matters ever since.

5) If the American public were to stop eating the food ingredient known as high fructose corn syrup (HFCS), its potential for recovery from the woeful effects of the Standard American Diet (SAD) would increase significantly.

appear on every piece of promotional material you include, every author's press kit should include the following items:

- A press release.

- An author bio, including at least one author photograph.

- A list of potential or "suggested" questions that interviewers may want to use when discussing your book with you.

- A page of blurbs and/or excerpted prepublication reviews, if your book has received any blurbs or reviews.

- For fiction, possibly an excerpt from your book that presents your best writing.

- For nonfiction, any facts, statistics, or quotes from the book that highlight its importance and any new information it provides.

The Press Release

The press release is the core of any media kit. It needs to provide much of the material about your book that appears on your sales sheet (see page 101 to learn about sales sheets), but the information should be focused on your pitch rather than providing a straight description of your title.

Your press release should, of course, be well-written and compelling, so if you feel confident in your writing ability, you can write your own press release. After all, you wrote the book and you know it well. Just keep in mind that because a press release is intended to generate interest in your book, and possibly even in you, it should include a "hook," or a newsworthy piece of information that immediately captures the reader's attention. For instance, you might immediately tie the book into an upcoming holiday or a breaking news story. Devising a hook is more difficult to do when publicizing a work of fiction, but even in that case, the release must make the media take note of the book.

Every press release for a work of nonfiction needs to answer these questions about your particular book:

- What is your book about?

- Why should the media or reader care about this book?

FOR IMMEDIATE RELEASE

Contact Info: Anthony Pomes, VP – Marketing/PR/Rights
Square One Publishers (www.squareonepublishers.com)

Think finding arsenic in baby food is bad? It's just the tip of the iceberg, according to former FDA investigator Dr. Renee Dufault.

Garden City Park, NY: A major study conducted recently by a new nonprofit organization, The Clean Label Project, has found alarming levels of arsenic, lead, and other heavy metals in approximately 80 percent of infant formulas. Some of the baby food brands found to have the largest amounts of these harmful toxins in their products include Gerber, Enfamil, and Plum Organics. According to the World Health Organization, arsenic in particular is associated with a higher occurrence of autism, ADHD, heart issues, diabetes, and cancer among children and adults alike.

If you are Dr. Renee Dufault—former FDA investigator and author of *Unsafe at Any Meal* (Square One, $16.95)—you know that the results of this study only scratch the surface of a much more disturbing and far-reaching picture in consumer health. Dr. Dufault's own research in this area actually dates back over a decade to 2005, when she was still working as a health investigator for the Food and Drug Administration. That was the year when she discovered that baby formula was comprised largely of corn sweeteners and vegetable oil. As she notes in Chapter Six of her book ("Spotlight on Autism and ADHD"), many baby formulas "contain corn sweetener in the form of corn syrup or corn syrup solids. Some formulas contain more corn sweetener than any other ingredient. I found one baby formula product in my local grocery store with a food ingredient label that claimed 54 percent of the product was made up of corn syrup solids and 26 percent of the product consisted of assorted vegetable oils."

Even though she has been aware of this problem for years and has worked diligently to alert the consumer public to it, she applauds the findings of The Clean Label Project and the force for change that the new study represents. "While they [The Clean Label Project] have tested and found results in cat food, dog food, and now baby food, the occasion of this study now sets the stage for further widespread mainstream investigation into more of our foods."

Unsafe at Any Meal
What the FDA Does Not Want You to Know About the Foods You Eat
by Renee Joy Dufault
BOOK SPECS: / $16.95 USD ($23.95 CAN) / 240 PAGES /
ISBN: 978-0-7570-0436-0 / 6 x 9-INCH QUALITY PAPERBACK

Square One Publishers • 115 Herricks Road, Garden City Park, NY 11040

FOR IMMEDIATE RELEASE
Contact Info: Anthony Pomes, VP – Marketing/PR/Rights
                    Square One Publishers (www.squareonepublishers.com)

To Be or Nto oT eB?
If You or Your Child Are Having Trouble With the Question Above, Then You May Have a Bad Case of *The Word Gobblers*

Garden City Park, NY: Millions of children and adults around the world cope with reading, writing, or depth perception problems, such as dyslexia. For one in every six, this problem is a result of a condition called **Irlen Syndrome**—the inability of the brain to process certain light waves or colors. Symptoms can include headaches and stomachaches when reading, sensitivity to light, poor sports performance, inability to focus, clumsiness, and low self-esteem.

The Word Gobblers ($15.95 USD, ISBN: **978-0-7570-0502-2**) is a handbook for parents who witness their child struggling to read and write. The book begins by explaining what the signs of Irlen Syndrome are. It then provides a questionnaire designed to alert you to the behaviors to watch for in your child. This is followed by exercises to help you determine if you should take the next step—having your child evaluated by a Certified Iren Syndrome Screener. *The Word Gobblers* will also show you a few modifications you can make immediately to ease your child's symptoms and discomfort.

Children who are poor readers or poor in sports are often teased, resulting in feelings of shame and low self-worth. *The Word Gobblers* offers **a medically-based reason why children—and even adults—struggle to read**. It shows them that they are not at fault, and their difficulties can be lessened or overcome. By identifying and relieving the symptoms of the problem, children can begin to enjoy and succeed at reading and math and sports, and all other endeavors that were once difficult due to Irlen Syndrome.

If you would like to review *The Word Gobblers* and/or wish to speak with Catherine Matthias, please feel free to contact Anthony Pomes Square One Publishers. Thanks for your consideration.

The Word Gobblers
A Handbook for Parents Working With Children Struggling to Read
by Catherine Matthias (Illustrated by Joan Gilbert) / *Foreword* by Helen Irlen
BOOK SPECS: $15.95 US ($22.95 CAN) / 80 PGS. / ISBN 978-0-7570-0502-2
9 x 7.5-INCH TRADE PAPERBACK

 Square One Publishers • 115 Herricks Road, Garden City Park, NY 11040

FOR IMMEDIATE RELEASE

Contact Info: Anthony Pomes, VP – Marketing/PR/Rights
Square One Publishers (www.squareonepublishers.com)

Introducing James A. Misko

Square One Publishers proudly presents the new book from acclaimed and up-and-coming, award-winning novelist James A. Misko

When Miles Foster received his teaching degree, he dreamed of obtaining a position in the highly respected and financially stable Portland, Oregon school system. Portland was where he and his wife called home—a place where everything a person could want or need was available. Soon Miles had to face the unwelcomed reality that there were no job openings in Portland. Even worse, the closest available position was in a remote lumber mill town nearly two hundred miles away in central Oregon. Far from the dream job he had anticipated, Miles took the position, which was in an impoverished school with forty students—students who had been passed along despite the sub-par education they had received. Adding to his challenge was a school board with a controlling superintendent—a jealous man who was intolerant of any teaching outside the box, and who became intent on destroying Miles and his teaching career. In *The Path of the Wind* (the fifth novel from acclaimed author James Misko), Miles must find a way to effectively educate his students and defeat the damaging control of the superintendent without losing his job, his marriage, or both.

ABOUT THE AUTHOR: *James A. Misko* was born in Nebraska, then moved to Oregon and Alaska, completing what for him was a natural bridge to the frontier. He has worked as an oil field roughneck, a logger, truck driver, saw mill hand, teacher, journalist, real estate broker, and writer. With numerous published articles and five novels to his credit, he continues to work at being the best author of fiction he can be. Jim and his wife Patti live in Alaska during the summer and California in the winter.

If you are interested in *The Path of the Wind* and wish to review the book and/or interview author James A. Misko, please contact Anthony Pomes at Square One Publishers. Thanks for your time and consideration.

The Path of the Wind
the new novel from James A. Misko
ISBN: 978-0-7570-0444-5 • BOOK SPECS: $17.95 ($26.95 CAN) / 304 PAGES / 6 x 9-INCH QUALITY PAPERBACK

 Square One Publishers • 115 Herricks Road, Garden City Park, NY 11040

- What is this book going to do for the reader?
- Who wrote the book, and why is this author qualified or credible?
- Why is this book coming out *now*?
- Why did you write this book?

When publicizing a work of fiction, the press release should focus more on plot and on the author's background.

Ideally, a press release should be one page in length. But if your press release is longer and you feel that all of the information you are presenting is necessary, always print "(turn over)" or "(more)" centered at the bottom of the first page. You might want to use a yellow highlighter to help ensure that whoever is reading the release will flip the paper over to see the second page. (See pages 165 to 167 for sample press releases.)

The Author Bio and Photo

Although the press release may end with one or two lines about the author—normally placed under the heading "About the Author"—a more in-depth author bio is generally included in a press kit. The bio should range from two to four paragraphs in length and should be no more than a page long. (See pages 169 and 170 for sample bios.)

The author bio is the perfect place to provide details about you and your life, including the city and state where you were born and raised and the place where you currently live. Your place of birth and current residence are important because local papers are usually among your best chances for getting media attention. If you are pitching to the national media, your present location will help outlets decide if you should appear in person or via satellite or online platforms instead. Keep in mind that a national media booking for a self-published author is usually improbable but is still worth pursuing. Your book might focus on exactly the topic that the media is interested in at that moment! If a media outlet is working on a segment that is a good fit for your book, you have a better chance of landing an interview than you would if you were trying to get a more general author interview on just you and your title.

In your author bio, you can include your undergraduate or graduate degrees and any professional work experiences that are

SAMPLE AUTHOR BIO FOR BOOK OF FICTION

James A. Misko was born in Nebraska, then moved to Oregon and Alaska, completing what for him was a natural bridge to the frontier. He has worked as an oil field roughneck, a logger, truck driver, saw mill hand, teacher, journalist, real estate broker, and writer.

It was his expertise in real estate that first brought him to the attention of Square One's president, Rudy Shur, who signed Misko to write a nonfiction book on the topic titled *How to Finance Any Real Estate (Any Place, Any Time)*. The book sold well and received good reviews, called "just the thing for investors" by *Publishers Weekly* and applauded by *Foreword Reviews* for "help[ing] investors think outside the box to land the property of their dreams."

Soon after, Misko became a first-time novelist who chose to self-publish his debut work of fiction entitled ***For What He Could Become.*** Over the next decade or so, however, Misko went on to write subsequent novels like ***The Most Expensive Mistress in Jefferson County*** and ***The Cut of Pride.*** After learning that Misko's fourth novel, ***As All My Fathers Were,*** had won the **Independent Book Publishers Association (IBPA) Benjamin Franklin Award™** in the "Best Fiction Title" category, Square One Publishers acquired the rights to all five of Misko's novels—including ***The Path of the Wind***, which went on to win "Best Fiction" awards from both the Feathered Quill Book Awards and the Los Angeles Festival of Books while also being named one of only three finalists for the prestigious PNWA Nancy Pearl Contest Award.

Having already established the Alaska Writers Guild by that time, Misko went on to give keynote speeches and conduct writing workshops at conferences both there and in California, together with his home state of Nebraska in April 2018. He also maintained author presence across several dozens of store appearances, both within the Barnes & Noble chain store system in both Alaska and California and a selection of key indie "brick 'n mortar" bookstores, including Mosquito Books at the Ted Stevens Anchorage International Airport, where he connected with all kinds of travelers. He even saw the first "Jim Misko Book Club" started this past year by a fan of his in the Philippines. And ***The Path of the Wind***, for which Misko was recognized as "a truly gifted novelist" by Midwest Book Review, was declared "an inspiring story, a classic tale of trying to expand a small town's rigid boundaries and change children's lives for the better" by The Seattle Post-Intelligencer.

Misko and his wife moved to Alaska in 1974—where they reside in the summer—and spend the rest of the year based in California. Jim likes whenever possible to meet his readers one at a time at his many book signings throughout the country.

SAMPLE AUTHOR BIO FOR BOOK OF NONFICTION

 **Pamela Wartian Smith, M.D., MPH, MS,** has been a medical doctor for more than 40 years. She spent her first twenty years of practice as an emergency room physician with the Detroit Medical Center, and then twenty-four years as an Anti-Aging/Functional Medicine specialist. Dr. Smith is a diplomate of the American Academy of Anti-Aging Physicians and past co-director of the Master's Program in Medical Sciences, with a concentration in Metabolic and Nutritional Medicine, at the Morsani College of Medicine, University of South Florida. An authority on the subjects of wellness and functional medicine, she is also the founder of the Fellowship in Anti-Aging, Regenerative, and Functional Medicine.

Dr. Smith has been featured on CNN, PBS, and many other television networks, has been interviewed in numerous consumer health publications, and has hosted two of her own radio shows. She is also the best-selling author of ten books to date, including *Max Your Immunity, What You Must Know About Vitamins, Minerals, Herbs & So Much More—Second Edition, What You Must Know About Women's Hormones—Second Edition,* and *What You Must Know About Memory Loss.* She is based in Michigan, but lectures frequently on a number of health topics throughout the US and abroad.

particularly relevant to your book. Any notable awards or accomplishments that would increase the media's interest in you should be stated as well. It is traditional to announce that a book is a first novel or, if there have been previous books, to state that, possibly providing the titles if they are pertinent to the new book. If you have a dedicated author website, the author bio can direct the media to your site for further information.

This section of the media kit can include one or two photos of you. One photo can be a standard author "head shot," and the second can be a photo of you "at work" or in a more informal pose. Some media outlets prefer to print an action shot rather than a head shot, which is why it makes sense to include both.

A List of Suggested Interview Questions

A list of potential interview questions is pivotal for an effective media kit. Many interviewers will rely on those questions for their radio or podcast interview even if they have read the book.

Provide a minimum of ten and a maximum of twenty questions. The most effective interview questions are the ones that cannot be answered with a simple "yes" or "no" response, but that allow for more interesting responses. The questions should afford you the opportunity to touch on all your main points so that you don't get lost while being interviewed.

You can include your answers to the interview questions, or you can leave them out. I recommend that you avoid providing the answers in the media kit. If you include the answers to someone in print media, it could tempt her to reprint your answers rather than interviewing you. If this happens too many times, you can have a number of repetitive answers floating around rather than fresh, new responses. Nevertheless, you might want to write out the answers for yourself as a way of orga-nizing your thoughts in advance.

Don't ask a question unless you can formulate a response that is likely to interest a potential reader. One standard question is, "Why did you write this book?" I just heard this question asked of an author who was being interviewed on a major network show. Although it was a great opportunity for her to talk about herself and her book, unfor-tunately, her answer was neither gripping nor especially convincing. Saying that others asked you to write a book is not going to generate the buzz that could have been created if you explained, for instance, that the topic was of great interest to you because of a childhood experience, your success in coping with a health challenge, or your family history.

While it is good to have your list of interview questions at the ready before you start your media campaign, there may be instances when you connect with a journalist or show host *before* you have sent out your press kit. If you find yourself in that situation, you may want to ask whether that individual would like to be provided with your prepared interview questions. Most journalists or show hosts will be pleased to have some of their work done for them, while those who wish to do their own research and formulate their own questions will nevertheless

Suggested Interview Questions for D. S. Lliteras
(*VIET MAN: A Novel*)

1. What is the meaning of your book's title, *Viet Man*?

2. Although technically a work of fiction, you have said that *Viet Man* is partially autobiographical. Tell us more about that.

3. How did you end up in the military?

4. How did you end up in Vietnam?

5. So much has been made over the past forty years about the lack of morality that seemed to permeate everything during the Vietnam War. Tell us about what you experienced, and how you, as a man still capable of love and emotion, struggled with moral conflict out there in the field.

6. Why did you write *Viet Man*—and why now?

7. What other, if any, Vietnam War books influenced you in the writing of your new book?

8. What particular body or area of literature has been an influence in your life as a writer?

9. What makes this book different from other books on the Vietnam War?

10. What kind of research did you do in preparation for this book?

11. How do you feel this new book now fits into the rest of your output as a writer?

12. Being a veteran yourself, how do you feel about the zealous military worship in most areas of the United States? That the military can do no wrong, etc.?

13. Your book, it seems, is less about being a soldier and more about being a veteran—which is something that alienates your character Doc from the civilians around him. Why is there such a disconnect between veterans and civilians who have never experienced military life?

14. In left-wing circles, there is a lot of growing skepticism about the term "support the troops"—accusations of it being a meaningless term with no real "support" backing it. Journalists particularly cite the lack of resources for veterans who come home wounded, suffering from post-traumatic stress disorder, and unable to find civilian jobs. What are your thoughts on this recent criticism of the slogan "support the troops"?

15. What is *Viet Man*'s intent—and how many drafts did you write of the novel before you considered it finished?

16. Over the past few months, many in our nation and throughout the world have purchased movie tickets to see Clint Eastwood's controversial new war film, *American Sniper.* As a man who has seen action while serving, how did you feel about the material set forth in the film? What kind of kinship—if any—did you feel with the sniper character, played by Bradley Cooper? Where does your book *Viet Man* fit in all of this?

17. You've also been a firefighter for 15 years. Given that you've put your life in danger before with your service in Vietnam—and made it out—why did you risk your life again by going into firefighting?

18. Where can folks go to purchase your book?

Answer: People can purchase *Viet Man* at Amazon dot com or Barnes & Noble or any fine bookstores located near you.

Interview Questions for Richard W. Walker, Jr., MD, author of *Black Health Matters*

1. As a physician now for more than 50 years, when did you first realize that the African-American population was at the highest risk for developing a deadly disease?

2. What diseases is the Black community most susceptible to?

3. What do you consider to be the biggest contributor in these statistics?

4. Do you think that enough of the African-American community is aware of this growing problem?

5. You speak in your new book about the importance of diet and nutrition in daily life. Historically, what kind of disadvantages or challenges have the Black community faced in this nation when it comes to their food and nutritional value therein—and how can it change for the better?

6. In your experience, what single vitamin and/or supplement do you think the Black community needs above all else—and why?

7. What are some of the better ways that you can recommend to promote overall wellness for the African-American community?

8. Do you lean towards traditional medicine, a holistic approach, or a combination of both?

9. If you had to share one piece of health advice for African-Americans, what would that advice be?

10. Are there are any especially good websites that folks can go to, in addition to learning from your new book?

11. Where can we buy your book?

Answer: People can purchase *Black Health Matters* by either going to "Amazon dot com" or by visiting the publisher's website at "Square One Publishers dot com." You can call Square One directly as well. The book is also available through Barnes & Noble or at your nearest local bookstore.

appreciate your consideration in offering the list. On pages 172 to 174, you will find sample interview questions for a fiction title and a non-fiction book.

Book Reviews and Blurbs, Assorted Press Coverage, and Excerpts

If you have already received reviews for your book by the time you actively pitch it to the media, be sure to include any assemblage you have of these items (either full reviews or review quotes) in your press kit. You want to avoid a media kit that is too long, so keep your reviews, excerpts, and blurbs to one page. Remember that anyone reading the media kit is pressed for time and probably inundated daily with media kits and information. Of course, if you've been lucky enough to receive a rave review from an important journal like *PW (Publishers Weekly)*, you want to include enough of the review to make the point that your book should be taken seriously. Similarly, if influencers, celebrities, or other newsworthy people have provided blurbs, you will want to include a selection of the best blurbs.

Make sure to include any media coverage that features your name or your book's title when you are putting together your press kit. Remember that you always stand a chance of receiving more publicity for your book as you continue to pitch to the media. If you do, be sure to scan and save copies of this new coverage as it is published so you can include it in your media kit. To paraphrase what they say in Hollywood, you're only as good as your most recent publicity.

An excerpt of a few lines from your book can be an effective addition to your media kit if the material you include is truly compelling. When legendary author Joan Didion died at the age of eighty-seven, most of the features about her began with the first lines of her best-selling memoir about grief, *The Year of Magical Thinking:* "Life changes fast. Life changes in the instant." If you visit the Amazon.com site for her book, you will find "Popular Highlights in this book," such as "Grief turns out to be a place none of us know until we reach it." These are the kinds of gripping lines that would add value to your media kit.

If you are unsure of which excerpts should be included in your media kit, ask your developmental editor, copyeditor, or proofreader what lines or paragraphs stood out to her as being especially well-written and memorable. Or skim your book again and pull out the lines that most resonate with you and that you think others would also find compelling.

Be aware that your media kit should change as you obtain additional positive reviews, as you get more media attention that would be of interest to journalists and other media people, and even according to what's happening in the news. As you learned in the section on press releases, depending on your book's subject and genre, world, national, or local events can suddenly make your book of greater interest to the media. In a case such as this, you would want to revise your press release accordingly. So even after you complete your media kit, you should not think of it as being "done." Instead, you should always be willing to change it to make it more appealing and relevant.

To "E" or Not to "E" Your Press Kit

When it comes to the media, many of its members prefer to receive their materials in a digital format as opposed to hard copies sent through the mail. Since you will always do better in promotion when you accept and embrace the preferences of those with whom you hope to connect, it is a good idea for you to use your press kit materials to create an electronic press kit, or EPK. Your EPK should include all the items associated with a traditional press kit, but in this digital version, you can add links to any websites mentioned, which, when clicked on, will take the reader directly to these websites. While there may always be a portion of the population, media or otherwise, who will want to read through your press kit in its printed form, the EPK is here to stay and should be used whenever a media outlet expresses a preference for receiving electronic material.

WHAT SHOULD BE SENT ALONG WITH YOUR PRESS KIT?

As you just learned, your press kit will provide fairly complete information about your book and you as an author. But at this point, you may be wondering if you should accompany the kit with a copy of your book and, perhaps, a customized letter such as the one you sent along with review copies of your book. (See page 128 of Chapter 8.) Let's consider each of these in turn.

Traditionally, a physical media kit should be accompanied by an advance reading copy (ARC) of your book. It makes sense that if someone's interest is piqued by your press release and the other materials in your kit, she will want to see your book before deciding whether to write an article about you or conduct an interview. By including an ARC in your mailing, you will avoid having to potentially send out another mailing to interested recipients.

The question of whether to send an ARC becomes more complicated when you are sending an electronic press kit (EPK). (See the inset on page 176.) As discussed earlier in the book, once you send an electronic form of your book to someone, it is very easy for it to become *pirated*—illegally copied and made available to others on the Internet. Therefore, I suggest that when sending out EPKs, you leave out the ARC and give the recipient the option of requesting one. You can then send her a password-protected PDF of your book as explained on page 124.

Should a personal letter—whether paper, or in the case of an EPK, electronic—accompany each media kit you send out? Whenever you have a specific name to which you will send your media kit, a personal letter is *definitely* a good thing to include. While the letter itself is usually a condensed presentation of what is covered in greater depth in your press release—together with the talking points and your "About the Author" page—its most crucial job is to help foster a direct connection between you and the letter's recipient. This could make the difference between the recipient tossing the press kit aside or giving you and your book the attention you deserve. (See the sample cover letter on page 178.)

WHAT MEDIA OUTLETS SHOULD YOU REACH OUT TO?

In Chapter 8, we looked at the media outlets that are most likely to write about or otherwise feature an author whose book was self-published, produced by a small press, or produced by a major house with a little-known author. These same media—local magazines, local newspapers, and local radio and television shows—should be on your list of people who will receive your media kit. (For more about this, see pages 137 to 143 in Chapter 8.) As described in that chapter, you should also consider contacting appropriate specialty publications, such as

SAMPLE COVER LETTER ACCOMPANYING PRESS KIT

Crestor – Double the Trouble,
Twice the Risk of Other Statin Drugs

Dear [Producer / Editor Name]:

In light of a new study that names Crestor as having at least twice the number of side effect risks already associated with a number of other cholesterol-lowering drugs such as Merck's Zocor and Pfizer's Lipitor, I'd like to offer you interview time with a leading expert in this area of medicine.

Jay Cohen, MD, a leading consumer advocate who monitors the pharmaceutical industry, has written the first book to explore the issue of statin safety, called *What You Must Know About Statin Drugs & Their Natural Alternatives* (Square One Publishers).

In his book, Dr. Cohen shows that most statin side effects are avoidable by using a precision method for identifying the right statin medication at the right dose for you. According to Dr. Cohen, the recent problems with Crestor and many of the other statin drugs have mostly to do with an industry-wide overload on prescribed dosage levels. Dr. Cohen contends that this atmosphere of rampant overdosage exists because drug companies value profit over patients, running contrary to the moral and ethical responsibilities of a medical community whose primary duty should be to serve the needs of the patient.

On your program, Dr. Cohen can tell your viewers:

1. Effective strategies for dealing with statin side effects

2. Practical ways to prevent statin side effects altogether

3. Special dosing guidelines for women, seniors, and patients with medical sensitivities

4. 6 ways to cut your statin treatment costs by 50 percent

5. Self-care strategies for reducing your cholesterol naturally

6. Medically proven alternative treatments for lowering cholesterol

7. Best foods, supplements, and nutrients for cardiovascular health

Please let us know if we can arrange a time for you to speak with Dr. Cohen directly.

Best regards,

Anthony Pomes
Square One Publishers
VP – Marketing/PR

journals and newsletters that are a good fit for your book because of your title's subject matter or genre, or because you are a member of the association that creates the publication. If a special circumstance has made your book especially newsworthy—for instance, if a news event ties in perfectly with the subject of your nonfiction book—you may decide to also send your media kit to a larger publication or show. As I've said before, it pays to remain aware of what is happening in the nation or abroad or, depending on your book, in your area of expertise. As far as Internet-based media, you can send your electronic media kit to any and all appropriate podcasts, bloggers, and online publications. (To learn more about appropriate digital media, see Chapter 4.)

As you select the media that will receive your press kit, you will have to locate the contact information for each publication and show. For information on gathering and recording the data, see page 144 of Chapter 8.

SENDING OUT YOUR PRESS KIT

Once you have your materials gathered together in a printed press kit, you will need to come up with the best method for sending it out in the mail—a.k.a. "snail-mail." Many authors, publishers, and publicists alike choose to use the United States Postal Service's (USPS) Media Mail method because it is more affordable than sending materials either through First Class or Priority Mail rates. When using Media Mail, remain mindful that there are guidelines in place for this rate. It is not uncommon for USPS workers to conduct random searches of what is contained in a Media Mail package to ensure that the contents are eligible. If an item in the package is deemed ineligible, the package may be returned to the sender, or the recipient may be asked to pay the increased cost for the next level of shipping, such as First Class or Priority Mail, resulting in your package being refused or abandoned. With that being said, over the years, I have had no trouble sending out the press kit items mentioned in this chapter using the lower Media Mail rate, as long as the contents was related to the enclosed book and I did not exceed the maximum weight for Media Mail, which is seventy pounds.

Can you send out your media kit using First Class or Priority Mail? If you are mailing out only a few packages and cost is not a major consideration, you can certainly use these services. The packages will get there faster and may even be taken more seriously. In general, though, you'll want to use Media Mail to send out large mailings and use First Class or Priority Mail only when a media contact has already expressed an interest in your book and is waiting for your package.

If you want to expand your reach beyond the media contacts you currently have, you might consider sending out your media kit en masse through a commercial press release distribution service. There are at least five press release distribution services that will do this for you, albeit for a fee. (You will find a listing of these services on page 256 of the Resources section.) Those services include, in alphabetical order: Business Wire, eReleases, Newswire, PR Newswire, and PR Web. In addition to the initial press material distribution fee, most of these service providers will also charge a fee if you want them to write your press material for you. There is usually a basic fee charged for text and then, on top of that, an additional fee if you add an image to your release. Since you are promoting your book, adding at least one image— ideally, your book's front cover—is recommended since it increases the likelihood that the cover will be included in any formally published synopses of your media release.

Before you choose the distribution service you will use, be sure to do your due diligence. Check out several websites, and call and speak to customer service representatives to get a better idea of which service would be best for you and your book. You might also network with other book authors—especially those who write in a similar genre—to learn about the results that were generated by the service they used. Always remember, though, that there are many variables at play when it comes to receiving press coverage. In addition to the basic effectiveness of the distribution service in question, the timeliness of your book's release, the topic or genre of your book, your perceived reputation as an author, the writing quality of the press materials, and the relative accuracy with which the media has been targeted can all affect your results.

The timing of your press release and/or media kit is particularly important to your promotion. In general, you would not want to send out your media release or press kit on a Friday afternoon in the summer- time. This is especially true of the media on the East Coast, where the lion's share of major media is based, because so many in this field have three-day weekends starting at the end of May—Memorial Day—and going through to Labor Day at the beginning of September. During this time of the year, many people in the media simply are not working on Fridays. (Many also take Monday off during the summer.) And if your emailed press kit or press release does go into someone's electronic in-box, by the time the recipient gets back to work, many more media releases may have arrived, and yours could get lost in the shuffle. The bottom line is that in the summertime, you should send out your press release between Tuesday and Thursday, and I actually favor sending it out on Tuesday or Wednesday.

The Power of Being Proactive

I know from experience that being proactive about possible media interviews really can work to your benefit. Yes, it takes a certain degree of effort, and a positive outcome is often a matter of timing or serendipity, but good things can happen when you try. For example, I once wrote to a producer at ABC's *The View* to pitch my book about friendships titled *Friendshifts*. The delivery of my letter happened to coincide with the program's decision to present an entire show devoted to friendship. Voilà! I was soon booked on a national TV spot!

Over the years, authors, publishers, and publicists have reported to me that these mass distributions to the media have yielded a variety of results—ranging from only a few cursory pick-ups to a veritable blast of well-timed coverage and time-sensitive interview requests. Unfortunately, there is no way to know in advance if your media kit will get enough hits to justify the cost. But if you want as many potential readers as possible to know about your book, the distribution of media kits to carefully selected media outlets can help you meet your goal.

HIRING A PUBLICIST

There is a reason why most trade book publishers either have PR experts employed in-house or work with outside publicity firms. It is because publicity is a tough and time-consuming job, especially when done right. Many people who have written books find that they don't have the time, the drive, or the dogged persistence necessary to promote their books. Also, book publicity depends on relationships that publicists build with the media over years, even decades. Most likely, you don't have these crucial relationships. There is nothing wrong with deciding that you do not want to handle the publicity for your book. But if you want the media to know about your book, you will need to hire someone to handle publicity for you, provided you can afford to do so.

You can either hire a freelance publicist or work with a part-time or full-time assistant who can pitch your book and manage your mailings. If you hire someone who does publicity full-time, she should have an extensive up-to-date list of media contacts to whom she could pitch your book. The advantage of hiring a publicist is that it is a more strategic approach than doing your own publicity and having to learn and improve upon the process at every step along the way.

Most publicity experts require a minimum time period of three months for any campaign they agree to handle. A good publicist will aim to book TV and radio segments for you from an established list of contacts and will send out review copies of your book or media kits to both traditional and online outlets. Some publicists concentrate on specific kinds of media coverage. The nature of your book should help you and any potential publicist determine whether she is right for the job.

When choosing a publicist, just as when hiring anyone else, it pays to check out the individual's experience and success rate, and also to make sure that you understand what she is offering. Here are a few tips for choosing a professional who can meet your needs:

- If possible, get referrals from book authors you know who have used a publicist and are pleased with the results. Make sure, however, that your book is comparable to theirs in terms of subject and genre. Be careful about comparing apples to oranges, as they say.

- If you cannot get referrals from other authors, turn to page 244 of the Resources section to find the Publicity Trends website, which features a contact list of freelance book publicists.

- Read the testimonials on each publicist's website, but also ask for the names and contact information for at least three clients whom you can contact if you wish to discuss how they feel about the services they received.

- Make sure you know what you will be getting for the price you're paying. For instance, how long will the promotional campaign last, and exactly what will the publicist do for you during that time?

- Ask if the publicist will be writing your press release and creating a press kit, and if that is included in the fee. If you prefer to write the media kit yourself, ask if your fee will be reduced.

- Ask how widely the company will be pitching. Will the publicist pitch to TV/cable and radio shows, podcasts, newspapers, magazines, online publications, and bloggers? Will you be given the list of contacts that are pitched or only a list of the results?

Rather than handing the promotion over to the hired publicist and assuming that it will be handled properly without your participation, it makes sense to keep in touch with the person you're employing, whether by phone, email, texts, Zoom conferencing, or in-person meetings. When you begin the relationship, decide how often you will be informed of the results of the publicist's efforts. Then follow up with regular communications to make sure that the campaign is staying on track.

CONCLUSION

In this chapter, you have learned how to create a relevant and timely publicity pitch, how to put together an effective press kit, and how to best deliver it to those media people who are most likely to find your book of interest. You have also considered whether you should do your own publicity or hire a publicist to handle it on your behalf.

The task of promoting your book can be a daunting one. The system has long favored well-known authors and large publishing houses that have experienced publicity departments. Moreover, there are more technological conveniences in our world than ever before, which means that changes in the industry occur at a rapid pace. The most effective means of publicity today may not be the most effective means of publicity next year or even next week, so it is just as important to be adaptable as it is to understand the tools currently at your disposal. The only thing you can truly control is the quality of your writing and the persistence with which you pursue the promotion of your title.

Throughout this book, I have mentioned the possibility of promoting your book through speaking engagements at bookstores, libraries, and other venues. If this is of interest to you, the next chapter will explore how you can secure speaking opportunities and, just as important, how you can make the most of them for you and your book.

10.

Speaking Your Way to More Sales

If you are a first-time author, you may be surprised to learn that a book can open up countless speaking opportunities for you, both free and paid. Although many speakers are authors, not all authors are speakers. During the fifteen years I was a member of the National Speakers Association, I used to say to other members, "I am a writer who speaks." The majority of the members, by contrast, were speakers who might have written a book—or even many books—but they identified themselves as speakers, and that's how they got the bulk of their income.

The simple fact is that authors who speak can gain attention for themselves and for their titles—which, in turn, can result in book sales and, for some authors, even some decent speaker fees. Famous American author Mark Twain sold a heck of a lot of tickets—along with books—by touring the country and speaking to groups of enthusiastic fans. And he was doing what many other authors had done before him.

Whether you get paid an honorarium for speaking or you simply profit from the sale of your book, there are many benefits to speaking. First of all, once you agree to be a speaker, your event will be promoted, which means free publicity for you and your title. You will also get to meet new people, whether it is the meeting planner who sets up the opportunity or those in the audience. If you speak at a conference, you will also meet fellow speakers. Interestingly, when talking to fans or others at your event, you might also get an idea for another title to write. This has happened to me on occasion, resulting in my writing a new book.

Of course, not everyone feels comfortable talking in front of an audience. If speaking does not come naturally to you, but you wish to develop your skills, there are many ways to improve both your confidence and your proficiency. Turn to page 197 for tips on being a better speaker as well as suggestions regarding groups that can provide you with training and experience.

I understand that public speaking is not for everyone. If it's not for you, you can still promote yourself and your book on a more limited basis at common speaker venues such as book fairs, association meetings, and library and bookstore author events. I recommend that you stick to book signings and avoid giving longer talks or workshops. But if you feel that you are a good enough speaker or that you are willing to work on your skills and give this promotional tool a try, this chapter is for you.

WHO WILL SECURE YOUR SPEAKING ENGAGEMENTS?

If you have been published by a commercial publisher, it is likely—but not guaranteed, unless it is specified in your publisher's agreement— that the publishing company will provide you with some form of publicity. This is normally done by an in-house publicist. While the focus of such promotion is based on the book's subject, as a rule of thumb, the publisher generally schedules signings at bookstores and/or interviews. Several of the major publishers, such as HarperCollins and Simon & Schuster, have even added speakers bureaus to the services they offer their authors. If your publisher offers these services, this is an option that you should explore.

If you are working with a hybrid publisher, depending on the specific company and what it offers its authors, the promotional service will probably be included at an additional charge, separate from the production, printing, and distribution services. If you are willing to pay for promotion, the publicist—just like a publicist from a traditional publishing house—will likely be open to arranging book signings and interviews for you.

If you are self-published, you already know that the task of publicizing your book will land squarely on your shoulders or, perhaps, on the shoulders of a hired publicist. However, surprisingly, not enough authors and their publicists place speaking engagements high on their

list of promotional goals. This is unfortunate, because speaking at various events can make a significant difference in the success of a title and,
of course, can sometimes provide speaker fees.

If you are interested in speaking but don't have the time or inclination to secure speaking engagements on your own, you might consider
trying to get listed with a speakers bureau or working with an individual who books speakers on a fee or a 25-percent commission basis. This
will keep your publicist—if you have one—focused on media pitches
and review copy distributions, which are most likely his areas of expertise. Keep in mind that celebrities and authors with more recognizable
names are going to have a better chance of getting listed and selected
for speaking engagements than an unknown author. Nevertheless, it is
worth a try, especially if your book focuses on a topic that is currently
of great interest to the public.

Despite the existence of speakers bureaus, the fact is that most
authors who are self-published are on their own when it comes to
finding and securing promotional speaking opportunities. Fortunately,
there are a number of venues that are open to enterprising authors who
are interested in talking to people about their book, their subject of
expertise, or themselves. In the following pages, we'll look at the most
promising possibilities.

BOOKSTORES

A successful bookstore book signing benefits everyone involved. The
bookstore and author benefit from the fact that, potentially, many copies
of the book will be sold. Book signings also increase the visibility of the
store, enhance public goodwill, and allow authors to get to know their
fans. And, of course, fans appreciate signings because they provide a
chance to see and meet a favorite author, to get a signed book, and to
even ask questions.

Bookstore signings can be conducted in one of two ways. The event
can be just a straight book signing, with the author sitting at a table for
the sole purpose of signing books. (In some cases, there may be more
than one author signing books in a store at the same time.) Alternatively, the author may be asked to speak before the signing. Normally,
signings of adult fiction and nonfiction authors are scheduled in the
evening, although weekend signings are also possible. Signings of a

children's book can take place in the middle of the day or on a Saturday or Sunday—whenever a parent is off from work and the children are not in school. Naturally, children may also be taken to these events by caregivers other than their parents.

When authors speak to the audience before the signing, their presentation partly depends on the nature of their book. A fiction author might talk about his interest in a specific genre, other fiction writers whom he finds inspiring, where he got the idea for the plot of his latest book, and how he researched his book. (For instance, if the book is set in Victorian England, he most likely researched that place and time period, and might even have traveled to London or other parts of the United Kingdom.) Often, a fiction writer will also read a passage from his book. Nonfiction authors are likely to discuss the subject of their book, such as tax preparation, local history, friendship, wellness, sailing—the possibilities are endless. Often, the author's presentation—which should be twenty to thirty minutes in length—is followed by a question-and-answer period with the audience. After this, members of the audience are given the opportunity to have their books signed.

When an author is well known and is guaranteed to draw a large audience, the stores normally work around the author's schedules. While bookstore events are usually free of charge, celebrities and high-profile authors may have such an impressive reputation that the bookstore is able to charge the patrons a fee, which usually includes the retail list price of the book.

In many bookstores, a Community Relations Manager, or CRM, has the job of setting up and coordinating such events. In smaller bookstores, the events are usually limited to just a book signing, because the lack of space makes it impossible to set up enough chairs for a speech. Occasionally, a small store will partner with a nearby venue, such as a local library, if the number of expected attendees justifies the cost of such a rental. Larger stores, of course, often have the space needed to accommodate a speaker's podium and seating. In order to get booked into such a speaking engagement, most stores have certain requirements that authors should be aware of beforehand. These may include the following:

- The author may be required to guarantee that he will arrange for at least fifty people to attend the event. The more people who show up, the more of the author's books will be sold, and the more likely it is that some of the audience members will browse the shelves and buy additional titles.

- The author or publisher may be asked to pay a fee for the event. This money may be used for "co-op" advertising of the event in a local newspaper, creating a window poster promoting the event, or the additional labor involved in setting up the space.

- The store will probably ask the author to help promote the event through both traditional and social media. Bookstores want to make sure that the event and the name of their store is made known to as many local people as possible.

- The store may require the author and/or the publisher to provide a better-than-standard discount for the books sold at the signing. Once the event has ended, the bulk of the unsold titles are likely to be

Remote Author Events

Since 2020, when the pandemic hit and forced many bookstores to close or reduce their hours, many author events moved to cyberspace and video conferencing services such as Zoom, Microsoft Teams, and Webex. Libraries, too, began hosting remote author interviews. Like many practices that started during the pandemic, remote author talks are still an option in some instances, although live author talks have been brought back as well.

Videoconferencing events are still an excellent way to promote your title—without traveling to a distant store or library. While they may not generate immediate bookstore sales or offer the opportunity for you to interact in person with your fans and actually shake hands, they can create word-of-mouth marketing for your book, which will lead to sales. When I do an online event, as a way of connecting with attendees, I often create a related handout or information sheet that I offer to email to participants if they contact me by email. With their permission, I also add them and their contact information to my publisher's or author's email mailing list as a way of maintaining a relationship with them.

returned for full credit, although some stores may commit to "pushing" the unsold books so that they don't have to deal with the returns process. (If the store decides to keep the unsold books, you may be asked to sign them so they can be displayed in a special "Signed by the Author" section of the store.) Payment to the author for the books sold may take place only after the event has concluded.

Making It Happen

Your first step in arranging a bookstore event is to get in touch with that store's CRM. This can be done by making a phone call, sending an email, or simply dropping by the store. If you do visit the store, make sure it isn't the busiest part of the day. If it turns out to be busier than you expected, politely excuse yourself and ask what would be a good time to meet with the CRM and discuss a possible event. Bring your book along with your press kit, but give the kit out only if you are asked to do so.

During your meeting with the CRM, ask what the store's procedure is for hosting an author talk. At that point, the CRM may tell you what his requirements are. He may also ask you a number of questions, such as: Do you think you can attract a large enough audience? Where else have you spoken? Do you live in that community? Do you work in that community? If your answers convince the CRM that you can help deliver an event that is a commercial success, he will be more likely to work with you.

If and when you are scheduled to do an author talk and/or signing, your contact for the event will be the CRM. While a good deal of the pressure for bringing in a decent-sized audience will be on your shoulders, the CRM also is responsible for making your event a success. His job includes letting the bookstore's customer base and community know about your author event in advance. Standard practice is to place a poster in the store's front window promoting the event, and to send out several email blasts to the store's in-house email list of customers. In some cases, the CRM may also have local media contacts. If the store has a website, all events should, of course, be listed there, as well. When you discuss the talk or signing with the store's representative, be sure to ask how he will promote the event.

Even if the CRM will promote the bookstore event, it's a good idea to reach out to friends, family, and social media contacts to ensure a good turnout. See the inset on page 193 for tips on attracting people to an author talk or signing.

The more successful your bookstore event is, the more likely it is that you will find other bookstores interested in hosting events that showcase your book. Try to learn from each experience. Keep track of the response you receive at each store, including the number of attendees and the number of books sold, so you will have that information at your fingertips. If the numbers are impressive enough, you can share them in your pitches to additional bookstores.

LIBRARIES

As you would imagine, libraries love authors, and authors love libraries. Public libraries can be stand-alone facilities or have a number of branches. While some libraries are of a limited size and budget, and some have relatively few patrons because they are situated in sparsely populated areas, many mid-sized and larger libraries are bustling with activity. These libraries offer the community a number of services and events, from lectures to movies to crafts demonstrations, and they usually have clear-cut departments that focus on children's books, young adult titles, and books for adults. Often, they have staff members who arrange events such as authors talks. In many libraries, in fact, author talks are regularly scheduled and include book signings or even one- to two-hour workshops.

Making it Happen

Each library has its own procedure for scheduling an author talk. To find the person who arranges these events, call the general library number and ask to speak to either the front desk or the reference librarian. One of these people should be able to provide you with the name, extension, and/or email of the right staff member. You might also check the library website and look for the person in charge of Adult Programming or Children's Programming—whichever is appropriate for your title.

When you speak to the staff member who arranges author talks, be prepared to provide as much information as possible about your book, the subject you would like to discuss, and yourself. That person may have to pass on your request to other committee members, so the more information your contact has to present on your behalf, the stronger your case. You may offer to send him a copy of your book and a press kit or to drop these materials off in person. If your book has been reviewed in any newspapers or prepublication trade publications such as *Library Journal, Booklist, PW, Kirkus Reviews, or Foreword Reviews,* be sure to include copies of the reviews, as librarians especially value the endorsement of these publications.

Because of limited budgets, most libraries expect authors to provide talks free of charge. However, some better-funded libraries do set aside funds for a speaker's honorarium. The typical library honorarium is not going to pay for your next European vacation, but you may be offered between $100 to $250, if you are lucky, and some might go as high as $500. Be sure to ask if there is an honorarium while keeping in mind that an opportunity to tell people about your book can be worthwhile even if you do not get a fee. Ask if the library will keep the money from the sale of the books, if the money generated by book sales will go soley to you, or if you and the library will divide the proceeds.

Be aware that some libraries ask authors or their publishers to pay for space as a reimbursement for holding the event. If this is the case, make sure you are allowed to sell books and that the money earned from the book sales will go to you or the publisher. Be practical, and consider how many attendees you can expect and how much money you stand to make on the sale of each book. You want to avoid spending more money on renting the space than you are likely to earn at the event.

As with author talks at bookstores, it is important to have a decent number of people attend your event. In most cases, the library will send out email blasts to their patrons announcing the talk, will post the event on their bulletin board or in their showcase, and will include a listing of it on their website and in their newsletter, if they have one. You should, of course, reach out to your own social media followers, friends, and colleagues. (See the inset on page 193.) With the permission of the library director or branch manager, you may also want to supply your own poster to place in the library.

The good news about libraries is that there are plenty of them, so you can find a wide range of places that will potentially offer to host an author talk. These days, your community is likely to have more libraries than bookstores, so be sure to make the most of the opportunities they offer. If one librarian likes the way your speech was received, ask him to let other libraries know. Library events can also help you hone your speaking skills and learn more about your audience.

Attracting an Audience to Your Author Events

In some situations, you will not be expected to attract attendees to your event. You will simply be asked to show up and speak. On the other hand, as already mentioned, some bookstores may expect you to bring in enough people to justify the time and effort it takes the store to put together an author signing. Some bookstores will not even schedule an event unless the publisher puts up funds that can be used for "co-op" advertising in local newspapers or on websites.

Libraries may have their own outreach programs, through local media as well as their email lists. Or, if you or your publisher prefers, the library may work with a local bookseller who will take care of the book sales part of the event.

Whether or not a library, bookstore, or other venue promises to promote your event, it is always a good idea to do whatever you can to help generate an audience so that the event is as well attended as possible. If you have established a social media presence as discussed in Chapter 4, you can easily get the word out about your upcoming talk or signing. If you have connected with a fan in the immediate vicinity of your event, he might show up to finally meet you. If your fan does not live nearby, he might get out the word to friends or relatives that live in the area. Once you have an event scheduled, tweet about it, post about it on Facebook, let your LinkedIn connections know about it, and keep posting now and then to help generate buzz. Just don't post so often about a particular upcoming author event that you turn people off.

CONVENTIONS, CONFERENCES, AND OTHER SPECIALIZED EVENTS

Each year, there are literally tens of thousands of specialized events occurring throughout this country and the rest of the world. These events can take many forms, including conventions, workshops, conferences, seminars, in-service programs, or just plain weekly club meetings. Their focuses can be highly specialized or absolutely freewheeling. What they have in common is that they bring like-minded people together, either in-person or online. Many of these groups, organizations, and associations look for speakers based on their particular interest. For example, natural product expositions look for speakers who can talk about a subject related to health, interior design conventions look for speakers who can discuss new trends in their field, and book clubs look for local authors who have written a good book. (Note that most book clubs prefer fiction, memoirs, and possibly thrillers and true crime, but some are open to an occasional self-help or other nonfiction work or a children's book.) All of these events can help authors gain visibility, grow their fan base, and sell books.

Consider the following organizations and events as potential opportunities for you to speak and sell your book at the end of your presentation:

- National, regional, and/or local conventions
- Professional association and/or educational meetings
- Local chamber of commerce meetings and other business groups
- Local hobby, religious, and/or cooking club meetings
- Book discussion groups
- Literary clubs

If you have a clear idea of who your audience is and where your potential readers may be found, the speaking opportunities listed above can pay off nicely. Some event sponsors pay fees, while others don't provide payment. But remember that even if you are not paid for speaking, you will have a chance to be seen and heard—and, hopefully, to sell your book. If you will be an unpaid speaker at a conference, ask in advance if you will be expected to pay to attend the event. If that is the policy, you will have to decide if it's in your best financial interest to accept the opportunity, especially if the event is out of town and you are paying your own way.

Making it Happen

While many organized meetings provide potential opportunities to authors, based on the organization and its purpose, you may find it relatively easy or quite challenging to get a speaking engagement there. At larger meetings, speakers may be hired by companies to talk about a product-related topic of interest to the attendees. These sponsoring companies pay speakers a fee and cover all their travel expenses. They also pay for a time slot and room for the speaker to lecture. Often, these speakers are also published authors, and the sponsoring companies buy copies of their books to be given away free to those people who attend their talks. At larger venues, the company generally reaches out to the speaker. At smaller venues, it is usually the speaker who reaches out to the group and requests an opportunity to talk.

Making the Most of Book Events

If you go out of town for a book fair or other book event, you will probably be spending a good deal of money on transportation, hotel accommodations, and meals. It is a smart practice to make the most of this opportunity.

As soon as you commit to attending the event, let local media know that you will be in town on those dates, and see if they want to interview you during your visit. You can also contact the local bookstore, library, and other likely venues for author events. For instance, if you have written a book about World War II, a local war or military museum might be a good fit, or you might contact the local chapter of the Veterans of Foreign Wars (VFW) or another veterans association. The media may be more likely to cover you and your book if in addition to being physically present in their town or city to attend a book conference, you offer an event that is open to the public.

Because of the varied nature of these group meetings, it is difficult to provide an overall approach to getting speaking engagements. Generally, nonfiction authors are more likely than fiction authors to find speaking opportunities at these meetings. However, opportunities for fiction authors do crop up. For instance, *any* author—of fiction or nonfiction—may become an invited speaker at his own college, high school, or professional or graduate school reunion, or at a local club meeting. For the most part, it falls on you, the author, to evaluate which groups are likely to value you as a speaker, and to then reach out to see if they are providing speaking opportunities.

BOOK EVENTS

The world of organized book events is a big one. It is composed of commercial publishers, librarians, bookstores, and writers groups that organize or sponsor meetings around the country and the world. These events are designed to highlight publishers, their books, and their authors.

While in the past, many of these events—which can take the form of conventions, meetings, or book fairs—were restricted to commercially published authors and their titles, over the last few years, things have changed. Now, many authors whose books have been self-published or produced by hybrid publishers or smaller indie presses are able to promote their books as well as conduct author talks at these events.

Conventions and meetings can be national, regional, or local. The book fairs are usually local, although a number of them have gained national attention, such as the fairs held annually in Miami, Brooklyn, and Los Angeles. These larger fairs attract much larger crowds and many potential book buyers.

Lots of book events sell space that allow booths and tables to be set up so that publishers and authors can display their titles, and authors can sign and sell books. (See Chapter 11 for information on setting up displays at fairs and conventions.) Many of these events also allow authors to talk about their books. Sometimes, but not always, authors have to pay a fee to speak.

Making It Happen

Each book event has a specific purpose and is focused on attracting a particular audience. Some are geared to reach bookstore owners or librarians, while others are designed to bring in the general public. Although you may find that you can display and sell your book at many of the events, you'll want to look for venues that will enable you to speak about your title.

In the Resources section, you will find a list of organizations that sponsor book events along with websites that list book events all over the United States. (See page 238.) This will give you a starting point for your search. Visit the websites set up for those events that seem appropriate for your book—and, of course, those in geographic areas that are convenient for you or that you might be traveling to anyway—and learn as much as you can about each event of interest. By considering the speakers that have been featured at a given event in the past, you will be better able to decide if the audience will be a good fit for you and your book. Once you have found an event that seems promising, you can look into the application process.

BECOMING A BETTER SPEAKER

Have you ever listened to a speaker who was absolutely terrific? Conversely, have you sat through a speech that was disorganized, boring, and of little substance? I still remember hearing Alex Haley—best known for his books *Roots: The Saga of an American Family* and *The Autobiography of Malcolm X*—when he was the keynote luncheon speaker at the American Society of Journalists and Authors (ASJA) writers conference many years ago. He was commanding at the podium, and his words were as mesmerizing as his books.

If you're introducing a colleague at an upcoming writers conference or you're giving a forty-five-minute speech to a room full of eighth graders, you may not feel that you should be judged by the same standards that might have been applied to Alex Haley. Nevertheless, you want to command your audience's attention and respect, and if you're discussing your new book, you definitely want to pique your listeners' interest.

If you are truly interested in honing your speaking skills, you might consider working with a speaking coach, joining the local Toastmasters to get practice speaking before a group, or attending monthly meetings of your local National Speakers Association (NSA) group. Toastmasters will offer you an opportunity to speak on a regular basis at its meetings, and the NSA will expose you to excellent speakers and can also provide a speakers' "boot camp"—usually referred to as the Speakers Academy—for aspiring speakers.

Whether you get formal training in giving talks or you want to work on your own to improve your speaking skills, there are several concepts to keep in mind. The following pointers can help you better connect with your audience, maintain your audience's attention, and more clearly share your ideas.

Helpful Tips for Becoming a Better Speaker

- Plan for each and every speech. Don't think you can "wing it." Prepare, prepare, prepare.

- If possible, learn about your audience ahead of time so that you can tailor your speech to the attendees. You don't want the audience members to get the feeling that you're delivering the same old speech you've given a dozen times before.

- Be aware of what was promised to the audience in promotional materials or write-ups, and make sure that your speech will meet your audience's expectations.

- Dress appropriately for both your audience and the venue. This is an important way to make a good impression and show your respect for the attendees.

- Arrive on time for the speech, or even better, get there ahead of time so that you can make sure that your microphone is in working order and also learn about your audience. If circumstances allow, mingle with the audience before the speech so that you can get a sense of their interests.

- While it's a good idea to bring notes with you for reference, do not keep your eyes glued to a sheet of paper or a stack of cards while you speak. Instead, try to talk directly to your audience, making eye contact with attendees whenever possible.

- When creating your presentation, organize your thoughts using this structure: Start with an interesting anecdote, example, or statistic. Then build on your opening statement by providing more information, usually making just two or three key points in your talk. Finally, wrap your talk up with a closing anecdote, example, or summary that ties everything you said together.

- Within your speech, share at least one idea that is memorable and useful. Think in terms of providing one "take-away" line that attendees will feel is important enough to write down in their notebook or record on their smartphones.

- Speak clearly and loudly. You want all the attendees to hear what you have to say without straining.

- Try to show confidence—after all, you are an expert on your book and, if you are a nonfiction author, in a specific field of expertise—but never behave in an arrogant manner.

- Regardless of your audience members' age or educational level, show respect for their intelligence and their investment of time. Never talk down to your audience.

- Be flexible and go with the flow. For instance, if an audience member asks a question, answer it to the best of your ability and avoid being dismissive. Also be willing to modify what you were going to say to suit the needs of your listeners.

- Don't hesitate to share appropriate personal examples or anecdotes that clarify the points you're making and help the audience learn from your past mistakes and triumphs. Personal anecdotes can also help keep a speech from being dull and dry.

- Do not hype your product. Of course, you want the attendees to buy your book, but telling them to do so will make them feel uncomfortable. It may even backfire! If you talk about yourself, your book, and your subject in an interesting way, you may be pleasantly surprised by how many people are more than willing to make a purchase.

- If you decide to use a PowerPoint presentation in your speech, use it only to enhance what you are saying. Never show slide after slide of text that will distract your audience from you, the speaker.

- Consider using handouts (information sheets) that reinforce or expand upon the information you're providing in your speech. If you are giving your talk through Zoom or another videoconferencing service, offer to email handouts to your audience or guide them to a website where they can find added knowledge and materials.

- At the conclusion of your speech, be available to answer questions, speak to audience members on a one-to-one basis, and shake hands.

- After each speaking event, ask yourself these questions: Did I do my best? Did I provide information, inspiration, and examples that made it worth my audience's time and money to listen to me? If the answer to either question is "no"—or if you're unsure—rework your presentation to improve it before giving another talk.

CONCLUSION

Although public speaking may not be for everyone, with proper preparation, some practice, and, if necessary, some coaching, an author talk can help you accomplish a number of goals. It is a respectable and time-honored way to promote yourself and your book. Through talks and appearances, you can help establish a fan base or, if you already have one, you can strengthen the connection you have with your readers so that their enthusiasm remains high. Getting out from behind your computer and talking about your book is also a great way to break out of the isolation that many writers—especially those who write full-time—experience. And, of course, speaking can be an effective way to make sales or earn extra income.

As you can see, there is no shortage of places where you can offer yourself as a speaker. Opportunities range from local libraries, bookstores, and book clubs to conventions and book fairs on the other side of the country. If you are not an experienced or confident speaker, you may want to start with small local venues, where you can work on your skills and build your confidence before moving on to larger audiences. You can set the pace and decide what is right for you.

In this chapter, we explored shows, meetings, and conventions where you could talk about your book. But many of these events also provide an opportunity to display and sell your book even if you are not going to speak to your potential readers. In the next chapter, we will discuss the details of booking and setting up a display table at some of these events.

11.

Exhibiting at Book Fairs and Trade Shows

n Chapter 10, you learned how to arrange speaking opportunities that will help you promote your title and generate sales. As you discovered, book fairs and trade shows are two of the many places where you may be able to deliver talks. What you may *not* know is that the majority of exhibitors at these events are not there to speak, but to show off their books. In fact, depending on the nature of the event, book fairs and trade shows are excellent places to get your book seen by bookstore buyers, librarians, the media, and the general reading public. They're also good places to meet and network with publishers and other authors.

WHAT ARE BOOK FAIRS AND TRADE SHOWS?

Before we begin exploring the subject of this chapter, it might be helpful to clarify what we mean when we talk about trade shows and book fairs. A *trade show* is designed for people in the industry—including not only publishers and booksellers, but also distributors, printers, and non-trade book buyers—so that they can promote their products and services to one another. Authors, librarians, and the media also often attend, but generally, these events are not open to the public. A *book fair* or *book festival* is organized by publishers and booksellers to sell their books, and anyone—including the reading public—may attend. Authors often attend, as well, and the media may be present.

There are also events that combine aspects of fairs and trade shows. For instance, the Guadalajara International Book Fair takes place every year in Guadalajara, Mexico at the end of November. A ten-day fair, the first couple of days are a trade show for professionals in the industry. During those days, book industry professionals meet to make deals for their titles. The remainder of the show is a public fair, with many of the professionals staffing booths to exhibit and sell their titles to the public.

HOW DO PUBLISHING HOUSES PREPARE FOR FAIRS AND SHOWS

As you might imagine, effectively displaying books at book fairs and similar events takes a great deal of effort. Experienced publishing houses, which regularly attend these shows, know how to stand out at both domestic and international trade shows and major book fairs. In preparation for each such event, they:

- Apply for a well-positioned space to set up a booth or table.

- Make arrangements for travel and accommodations.

- Prepare promotional materials—which may include ARCs (advance reading copies), imprinted giveaways like mugs or pencils, posters, and catalogues—to be handed out to people who visit the booth.

- Arrange to have promotional items, books, booths, and other materials shipped to the event.

- Advertise titles in promotional spaces made available at the event.

- Determine special show discounts on books that will be sold at the event.

- Assign sales people and editors to attend the event so they can discuss their titles with those they meet, and also record the contact information of people who stop by the booth.

- Bring in various authors to sign books and talk to the media, when possible.

- Decide what will be done with the display books at the end of the fair.

While these preparations may be routine for big publishers, the process can be overwhelming for authors who are doing it entirely on their own, even if they have the help of a hired publicist or assistant. This chapter is designed to lay out the basic steps you will need to follow as you prepare for these events. As you consider attending trade shows and book fairs, keep in mind that a comprehensive list of associations and websites that offer book events begins on page 238.

THE BASIC PREPARATIONS

The preparations for attending either a trade show or a book fair are very similar to those carried out by any experienced publishing house, as outlined above. The only difference is that you will be doing all the work yourself without a team of editors and sales people. Of course, if you have a publicist or an assistant, that might make your job easier, but it's still likely that a good deal of the work will fall on your shoulders. So, let's look at what you need to do to make it happen.

■ THE APPLICATION

Once you have decided on the event at which you wish to exhibit, you should carefully review the application. It is likely to be available on the website of the organization that's running the show. While the basic application questions are generally simple, there may be some questions that will require more consideration. For example, you might be asked who will take care of selling your books. In this case, depending on your situation, you might provide information about a local bookseller who is affiliated with you or with your publisher, if you have one. Of course, you may be selling your books yourself. If the application requests reviews or blurbs, be sure to include them with your application. You may also be asked if you have been on any author panels at previous shows. If you have, you will need to provide names and contact information in case the event organizers want a recommendation about your speaking abilities. You may also say that you choose not to be a speaker. (To learn about promoting your book through speaking, see Chapter 10.)

If you don't know how to answer some of the questions posed in the application, don't be afraid to call or send an email asking for clarification. Make sure to provide all the information that was requested and to fully understand what your responsibilities will be as an exhibitor.

■ LOCATION, LOCATION, LOCATION

Many events provide potential book exhibitors with a map showing the locations of the confirmed exhibitors as well as the spots that are still available for their table or booth. Getting a good position at smaller shows is normally not an issue because visitors at these events have a more limited space to traverse, so they usually end up seeing all or most of the exhibitors. At larger shows, however, position can be very important.

In some cases, larger shows include a big central hall along with smaller rooms that accommodate any overflow of exhibits, and in some cases, shows may occupy several different floors. As you might expect, small additional rooms and any floors other than the main floor tend to get fewer visitors. There may even be poorly positioned spaces in the central hall, such as those areas that are far from the hall's entrances. I have found that to receive the most visitor traffic, it is best to be located near the entrance of the main hall, near the bathrooms, or near a refreshment stand.

It's a good idea to know who will be your neighbors at the show. Being positioned near or in the same aisle as a large publisher or other vendor who's sure to draw a lot of traffic can be helpful, as it means that a great many people will be walking past your stand and might stop by to learn about you and your book.

People who display at the exhibit every year tend to get most of the prime spots because they have seniority and they know to register early. Be sure to register as soon as possible to secure a good location.

■ SETTING UP YOUR SPACE

Before we cover some of the other considerations involved in becoming an exhibitor, it is important to know how you intend to fill your space at the event. Remember that you want to make your space eye-catching and inviting, so that people will stop to look at your book (or books) and to chat, but you also have to provide yourself with the materials you will need to sell your books, to record the contact information of people whom you may want to get in touch with in the future, and to provide other people with your own contact information. Below, you'll find a listing of the most important items you'll want to have on hand.

- *A table and chair.* As an exhibiting author, a single six-foot-by-thir-ty-inch table and a single chair will probably be sufficient for your needs. If you choose to bring along an assistant or companion, you will want to have two chairs. In most cases, tables and chairs can be rented through the show's organizers. Some shows or associated companies rent full booths, but these can be expensive, and if you have only one or two books to display, it may not be worth the invest-ment. If the show is small and local, you may be able to bring in your own table and chair.

- *A tablecloth and binder clips.* Consider taking along a black or red cotton tablecloth that is big enough to cover the table top. Since these are normally not made available for rent, you will have to purchase one in advance. Also take along large binder clips or tablecloth clips (often available at party stores) to keep the cloth in place so that it doesn't shift around and look sloppy. The cloth on your table will make it stand out from the other tables next to you. In addition, it will make the promotional materials you place on the table that much more noticeable.

  You might consider investing in an imprinted cloth cover for your table top. In the Resources, you will find a listing of several companies that imprint table coverings for trade shows. (See page 247.) Publishing companies usually have the name of the company imprinted on the cover. If I were exhibiting at a show to promote this book, I would have the table cover imprinted with: *How to Promote Your Book* by Jan Yager.

- *Pens.* Be sure to have on hand several black ink ballpoint pens that leave a nice dark line. Do not use felt tip markers. The ink in some markers will bleed through to the back of the book you have signed or the sheet you have filled out. Over time, a marker may also create a yellowish outline around your signature.

  Consider also bringing imprinted pens that you can use as promo-tional giveaways. These can be ordered in small or large quantities. (See page 248 of the Resources section for a list of companies that can imprint pens and other promotional items.) Imprint the pen with the name of the book you are promoting, your name, and the URL of your author website or your publisher's website.

- *Book stands.* Be sure to bring several book stands along with you, not only to hold the books you are displaying, but also to hold up a small poster of your book cover on your table. Make sure that one stand is strong enough to hold up the poster without tipping over. If necessary, take some tape or Velcro along so that you can secure the stand to the table. (To learn more about posters, see page 208.)

  Be aware that some trade shows and fairs may require you to rent your book stands from them. Before buying a book stand, read your exhibitor agreement to learn what you can and cannot supply on your own.

- *Notepads.* Make sure you take along either a pad of paper or printed forms you can use to record the names and email addresses of people who are interested in following you on social media, as well as booksellers, librarians, the media, and others who can be helpful to you and your book. You might also want to download an app or purchase a system that allows you to scan the badges of the people you meet with your phone and convert the scans into contact information. Even if you store information electronically, however, it's a good idea to have a paper backup copy, even if you jot down just names, companies or affiliations, and email addresses. Electronic systems can fail, and you don't want to lose the important contacts that you've gathered.

- *Velcro and tape.* Having Velcro and tape handy will help you secure various items—such as posters—to the table, the book stand, or the wall behind you, if there is a useable wall. Having exhibited my books at many shows and fairs, I have learned that Velcro and tape are my friends.

- *Portable rolling cart.* Based upon the number of books you will be taking to the show along with other material, you may want to take a sturdy rolling cart with you to help transport your materials. Once again, make sure that you know the rules of the show you're attending. Some shows don't allow you to bring in a rolling cart, and in that case, you can transport your books in a tote bag that you carry on your shoulder. If you're bringing too many books to easily carry, consider shipping the books in advance of the show. (You'll learn more about shipping on page 211.)

- *Credit card reader.* Since many people no longer pay for goods and services with cash, consider setting up a Venmo, PayPal, or Zelle account or attaching a mobile credit card reader to to your smartphone.

  If you do decide to accept only cash payments, find a way to safeguard your cash. Depending on the show's facilities, you might be able to rent a locker where you can store your cash if you are able to get coverage for a quick break. You might also consider using a wearable money belt or pouch that you can position under your clothes. (Be careful not to let anyone see you putting your cash away, since you don't want to set yourself up for a robbery.) Of course, you'll want to keep enough small bills on hand to make change.

- *Name tag.* At many shows, the organizer provides name tags attached to cords to be hung around your neck. Make sure to provide the show with the exact name and other information you want printed on the tag. For instance, if I was promoting this book at a show, I would want my tag to read as follows:

  Dr. Jan Yager
  Author
  How to Promote Your Book

  If I was at the show on behalf of my publishing company, rather than one book, I would request the following wording on the tag:

  Dr. Jan Yager, CEO
  Hannacroix Creek Books, Inc.

  The information on your name tag is actually quite important. When attendees don't have an appointment but are strolling around the show, they may make the decision to stop and talk to you based on what they've read on your tag. So, if the show does not provide a name tag for you, create one for yourself as well as for anyone who is assisting you.

- *Other considerations.* In addition to the items discussed above and those suggested later in the chapter, you should take along whatever you think will make your time there as an exhibitor more productive and comfortable. For instance, you might include a stapler that will allow you to attach business cards to the pages of your notebook, and you might take along a bottle of water and a granola bar, as taking breaks is usually challenging unless you have an assistant.

■ SELECTING PROMOTIONAL MATERIAL AND BOOKS

Once you have decided what you will need to make your space functional, you'll want to consider the items you should have to attract the attention of those who pass by, to provide information about your book (or books), and to otherwise promote your title as well as you as an author.

- *Sales sheets.* In Chapter 6 (see page 101), you learned how to create an attractive sales sheet that presents a one-page summary of your book's basic information. Before each show, make as many copies as you think necessary. Remember that not everyone who passes your table will pick one up, so if you prepare fifty copies to give away, that will probably be adequate. Also have a PDF of your sales sheet stored in your phone or tablet so you can easily email it to attendees who don't want to add a physical sales sheet to the materials they're carrying around the show.

  If you do run out of sales sheets during a show, find a duplicating machine close by, and run off the additional copies you need. Most trade shows have a business center where you can make your copies, but because these centers charge premium prices, you will want to bring a reasonable number of copies with you. Even if you think you're well stocked with promotional materials, it's a good idea to bring a flash drive with you so that you can print off your flash drive rather than copying a printed sheet, which will result in handouts that are lower in quality than the original.

- *Press kits.* Because of the potential opportunities to meet people from the media, it is important to have at least three or four copies of your press kit with you. (To learn about press kits, see page 161 of Chapter 9.) A good press kit can convince a media person that you're worth interviewing or that your book is worth reviewing.

- *Posters.* Creating a poster of your book cover is a great way to catch people's attention. A number of office supply stores, such as Staples and Kinko's, can produce a poster for you at a reasonable price. The thirteen-by-nineteen-inch size is usually just about right for the space you'll have at a show. Just remember to have the poster glued onto a foam board backing and then laminated to guard it from scratching. Packing and unpacking materials for different shows can easily damage an unprotected poster.

As described earlier, you can best display your poster by placing it in a book stand on your table and securing the stand to the table with tape so that it doesn't tip over. If you can afford to print and mount two posters, consider hanging the second one on the wall behind you.

- *Signs.* In addition to the poster of your book cover, you may want to have your office supply store produce a narrow six-by-thirty-inch white cardboard sign that features the name of your book and/or the name of your publisher, if you have one. The sign can be attached to your table by tape or Velcro so that it hangs off the front edge. It's very important to identify who you are among the other tables at the event. Be aware that some shows provide each exhibitor with such a sign, so check your agreement or speak to the show's organizer before ordering the sign.

  If I were promoting this book at a show, I would have "HOW TO PROMOTE YOUR BOOK" printed on the sign.

- *Books.* Since you will be at the show to promote your book, you will, of course, want to bring a number of copies with you. Unfortunately, it's not always easy to know just how many copies you'll need. There are many factors to consider, including the specific venue, the number of attendees, and whether or not the topic of your book is popular enough to garner the attendees' attention.

  If you have never done this before, perhaps you can get the names of past author exhibitors who have had the experience of selling books. Ask them how many books they brought with them, how many copies they gave away, and how many they sold. You might also consider attending a similar event to see how well the authors fare in selling their books.

  If you don't know any author exhibitors and you won't have the opportunity to visit a comparable show before you exhibit, I suggest bringing between twenty-four and thirty copies to the event. You may want to include a backup box of copies just in case, but until you have greater experience, don't overdo it, since any books that remain will have to be shipped back home. Be aware that some trade shows offer the option of donating unsold books to a charity so that you can avoid the cost and bother of shipping them home. Before doing that, you'll want to consider the cost of shipping the books versus the inventory you'll lose by donating them.

- *Business cards.* When you attend various book events, you may be asked for a business card for any number of reasons. Of course, you can always provide people with sales sheets, since they should include your phone number and email address, but a well-designed business card always looks professional. These cards can be printed up quickly at most office supply stores and through online business card services. (See page 248 of the Resources section.)

  Keep in mind that younger attendees—especially those thirty-five and younger—consider business cards an old-fashioned way of sharing contact information. Instead, they use their smartphones to instantly add the information to their phone's Contacts list.

■ MAKING TRAVEL AND ACCOMMODATION ARRANGEMENTS

Unless the event you're attending is only a few hours' drive from your home, you'll have to make travel arrangements and find convenient and affordable accommodations near the show. In general, you should make all your reservations—for both transportation and lodgings—as far in advance as possible, as this can save you money and also help ensure that you get what you want. To exhibit at some major shows—like the Frankfurt Book Fair, which is held every October in Frankfurt, Germany—you have to book a hotel room as much as one year in advance of the show.

- *Local events.* If your event is going to be held locally or is just a drive away, all you have to do is fill your car up with what you need and drive to the venue. Unless you want to get there the night before, or an extended stay is necessary for another reason, you won't have to spend money on a hotel. Make sure to take along a sturdy rolling cart that will allow you to transport all your exhibit materials from your car to your booth or table, if this is allowed. If such a cart is not allowed on the show floor, you will have to make other arrangements, such as shipping your books and other materials in advance.

- *Air travel.* If your event requires air travel, book your tickets well in advance to get the best rates. Do not wait until the last minute.

   Although you may be fully committed to attending a show, consider purchasing refundable plane tickets. Although higher in price than nonrefundable tickets, if you are unable to take the trip due to an unforeseeable event such as an illness or a family emergency, the price of your ticket can be fully refunded. If you don't choose refundable tickets, another option is to purchase travel insurance that includes trip cancellation protection. Since these arrangements can vary, when you make your purchase, be sure you understand the circumstances in which you can get a full refund.

- *Accommodations.* If travel requires you to stay overnight, some events provide exhibitors with a reduced hotel rate. Check with the event organizer to see if your show offers such a discount.

   Most shows actually indicate the distance in terms of miles or even the walking time from the event venue to a particular hotel. This will help you choose a hotel that is a reasonable distance from the show. Just remember this rule of thumb: The closer the hotel is to the event, the higher the rate; the farther the hotel is, the lower the cost. If no discount is available for the closest hotel, check to see if the show offers free transportation—such as a chartered shuttle bus or a pass for public transportation—from other hotels to the event.

   Again, you'll want to be sure to book your accommodations well in advance. A convention or show—especially a large one—fills up hotel rooms quickly.

■ SHIPPING

Sometimes, transporting your books and material by car to an event is not an option. In this case, you'll need to have everything shipped.

- *Sending books and materials to the event.* If shipping is a necessity, ask the event organizers if you can ship the books and whatever other materials you need directly to the venue to be placed in your space. They will normally give you an address to ship it to, the date by which it needs to arrive, and the appropriate booth number. You can then ship the items by UPS—or another carrier that provides track-ing—making sure you can have it traced.

Note that Media Mail (first discussed on page 179) is the cheapest way to ship books, and it will allow you to insure and track your boxes. It will take longer for the books to reach their destination than it would if you were using UPS, FedEx, or Priority Mail, but if you mail the packages out early enough, you'll be able to save some money. To prevent damage, I suggest that you carefully pack the books with shock-absorbing packing material or even double-box the books you send.

- **Sending books and materials to your hotel.** If your hotel is open to this option, instead of shipping materials to the venue, you can have books and other items sent to your hotel to be held until your arrival. Always check with the hotel first to confirm that it has a safe place in which to store your packages. Also make sure that you will have a way of transporting the boxes from the hotel to the show.

- **International transportation.** When transporting items to interna-tional events, you may, again, have the option of shipping materials directly to the show or to your hotel. Be sure to find out if the country you're shipping your materials to will charge customs fees when items arrive. In some cases, it may be less expensive to bring as many items as possible along with you in your suitcase. Alternatively, you may consider contacting a company that specializes in international shipping to handle these details for you. (To find these companies, see the introduction to the Resources, which begins on page 233.)

In these pages, it is impossible to cover every potential obstacle you may face as you prepare for a book event, as there may always be new problems that arise. However, by keeping in mind all the key suggestions covered here, you should be good to go. And once you have experienced preparing for and setting up your first show, you will better know what to expect and how various tasks can be best handled.

GUIDELINES FOR SUCCESS

It is essential to have a clear idea of what you want to accomplish when you exhibit at any book-based event, and what you can do to best meet your goals. Based on the type of event you have chosen to participate in, you will want to keep the following guidelines in mind.

Before the Show

So far, the preparations discussed in this chapter have mostly concerned choosing and transporting materials you will need to have with you at the fair or show. But other types of preparation are just as important.

- *Set clear goals that are manageable and realistic.* Do you want to make deals with booksellers or librarians, or just network with other authors or publishers? Do you want to collect business cards for your growing database, or do you want to contact specific buyers? Do you want to see what other publishers are doing to garner attention for their titles, or are you trying to interest a publisher in the paperback rights to an in-print (backlist) or forthcoming title? Book events tend to be busy and potentially distracting, so it's important to keep your chief goal or goals in mind so that your efforts are appropriately focused.

- *Learn your product details.* Make sure that beyond knowing about the book you have written—its point of view, its contents, its intended audience, etc.—you also know about the title's retail list price, how it's being distributed, discounts, and more. If someone else will be helping you at your table, make sure that she also can answer any questions that might be posed by publishers, booksellers, readers, and the media.

- *Create handouts geared to each particular show.* Too many authors make the mistake of having one "boilerplate" handout that they bring to every book event. Instead, take a few moments to customize your handout or flyer for a particular event. What is the target audience? What information about you or your book should be emphasized to make your book appealing to these particular attendees?

  If you are promoting one book, a customized sales sheet can be an effective handout. As explained earlier, in addition to physical copies of your sales sheet, you should keep a PDF of your sales sheet on your smartphone or tablet so you can send it to an attendee's email address.

If you have written more than one book, a catalogue that includes all of your titles—and also includes information on shipping and the like—might be a better idea than a sales sheet. If you cannot afford to have a number of catalogues printed up, you can print up the pages of a single catalogue on your home printer, and secure the pages in a binder that visitors to your table or booth can browse through. If someone shows an interest in having their own catalogue, you can always offer to send her a catalogue after the show. (If you make such a promise, however, be sure to follow through!) Another good option would be to refer the individual to your author website, assuming that it provides information on all of your titles.

- *Plan to dress professionally but comfortably.* You want to look neat and professional, so a suit or an outfit with a jacket is a good bet. Appropriate dress, of course, depends on the specific book event. If you were exhibiting at the *Los Angeles Times* Festival of Books, for instance, you might aim for a more casual and stylish look. Just remember that you'll be at the show for many hours a day, and much of that time, you will be standing and walking—probably more than you can imagine. Be sure to wear or bring comfortable shoes so you can keep your focus on selling books and networking rather than on your sore feet.

- *Contact the media.* Once you commit to attending a book show or fair, be sure to alert the local media. They might want to arrange an interview with you that can be published or aired before or during the event, or they may want to interview you when you're in town for the show.

During the Show

During the book event, you may be overwhelmed by all the activity around you. To stay focused and make the best possible use of your time, keep the following tips in mind.

- *Be friendly, not pushy.* The next person who comes by your space may be able to provide you with additional media, a sales opportunity, or simply a book purchase. You never know, so keep a smile on your face and be willing to listen and to answer questions. On the other hand, you don't want to be pushy or too aggressive in your approach, as that can turn people off.

- *Keep track of the people who you think can help you moving forward.* If someone stops by your space and you have a conversation that seems promising—for instance, if an individual has a store and seems interested in stocking one or more of your books—make notes on the back of the business card she gives you to serve as a reminder of your conversation when the show is over. Have a system for keeping track of the cards, whether you file them in a business card holder, you staple them to sheets in a notebook, or you drop them into an envelope.

  Occasionally, a person of interest will not supply a business card. In that case, simply write her name and contact information on a pad, along with a reminder about what you discussed with her; or add a note in your smartphone, along with the individual's name, affiliation, and email address.

- *Pace yourself.* There will be lots of possibilities for additional networking at the show, but you have to decide just how much socializing you can do and how little sleep you can function on for the duration of the event. If you have boundless energy and enthusiasm, you can set up a breakfast meeting before the show and arrange a drink or dinner meeting after the show. These before- and after-show get-togethers can be a great way to get to know and make deals with publishers and booksellers, and to meet with the media. If, however, you know you need a certain amount of time to rest and recuperate each day, skip the extra meetings or choose them very selectively.

- *Enjoy yourself!* A show can be hard work. It can feel competitive and sometimes overwhelming. But it can also be a wonderful place to meet new people who can offer you further promotional and sales opportunities. Whenever you can, take a step back and enjoy the experience of being with other people who share your interest in books.

After the Show

When the event is over, you may be tempted to take a day or two off to rest and relax. But trust me when I say that your work is not done!

- *Follow up on your leads.* Be sure to allot at least a few days in your schedule for immediate follow-up, especially with your hottest leads. If the person you are contacting is in the position of making buying decisions, you will want to get to that person as quickly as possible. She may have a budget that enables her to spend only so much money, and once it is spent, further purchases may be pushed to another season. That's why it's crucial to contact potential buyers without delay. Also, if you wait too long, the individual may think you are indifferent and that your initial meeting was not that important to you, or the memory of your conversation may fade from her memory. Follow up on your meetings while the experience of the show is still fresh in everyone's mind.

- *Consider what you have learned from the experience.* After the show, consider whether the event met your expectations. Was it worth the cost of exhibiting? Is it something you would want to do again? If you do plan to attend this show or similar shows in the future, would you handle it any differently?

    Over the years, I have exhibited at and attended both lively, well-attended events and poorly attended shows. During that time, I have learned which shows work best for my titles; whether they are likely to provide promotion, sales, or just plain visibility; and how I can best prepare for each one. I have also learned which shows

Having the Show Exhibit Your Books for You

If you are unable to personally attend and exhibit your books at a show, consider having the show display your materials for you, for a fee. Of course, this is not going to be as effective as being there in person, as you won't be able to talk to and network with buyers, distributors, and others who might be of help to you. But this can add to your book's visibility and—especially if the show's organizers will send you a list of anyone who showed interest in your book or even those who attended the show—it may be worth the fee that they charge as well as the time, effort, and costs involved in sending at least one display copy of your book to the event. (See page 242 for more information.)

involve too much investment for too little return. As you attend shows, you'll want to make the same evaluations so that you can wisely spend your money and your time in the future.

CONCLUSION

Both trade shows for the book industry and public book fairs can be an excellent means of expanding your network and giving yourself and your book additional visibility. They can also attract interest from the media if you are serving on a panel, listed as a sponsor, or attending as an exhibitor. Like all promotional activities, sometimes you will not know in advance if the time, expense, and effort of being an exhibitor will be worthwhile. But these book-related events provide one more way to promote your book and bring attention to yourself as an author in your field of expertise or genre.

A list of many of the most prominent book-related events held in the United States and around the world begins on page 238. I suggest that you spend some time reading the list and visiting the suggested websites to see if there is a show close by at which you might want to exhibit, or even a show far away that you might choose to participate in because of the appealing location. If you don't want to exhibit at a particular show, consider attending it as a visitor to determine if it would be a good place for you to promote your book.

Conclusion

Whether this is your first book, and you are learning about book promotion from scratch, or your fifth, and you want to brush up on techniques—including some of the newer trends—book publicity is an ongoing and necessary part of the publishing process. Promotion is demanding, time-consuming work, and unless you love talking about your book and being interviewed, it is going to be a challenge at times. But you have to keep reminding yourself that it can make the difference between a book that gets just a little bit of attention versus a book that keeps receiving attention and sales week after week, month after month, even year after year.

An author and speaking colleague, Laura Stack, shared on Facebook recently that she was interviewed by a major cable news show, and her segment was going to air that night. Good for her! This author has been working tirelessly for two years writing blogs, getting interviewed by all sorts of media, big and small, even speaking twice via Zoom for college courses that I teach. She shared a thank you in her Facebook post stating that the emails and letters that so many had written to that show suggesting she should be a guest had finally paid off. Laura Stack's book, *The Dangerous Truth About Today's Marijuana*, was not published by a major house, but she is still getting air time on a top cable news show. The subtitle of her book is *Johnny Stack's Life and Death Story*. These interviews are probably tough on Laura, whose nineteen-year-old son Johnny died by suicide two years ago. But she pushes on because she has a message that needs to be heard.

If you need motivation to start promoting your book, ask yourself why you wrote it. Did you write that novel to entertain readers? Did you write a collection of poetry to inspire others? Or did you write that nonfiction book to share your expertise with the rest of the world, or maybe even because you want to change the world for the better?

Call up that burst of enthusiasm you had when you first decided to write your book, as well as the excitement you felt when you had that first copy in your hands or when you saw your e-book displayed on your smartphone or laptop for the very first time. Now put that same passion into promoting your book, not just for a few days but on a continuous basis. You might even find yourself enjoying it.

Illinois-based Marilyn Brant, author of twenty-two books, including eighteen romance novels, told me that the ultimate goal of promotion is to help the right book find the right reader. "Even if promotion is not my favorite part of the writing and publishing process, I love being introduced to new readers, and publicity is the way to make that happen," she added.

If nothing else, I hope that *How to Promote Your Book* has convinced you of the importance of giving your book a publicity timeline of at least six months. There are so many prepublication tasks that you, your publisher, or your freelance publicist needs to do to set your book up for as much success as possible. A book publicist recently told me that she prefers to hear from an author *one year* before publication. That shows you the importance of advance planning.

Finally, you need to manage your expectations. You can do a lot of promotion on your book and not get the results you hoped for. There are no guarantees with publicity, other than the guarantee that if you do not do any publicity or you do only a minimal amount, your book is unlikely to get the attention it deserves and needs. This, in turn, will translate into getting fewer readers. So, make the effort, and hopefully you will get rewarded with visibility and even sales.

Good luck and happy promoting!

Glossary

Please note that all terms that appear in *italic type* are defined within the Glossary.

academic books. Books that present scholarly research intended for an academic audience.

academic publisher. A publisher that produces books and/or *journals* designed for the college, graduate-level, professional, or scholarly market. Like *commercial publishers,* academic publishers underwrite the cost of producing and distributing their books.

acquisitions editor. An editor responsible for acquiring and developing books for a *commercial publisher, academic publisher,* or *hybrid publisher.*

advance praise. *See* blurb.

advance reading copies (ARCs). Bound typeset pages of a forthcoming book, sometimes referred to as bound *galleys,* that are given out prior to a book's publication, usually for review or promotional purposes. When appropriate, *digital review copies (DRCs)* are used in place of physical ARCs.

ARCs. See *advance reading copies.*

audience. A book's intended readership.

audiobook. A recording of a text being read aloud by the book's author or by a hired narrator.

author bio. The component of the *media kit* that provides an in-depth author biography ranging from two to four paragraphs in length.

author platform. Also referred to as a media platform, the degree of visibility of an author on *social media* that may predict the author's ability to connect with his or her audience.

author tour. See *book tour*.

backlist. A publisher's titles that are more than six months old but still in print. By comparison, newly published titles are sometimes referred to as the frontlist.

BISAC (Book Industry Standards and Communications) subject listing. A collection of industry-approved categories created and maintained by the Book Industry Study Group (BISG). These categories enable publishers to classify their books for the benefit of bookstores and libraries.

blog. Short for "weblog," a regularly updated personal website or web page that is the Internet's equivalent of a journal or diary, and may include reviews, stories, and articles.

blogger. A professional journalist or a nonprofessional who regularly writes for a *blog*.

blurb. A brief written advance endorsement of a book—usually one to three lines in length and written by a well-known author or expert—that praises the book and/or the book's author. Sometimes referred to as testimonials, blurbs are used in book promotion. See also *published endorsement* and *unpublished endorsement*.

board books. *Picture books* that are small in size and constructed with thick, sturdy covers and pages, and are therefore appropriate for babies and toddlers.

book fair. Also called a book festival, an event organized by publishers and booksellers for the purpose of selling their books. Generally, anyone, including the reading public, may attend a book fair. Some book fairs are organized by schools, which may invite authors to speak at the event.

book publicist. See *publicist*.

book review. An evaluation of a book that is both descriptive and critical.

book review editor. An editor who assigns books to reviewers for a publication.

book reviewer. A staff writer or freelancer who writes reviews of books for a publication.

book tour. Sometimes called an author tour, a promotional tour—which may be in-person or virtual (online)—in which an author tours one or multiple cities to present a newly published book to the media, including print media, TV/cable, radio, etc.; speak at events; and meet potential readers.

books columnist. A writer who covers the subject of books for a print or online media outlet such as a *newspaper, magazine,* or website.

bound galleys. See *advance reading copies; galleys.*

brick-and-mortar bookstore. A physical retailer you can visit.

bridge books. Children's books that have fewer graphics and more text than *picture books* and are designed as a "bridge" between picture books and *early readers.*

broadcast media. A means of transmitting communications electronically, which generally includes television, cable, and radio.

Cataloging-in-Publication data (CIP data). A block of information, provided by the Library of Congress prior to a book's publication, that includes the title and author of the book; the ISBN number; subject headings; and library classification numbers.

chapter books. Books to be read by children who are seven to ten years of age and tell their stories primarily through text, although some illustrations are included.

CIP Data. See *Cataloging-in-Publication data.*

commercial publisher. A publisher that buys the rights to publish an author's work, and then edits, designs, markets, and sells the book. Also called a traditional publisher, a commercial house underwrites the cost of producing and marketing the book, may offer the author an advance upon signing the contract, and also awards the author a *royalty* based on sales.

copyediting. Editing that corrects errors in grammar, spelling, syntax, and punctuation; technical inconsistencies in capitalization and numerals; errors in continuity; factually incorrect statements; and inconsistencies in content.

copyeditor. Sometimes called a line editor, an individual who performs *copyediting.*

copyright page. A page that typically appears on the back of the title page and may begin with a list of the individuals responsible for putting the book together, such as the cover designer, editor, and typesetter. Beneath these names should appear the name of the publisher, the publisher's address, the publisher's phone number, and the publisher's website. This contact information should be followed by Library of Congress *Cataloging-in-Publication data (CIP data)* or a *Library of Congress Control Number (LCCN).*

crowdfunding. The practice of funding a project—such as the promotion of a book—by getting relatively small contributions from a large number of people via the Internet. Well known crowdfunding platforms include GoFundMe, Kickstarter, and Indiegogo. See also *reward-based crowdfunding.*

customer reviews. Comments about a book posted by readers on the online sites of retailers such as Amazon and Barnes & Noble.

developmental editor. An individual, sometimes called a substantive editor, who works with a writer to help develop, flesh out, and improve the themes and structure of a fictional story or the organization of information provided in a nonfiction work.

digital review copy (DRC). An electronic version of an *advance reading copy. PDFs* can usually be used as digital review copies.

distributor. Traditionally, a company that has an exclusive agreement with a publisher to sell its books to bookstores, libraries, or wholesalers. Today, some distributors sell books on a nonexclusive basic. See also *wholesaler.*

early readers. Sometimes called easy readers or independent readers, books geared to be read to or by children from ages five to seven.

e-book. A book-length publication in digital form that can be downloaded from online retailers or directly from publishers and read on electronic devices, such as electronic tablets and smartphones.

electronic press kit (EPK). A digital version of a press kit (or *media kit*).

e-newsletter. A *newsletter* that is sent out via email.

EPK. An electronic press kit or *media kit*.

fiction. Literature that is created from an author's imagination and is not presented as fact. Fiction includes many *genres*, including fantasy, *graphic novels*, historical fiction, horror, literary fiction, science fiction, mysteries, thrillers, romance, and more.

font. A specific size and style of a *typeface*. See also *typeface*.

foreword. A section of a book's *front matter* that has been written by a third party whose reputation lends credibility to the book and its author.

front matter. The opening sections of a book, also known as preliminaries or prematter, which include the *title page, copyright page*, and optional sections, such as the *half-title page, foreword, preface*, and introduction.

frontlist. See *backlist*.

galleys. A rough advance version of a typeset book. As promotional tools, galleys have largely been replaced by *advance reading copies*, or ARCs, which are sometimes referred to as bound galleys. See *advance reading copies*.

genre. A category of literature that may be determined by form, content, style, and length. For instance, in *fiction*, popular genres include romance, mystery, science fiction, and more.

graphic novels. Books written in comic-book style, composed of panels made up of sequential images and text. Graphic novels are available for different reading levels, from age five up. Some are designed for children, and others, for adults.

half-title page. The page that comes before the *title page* in some books and features the title of a book without inclusion of its subtitle, author's name, or publisher's logo. Half-title pages are often used to display *blurbs*.

head shot. A tightly cropped photo of the face, from the shoulders up.

honorarium. A token payment made to an individual in exchange for services for which compensation is not actually required. Because there is no set fee, payment to the person providing the services is at the discretion of the payer.

hybrid publisher. A business that performs many of the same tasks of a *commercial publisher*—such as editing, typesetting, proofing, and printing—but requires the author to underwrite the cost of producing the book, usually by committing to the purchase of a specified number of copies of the finished book. Like a *commercial publisher,* a hybrid publisher gives the author a *royalty* based on sales. Marketing, distribution, and promotion may be provided at an additional cost.

index. An alphabetical list of important words, terms, phrases, names, or concepts mentioned in a book and the corresponding pages on which they appear.

influencer. An individual who may be able to stimulate purchases of a product (such as a book) by recommending the product to his or her followers on *social media* or through appearances on traditional broadcast media.

International Standard Book Number (ISBN). A thirteen-digit number that acts as a unique identifier of a book for booksellers, libraries, book wholesalers, and book distributors. In the United States, ISBN numbers are available only through R.R. Bowker or a company authorized to sell ISBNs on R.R. Bowker's behalf.

ISBN. See *International Standard Book Number.*

journal. A periodical publication that is focused on one specific topic or professional activity, and is therefore read by professionals in a particular field of study, such as medicine or education.

launch party. An event, usually a party, that celebrates the release of a book. Media, friends, and family may be included.

Library of Congress Control Number (LCCN). A number issued by the Library of Congress to a book in advance of publication to help libraries find and acquire it. Self-published authors often use LCCNs instead of *Cataloging-in-Publication data.*

line editor. See *copyeditor.*

magazine. A periodical publication, geared for the general public, that can contain different types of articles—such as essays, news stories, interviews, book excerpts, and *book reviews*—as well as illustrations.

marketplace. An outlet or venue through which books can be sold. Book marketplaces can include trade bookstores, specialty bookstores, non-bookstores that sell books, libraries, speaking engagements, special sales, direct mail, and online marketplaces.

media kit. A package of key information about a forthcoming book and its author designed for people in the media who might want to feature the title on their website; in their magazine, newspaper, or other publication; on their television or radio show; or on another media outlet. Also called a press kit, it generally includes a *press release,* an *author bio* and photograph, a list of potential interview questions, and possibly excerpts from the book.

Media Mail. A way to send media items—including books—through the United States Postal Service at a reduced rate.

media training. A specialized form of training that prepares people, such as authors, to effectively deal with the media during interviews and other interactions so that they can better deliver their key messages.

metadata. A book's specifications (sometimes called specs), which include a description of a book as well as its title and subtitle, author's name, ISBN number, retail price, page count, format (*trim size* and whether paperback, hardback, or audiobook), and *BISAC* subject heading.

middle grade books. Sometimes considered a subcategory of *young adult (YA) books,* these are books designed for the middle grade audience, including children ages ten to thirteen.

newsletter. A brief publication—such as a leaflet or bulletin—containing news that is of interest to the members of a society, business, or organization. Electronic versions of newsletters are called e-newsletters.

newspaper. A periodical publication—usually daily or weekly—that is of general interest and presents news, feature articles, *book reviews,* advertisements, and correspondence.

nonfiction. A category of books based on facts, real events, and actual people rather than on invented stories and characters. Popular categories include art, biography, cookbooks, crafts, health and wellness, history, relationships, self-help, true crime, and more.

non-trade. Any bookseller not considered part of the book trade marketplace.

out of print (OOP). A term describing a book that is no longer available from a publisher.

online retailer. An organization or company, such as Amazon, that sells products through a website on the Internet.

PCIP (Publisher's Cataloging-in-Publication) data. A block of information identical to *Cataloging-in-Publication data*, but created by a professional librarian on a fee basis at the request of a publisher.

PDF. Short for Portable Document Format, a file format that provides an electronic image of text or text and graphics that looks like a printed document. A PDF can be viewed, read, printed, and transmitted. PDFs are often used as digital *advance reading copies*.

permissions editor. An editor whose job is to secure copyright-protected text, illustrations, and photographs for use in a physical book or an e-book.

picture books. Large-format books that tell their stories through pictures and brief text. They are designed for preschool children.

pirated material. Material, such as an electronic book under copyright protection, that has been illegally copied and made available to others via the Internet.

pitch. A description of a book used to seek out promotional opportunities by expressing what the book is about and why people should be interested in reading it. A pitch can be delivered in person, by phone, via email, or in writing.

POD. See *print-on-demand (POD) book*.

podcast. A program—similar to a radio program, and usually part of a themed series—that is made available in digital form through the Internet for downloading.

PowerPoint. A software system developed by Microsoft that creates a slide show of key information, charts, and images for use in presentations.

preface. Written by the author, this section of the *front matter* briefly outlines the story behind or inspiration for the writing of a book.

prematter. See *front matter.*

prepublication trade journals. In the world of books, a *journal*—such as *PW, Kirkus Reviews, or Library Journal*—that publishes reviews of books prior to their release date.

press kit. See *media kit.*

press release. A document prepared for the press (or media) with the goal of generating press coverage. Usually included in a book's *media kit,* it provides much of the material that appears on a *sales sheet,* but is focused on the book's *pitch* rather than providing a straight description of the book.

print media. A means of transmitting information in physical form, including *newspapers, magazines, journals,* and *newsletters.*

print run. A requested number of copies of a book to be printed.

print-on-demand (POD) book. A book printed as a single copy or in small numbers by a service that keeps an electronic version of that book on file to print and bind copies as needed.

professional books. Books designed to develop the skills of people who are working in a specific profession—such as education or health—or are training for work in that profession.

proofreading. Sometimes called "proofing," the process of reviewing the final draft of the manuscript—after it has been copyedited—to ensure that there are no remaining errors. A proofreader will look for and correct spelling errors, punctuation errors, typographical errors (typos), missing words, and other problems that may have been missed during previous stages of editing.

publicist. An individual who has expertise in getting attention from *traditional media* and/or *social media* for a product, person, or company. A book publicist specializes in garnering publicity for authors and their books.

publicity department. In the publishing world, a department within a publishing company that is tasked with promoting its company's books.

published endorsement. An endorsement or *blurb* that comes from an established publication. See *blurb*.

quotation. A positive statement that offers the reader an understanding of what is in a book. See *blurb*.

radio tour. A series of short, back-to-back radio interviews—usually scheduled around a book's *release date*—intended to get optimal radio exposure for the book and its author.

release date. Sometimes called a launch date, the date on which physical books are shipped to stores and become available to readers and/or e-books are made available online.

review quote. A significantly abridged version of a review used to focus on its positive points. See *blurb*.

reward-based crowdfunding. A type of *crowdfunding* in which people give an online contribution in exchange for a reward, such as a copy of a new book, an invitation to a book *launch party*, or mugs imprinted with the name of the book.

royalty. An agreed-upon portion of sales revenue paid to an author.

sales seasons. One of the three seasons of the year—fall, spring, and summer—in which publishers schedule their new books for release.

sales sheet. Sometimes called a sell sheet or tips sheet, a one-sheet presentation of a book's basic information, including an overview of the book, About the Author information, the book's *metadata,* and contact information for the person handling publicity.

secondary title. See *subtitle*.

self-publishing. A publishing option in which an author arranges and pays for every stage of the publishing process, from editing and typesetting to printing and binding, as well as the promotion, distribution, and sales of a book.

social media. A collective term for websites and applications that make possible the sharing of ideas and information through virtual networks and communities. Well-known examples of social media include Facebook, Twitter, Instagram, Pinterest, TikTok, and LinkedIn.

speakers bureau. An organization that books professional speakers—some of whom are book authors—for *trade shows,* conferences, and other events.

special sales. Sales of books in large quantities to companies that will not resell them to the book trade marketplace. Examples include warehouse clubs such as Costco, pet stores, health food stores, and more.

specifications. See *metadata.*

subsidiary rights. All rights related to a book beyond its initial print or e-book publication, including movie or TV rights, book club rights, foreign rights, and various other rights.

substantive editor. See *developmental editor.*

subtitle. A secondary title that clarifies the subject matter of a book or otherwise enhances the book's title.

talking points. Topics or key ideas to discuss in relation to a book during its promotion.

textbooks. Books written and organized in a manner that makes them useful as a resource for people studying a specific subject, usually in a school setting, such as grade school, college, university, law school, or medical school, for example.

title page. The page of a book that bears the book's title; the *subtitle,* if any; the author's name and credentials, if any; the name of the publisher; and sometimes the place of publication. This is the first page of the book unless a *half-title page* is included.

trade. Bookstores and libraries to which publishers sell their books.

trade show. In the book world, a show designed for people in the industry—including not only publishers and booksellers, but also distributors, printers, and non-trade book buyers—so that they can promote their products and services to one another.

traditional media. Any form of mass communication that was available before the advent of the Internet, including television, radio, *newspapers,* and *magazines.*

traditional publisher. See *commercial publisher.*

trim size. The height and width of the finished book. Common United States trim sizes include but are not limited to 6 by 9 inches, 5.5 by 8.5 inches, and 8.5 by 11 inches.

troll. Someone who intentionally antagonizes others online by posting nasty or abusive comments about someone else's *social media* comment or activity.

typeface. A specific style of lettering. Each typeface includes different *fonts,* each of which is specific in thickness, size, level of condensation, and other features.

typesetter. A person who typesets text, turning a manuscript into a properly formatted book.

unpublished endorsement. An endorsement, or *blurb,* that is derived not from published reviews but from individuals, including authors of similar books or, in the case of nonfiction, experts in the book's subject. See *blurb.*

wholesaler. A company that has an arrangement with a publisher to sell a publisher's books to bookstores and libraries on a nonexclusive basis at a specified discount. See also *distributor.*

writers group. An informal group of writers who meet periodically—usually, once a month or more frequently, in person or online—to share their writing and to provide advice, criticism, and support for one another.

young adult (YA) books. Books written for teenagers from age twelve and up. YA books reflect many areas of interest of adult audiences, but are written to appeal to teen readers.

Resources

Regardless of whether your book is being produced by a commercial publishing company or is being self-published, there are a range of resources that may be helpful to you as you finalize and promote your book: professional editors and proofreaders, trade journals that publish book reviews, services that can help you create effective websites, and so much more.

The following resources may prove useful during your efforts. While many of these lists are extensive, they are by no means complete, because new resources of all types become available all the time. Do not hesitate to scout out resources on your own, with the help of your local librarian, or with the help of contacts you make through a writers group; or to ask your network of authors. Also be aware that the inclusion of a resource on this list should not be considered an endorsement. Furthermore, since companies change their policies and go out of business without warning, the accuracy of these listings cannot be guaranteed. You need to do your due diligence to evaluate any resource and see if it is right for you and your book.

The list below includes resources in the following categories:

- Audiobook Reviews and Promotion
- Author and Publisher Groups and Organizations
- Book Fairs and Events in the United States
- Book Fairs Around the World
- Book Fairs—Companies That Display Authors' Books
- Book Promotion and Marketing Information Websites
- Book Publicists
- Book Reviews from Fee-Based Services
- Book Reviews from Prepublication Trade Journals
- CIP Data, PCIP Data, LCCN, and ISBN Information

- Companies That Imprint Promotional Materials
- Crowdfunding Platforms
- Email Management Programs for Sending Out E-Blasts
- Foreign Rights and Translations
- Free PR Leads
- Freelance Editors, Proofreaders, and Other Publishing Professionals
- Media Outlets
- Online Services for Sharing Digital Review Copies
- Online Sites Where You Can Sell Your Books
- Press Release Distribution Services
- Social Media Websites
- Training in Media Skills
- Training in Speaking Skills
- Website Builders, Do-It-Yourself

On the publisher's website https://squareonepublishers.com/Title/9780757004742, you will also find resources in the following categories:

- Books Related to Publishing and Promotion
- Companies That Offer International Shipping
- Photograph Services
- Print, E-Book, and Audiobook Self-Publishing Services
- Wholesalers and Distributors

AUDIOBOOK REVIEWS AND PROMOTION

If your publisher or you have produced an audiobook version of your title, the following resources may be helpful in making both audiobook lovers and the media aware of you and your title.

Audiobook Boom!

Website: https://audiobookboom. com

Audiobook Boom! subscribers can opt to receive free review copies of audiobooks from Audible, Downpour, and CDBaby, which they may review within thirty days. The reviews are available to those who visit the site.

Audiobook Reviewer

Website: https://audiobookreviewer. com

Audiobook Reviewer currently reviews only specific genres of fiction, including sci-fi, horror, game-lit, mystery, and thriller. You can also submit your audiobook for consideration in the ABR Awards program.

AudioBookRadio

Website: http://audiobookradio.net

AudioBookRadio.net is a free Internet radio station that broadcasts a varied range of spoken word content. Getting your audiobook heard could be an excellent way to attract the attention of media, fans, or buyers.

The Audiobookworm

Website: https://theaudiobookworm. com

The Audiobookworm is a review blog that offers audiobook reviews and promotional services. This is a useful site for authors who are seeking more exposure for their audiobooks.

AudioFile

Website: www.audiofilemagazine. com

A magazine dedicated to audiobooks, AudioFile reviews and recommends audiobooks that are worth your listening time.

AudioGals

Website: www.audiogals.net

AudioGals is made up of volunteer reviewers focused on the Romance genre.

AUTHOR AND PUBLISHER GROUPS AND ORGANIZATIONS

There are many ways that associations or organizations can help you with your book promotion efforts. Writer and/or publisher associations often allow you to participate in marketing programs at a reduced rate. Some create co-op exhibits at various trade associations or book fairs that you can join at a much lower cost than exhibiting on your own. Many have local or annual conferences that provide speaking opportunities on a free or paid basis. And, of course, as a member, you'll be able to network with the dozens, hundreds, or thousands of other members who may be willing to support and promote a book by a fellow member in the interest of camaraderie.

Alliance of Independent Authors (ALLi)

Website: www. allianceindependentauthors.org

The Alliance of Independent Authors is a nonprofit professional membership association for self-published authors. It provides advice on going digital, learning publishing and business skills, and publishing in a variety of formats. ALLi offers different levels of membership.

American Society of Journalists and Authors (ASJA)

Website: https://ASJA.org

Through the ASJA, authors and content writers may find opportunities for networking and professional development. The ASJA also holds an annual conference that provides further opportunities for book authors. (For more information, see the ASJA listing on page 239.)

Association of Ghostwriters (AOG)

Website: http://
associationofghostwriters.org

The Association of Ghostwriters is a professional organization that offers professional or associate memberships for ghostwriters of books, articles, speeches, blogs, and social media content.

Association of Publishers for Special Sales (APSS)

Website: http://community.bookapss.
org

APSS is a membership association that offers educational materials and marketing opportunities to book authors, publishers, and self-publishers who want to explore special sales— opportunities other than bookstores and libraries. It has partnered with Combined Book Exhibit (see page 242) to offer members co-op display opportunities at a range of book events, including international fairs.

Audio Publishers Association (APA)

Website: www.audiopub.org

This membership organization of audiobook publishers and narrators promotes its members' business interests. It gives annual awards to the best audiobooks of the year and hosts educational webinars and networking events.

Authors Guild

Website: www.authorsguild.com

Offering legal and web services to writers, the Authors Guild invites all published book authors, including

self-publishers, to apply for membership. Self-publishers are assessed for membership on a case-by-case basis. A members' bulletin offers a place to announce your book's publication. Members may also purchase a website that authors can update on their own through the Author Services division. Dues are charged on a sliding scale that is based on annual income from writing.

Book Marketing Works

Website: www.bookmarketingworks.
com

Created by Brian Jud, this company provides publishers with information related to special sales markets.

Book Publicists of Southern California

Website: https://www.thebookfest.
com/book-publicists-of-southern-
california/

In 1976, book publicist Irwin Zucker founded this membership association, which includes publicists as well as authors and experts. In addition to holding monthly meetings in California, the group sends out a newsletter that shares news about members' books and publicity-related accomplishments. Some of the members share media contacts at monthly meetings and through networking between meetings. They are also a potential source of advance endorsements.

BookWorks

Website: www.bookworks.com

BookWorks is an international organization of self-publishing authors and the professionals who serve them.

Florida Authors & Publishers Association

Website: https://fapa.org

This membership association holds an annual conference in Orlando with speaking opportunities, including compensation and free air fare for those chosen to speak. Florida-based authors and publishers may find the association's networking opportunities useful in their book promotion efforts.

Independent Book Publishers Association (IBPA)

Website: www.ibpa-online.org

Membership in the IBPA offers independent publishing companies, book authors, and self-publishers the opportunity to network and learn more about the process of publishing. The annual IBPA Benjamin Franklin Awards have become a popular way to promote independent titles. Membership also provides several discounts, such as discounted subscriptions to NetGalley and Edelweiss, which make digital ARCs available to reviewers. (See page 254.) Through its Media Outreach Program, for a fee, the IBPA will enable you to send a targeted email offering a complimentary review copy of your book to a customized media list. (See also page 243.)

National Association of Memoir Writers (NAMW)

Website: https://www.namw.org

This membership association offers information about memoir writing, networking with other memoir authors, and related author services. Members are provided with articles as well as coaching and classes to help them launch and promote their memoir.

National Writers Union (NWU)

Website: https://nwu.org

With chapters in cities throughout the United States, the NWU is the only union that represents freelance writers working in all formats, genres, and mediums. Its services include author advocacy and legal assistance. Members may help each other by sharing media experiences and contacts.

Nonfiction Authors Association

Website: https://nonfictionauthorsassociation.com

The Nonfiction Authors Association provides nonfiction authors with a community of writers in which they can exchange ideas and learn how to write, publish, promote, and profit. The Association offers different levels of membership, the basic version of which is free of charge.

Publishers' Publicity Association

Website: https://publisherspublicityassociation.com

Facebook group website: https://www.facebook.com/groups/PublishersPublicityAssociation

This free closed group is now a Facebook group, and it is a unique and useful place for the group to announce its events with book publicity experts and service providers. There used to be a charge for the in-person events, which were held at restaurants in Manhattan, but now the events for members are free and accessible via Zoom. The follow-up notes related to the events—which usually feature representatives of broadcast, print, and online media who review or feature book authors—provide useful promotional information.

Publishing Trends

Website: http://www.
   publishingtrends.com/

Publishing Trends provides up-to-date information on the publishing world, including new markets, digital publishing, deals, events, retailing, technology, and distribution. It also publishes a list of freelance book publicists.

Society of Children's Book Writers and Illustrators (SCBWI)

Website: www.scbwi.org

One of the largest associations of writers and illustrators, SCBWI's membership includes individuals who write or illustrate works for children and young adults. The group provides members with opportunities to market and promote their work.

Women's National Book Association (WNBA)

Website: www.wnba-books.org

The Women's National Book Association is an organization of women and men who work with and value books. Networking with other members of the association—which include authors and editors—can help you get the word out about you and your book, and may also make you aware of useful media contacts.

Writers and Publishers Network (WPN)

Website: https://
   writersandpublishersnetwork.com

This membership association provides information, resources, and opportunities to authors, freelance writers, artists, and publishing companies. The website shares information on writing, marketing, and publishing.

BOOK FAIRS AND EVENTS IN THE UNITED STATES

The number of book events that are scheduled each year in the United States is truly staggering. The list below looks at various associations that sponsor conferences. This is followed by a list of regional booksellers conferences followed by a list of websites that provide extensive listings of fairs, conferences, and other book events. In many cases, when you visit the website for an individual show, you will find an application that you can submit if you want to speak at a show or if you would like to exhibit your books there.

Association-Sponsored Conferences and Fairs

A number of associations sponsor book conferences and fairs. As you will see below, some events, like the yearly ALA conference, are broad in scope, including a wide range of authors and published material. Other events focus on specific types and genres of books.

The American Library Association (ALA)

Website: https://www.ala.org/conferencesevents/

Every year, the ALA conference is held in a different city, usually towards the end of June. Librarians from throughout the country attend, along with publishers (who are usually the exhibitors), authors, and the media. In addition to this large annual conference, there is a mid-year conference—also held in a different city each year—which has a smaller number of librarians and exhibitors. Check the ALA website for details.

American Society of Journalists and Authors (ASJA)

Website: www.asja.org

The ASJA holds an annual conference, mostly focused on nonfiction writing, usually in New York City some time at the end of May. One day is for just members of the association, and the following day is the public conference. Members of the media may be participants on panels for the public conference or be in attendance at the cocktail party held at the end of the day. In 2022, they introduced virtual conferences, as well.

The ASJA conference usually includes an on-site bookstore where those who speak are able to sell their books. Book orders are handled by the association and a local bookstore.

Association of Writers & Writing Programs (AWP)

Website: https://www.awpwriter.org/awp_conference/

This conference and book fair takes place every year in a different American city. There are literally hundreds of panels

as well as a huge exhibit hall where publishers (and authors) display their books. For four days, more than 12,000 attendees assemble in what is referred to as the largest literary conference in the country.

You have to apply well in advance of next year's conference to be considered for moderating a panel. However, once the panels are chosen and posted in August—the conference usually takes place the following March or April—you can see who the moderators are. If a panel has an open spot, you can apply directly to the moderator to be added to that panel. You or your publisher can also buy space in the exhibit hall.

Florida Author and Publisher Association (FAPA)

Website: https://myfapa.org

Every July, the FAPA holds a conference for authors and publishers in Orlando, Florida. Visit the website to find the application for speaking at next year's meeting.

Public Library Association (PLA)

Website: placonference.org

A division of the ALA, the Public Library Association—an association of thousands of public libraries—holds its conference biennially. Like the ALA conference, the PLA conference moves around to different cities in the United States. The website above provides information on the next scheduled conference.

Romance Writers of America (RWA)

Website: www.rwa.org

This international conference attracts romance writers and fans every year. It is an opportunity to network with

other authors and to meet fans, editors,   *there are opportunities for speaking and*
publishers, and any media people who   *exhibiting. You might also be selected to*
are in attendance. Like most conferences,   *moderate or appear on a panel.*

Regional Booksellers Conferences

Regional booksellers conferences are usually held in September or October through the different regional booksellers associations. The dates and locations change every year, so check each association's website for the upcoming conference as well as the deadline by which you must apply to have an author signing. Many regional booksellers associations have added spring events to their schedules, providing further opportunities for book authors to speak.

California Independent
Bookseller Alliance
Website: caliballiance.org

Great Lakes Booksellers
Association
Website: www.gliba.org

Midwest Independent Booksellers
Association
Website: https://www.
   midwestbooksellers.org/

Mountains and Plains
Independent Booksellers
Association (MPIBA)
Website: https://www.
   mountainsplains.org/

New Atlantic Independent
Booksellers Association (NAIBA)
Website: https://www.naiba.com/

New England Independent
Booksellers Association (NEIBA)
Website: https://newenglandbooks.
   org/

Pacific Northwest Booksellers
Association (PNBA)
Website: http://www.pnba.org/

Southern Independent
Booksellers Alliance (SIBA)
Website: https://sibaweb.com/

Websites That List Book Events

The following websites will guide you to book fairs, festivals, and conferences throughout the United States and sometimes in other countries, as well. (For information on international book fairs, see page 241.)

The African American Literature Book Club
Website: https://aalbc.com/events/list.php

Association of Writers and Writer Programs (AWP)
Website: https://www.awpwriter.org/wcc/directory_conferences_centers

Book Reporter
Website: https://www.bookreporter.com/book-festivals

Book Riot
Website: https://bookriot.com/2017/01/16/awesome-book-events-in-every-state/

Center for Book Publishing
Website:http://centerforbookpublishing.org/writers-conferences-and-book-festivals/

Publishers Weekly (PW)
Website: https://www.publishersweekly.com/pw/by-topic/industry-news/trade-shows-events/index.html

BOOK FAIRS AROUND THE WORLD

If you are interested in getting your book into the hands of readers who live in other countries and possibly speak different languages, you should consider attending foreign book fairs. It might also provide the visibility that leads to interest by a foreign publisher for a translation of your book. Below, you'll find a list of some of the most important book fairs in the world. If you want your book displayed at one or more of these shows but don't want to actually attend, turn to page 242 to find companies that will display your book for you. If you're interested in getting help with foreign rights and translations, see the list on page 250.

Beijing International Book Fair
Website: www.combinedbook.com
This major Asian book fair—attended by over 30,000 industry professionals—takes place over three days in August. The Combined Book Exhibit (whose website is listed on page 242) organizes exhibitors from the United States.

Bologna Children's Book Fair
Website: www.bolognachildrensbookfair.com/
This fair—which usually takes place in Bologna, Italy for several days in March—is considered the major international book fair for selling children's books through YA (young adult) titles.

Frankfurt Book Fair

Website: www.buchmesse.de

This major international fair has been held annually for more than fifty years, always in Frankfurt, Germany towards the beginning of October. It is considered by many to be the most important book fair in the world for international deals and trading, attracting thousands of exhibitors and hundreds of thousands of attendees.

Guadalajara Book Fair

Website: www.fil.com.mx

The largest Spanish language international book fair, with more than 500,000 visitors, the Guadalajara Book Fair is held over ten days beginning at the end of November. The first few days are for professional *"trade" business, but then it becomes a public fair.*

London Book Fair

Website: www.londonbookfair.co.uk

Although not nearly as large as Frankfurt, the London Book Fair—which takes place in mid-April—is considered a major international fair for selling foreign rights.

Sharjah International Book Fair

Website: www.sibf.com

Located in the United Arab Emirates (UAE), about forty minutes from Dubai, this is a large public book fair. Taking place in the fall, it attracts over 2 million reader attendees, as well as agents, publishers, distributors, and other professionals from around the world.

BOOK FAIRS— COMPANIES THAT DISPLAY AUTHORS' BOOKS

Although international book fairs can be an excellent means of making your book known to readers in other countries, you may not be able to travel internationally and exhibit your books yourself. Fortunately, several companies and organizations can display your books for you.

The Combined Book Exhibit (CBE)

Website: www.combinedbook.com

The Combined Book Exhibit showcases authors' books at the book fairs it attends worldwide, including the London Book Fair, Frankfurt Book Fair, and Beijing International Book Fair. The CBE also displays e-books on large monitors at these fairs.

Foreword Reviews

Website: www.forewordreviews.com

Foreword Reviews offers to display books at different trade shows, including the China Children's Book Fair, American Library Association Midwinter Meeting, Beijing International Book Fair, Frankfurt Book Fair, and Bologna Children's Book Fair. Click on "Marketing Services" on Foreword's website.

HBG Productions

Website: www.hbgproductions.com

HBG Productions, run by Deanna Leah, aims to bring authors to the world through its co-op exhibit at the Frankfurt Book Fair.

Independent Book Publishers Association (IBPA)

Website: www.ibpa-online.org

The IBPA has a co-op stand at the Frankfurt Book Fair and resells booth

space in its aisle to those who would like to have their own stands. IBPA executives attend the fair and meet with potential buyers—foreign agents and publishers. The association also creates a catalog that is emailed to a network of several hundred global contacts. (See page 237 to learn more about the IBPA.)

BOOK PROMOTION AND MARKETING INFORMATION WEBSITES

Many online resources provide a wealth of information on promoting your book, as well as information on writing, publishing, and self-publishing.

Bookmarket

Website: www.bookmarket.com

Run by book marketing expert John Kremer, author of 1001 Ways to Market Your Books, this website provides resources on writing, publishing, and marketing print books and e-books, and offers a newsletter with helpful tips and advice for authors.

The Creative Penn

Website: www.thecreativepenn.com

Written by best-selling author Joanna Penn, The Creative Penn provides information and inspiration on writing, self-publishing, book marketing, and how to make a living with your writing through articles, podcast episodes, videos, books, and courses.

Kindlepreneur

Website: https://kindlepreneur.com

Founded by Dave Chesson, Kindlepreneur is a free resource offering marketing tips for authors.

Publishing Perspectives

Website: https://publishingperspectives.com

Publishing Perspectives is an online business magazine that covers the global book industry and provides information that publishing and media professionals need to connect, cooperate, and work together. It also offers a free daily e-newsletter about the international publishing scene.

Reedsy

Website: https://reedsy.com

Click on "Marketing" on the Reedsy home page, and find the Reedsy Blog, which shares the latest book marketing trends as well as information on using social media to promote your book, planning a successful book launch, handling bad reviews, and more. The website also offers free courses on book marketing.

The Hot Sheet

Website: https://hotsheetpub.com

The Hot Sheet is a biweekly publishing industry e-newsletter that will fill you in on trends in the industry. Annual subscriptions may be purchased for a fee, and potential subscribers are offered a free trial.

Writer's Digest

Website: www.writersdigest.com

Writer's Digest is designed to help authors improve their writing and publishing skills, as well as their promotional campaigns. Type "book publicity" into the search engine, and you will find useful articles related to that topic.

BOOK PUBLICISTS

If you've decided to hire a publicist to help you promote your book, it would be ideal to get referrals from other book authors you know or perhaps from authors that you've met through a writers group (see the list of groups that starts on page 235). Just be aware that some publicists specialize in certain genres or subjects, and you should find one who is a good match for your book. Before signing on with a professional publicist, make sure that you know what you'll be getting for the price you're paying. (See the discussion on page 181.) The following resource can help you get started in your search for a good publicist.

Publishing Trends

Website: http://www.
  publishingtrends.
  com/?s=book+publicists

Publishing Trends—a monthly newsletter that provides news and opinion on the changing world of book publishing— features a contact list of freelance book publicists, including several firms and individuals that specialize in a wide range of genres and approaches.

BOOK REVIEWS FROM FEE-BASED SERVICES

Controversial when first introduced, fee-for-review services have proven to be a valuable additional source of reviews, especially for those who have not yet received a positive review from one of the major prepublication trade review journals. This can help jump-start the publicity process. Most fee-for-review services allow the buyer to decide if he or she wants the review to be posted, but check out the rules with any service.

Blueink Review

Website: www.blueinkreview.com

This pay-for-review service offers several review options and packages, each with its own turn-around time and price: the Standard Review; the Fast Track; and the 2-Review Package, which includes a BlueInk Review and a Foreword Clarion Review.

Booklife Reviews

Website: https://booklife.com

Launched by Publishers Weekly in 2014, BookLife Reviews are written by PW reviewers and paid for by authors. When you submit your book and purchase a review, a 300-word review is guaranteed and will be sent to you six weeks after the purchase date. Expedited reviews are available for an additional fee.

Clarion Reviews

Website: www.forewordreviews.com/ reviews/clarion

The sister company of Foreword Reviews, Clarion Reviews is designed primarily for independent publishers and self-publishers who missed submission deadlines or who need a review from qualified professionals.

IndieReader

Website: www.indiereader.com

IndieReader was created by author Amy Edelman with the goal of leveling the playing field for self-, hybrid, and small-press published authors. Costs of reviews vary according to the turn-around time.

Kirkus Indie

Website: www.kirkusreviews.com

The paid review service of Kirkus Reviews, Kirkus Indie's reviews are written by qualified professionals, such as librarians and journalists. Fees are based on turn-around times.

Self-Publishing Review

Website: www.selfpublishingreview. com

Established in 2008, Self-Publishing Review offers various book review and related book marketing services. Four book review options are available— Editorial, Jump Start, Classic Review, and Lead Story—each of which has its own fee, word count, turn-around time, and associated benefits.

Online Book Club

Website: https://onlinebookclub.org

Created in 2008, this service will review your book and post the review on its website. There, it can be seen by Online Book Club's members.

BOOK REVIEWS FROM PREPUBLICATION TRADE JOURNALS

The following are the key prepublication trade journals in which all commercial book publishers hope to have their books reviewed. While it's tough to get a self-published book reviewed in these journals, if your book looks and reads like a professionally produced book, and if it is in line with the publication's focus, you stand a chance. Keep in mind that submission requirements change all the time, so be sure to check the current guidelines listed on the publication's website before making a submission.

Booklist

Website: www.booklistonline.com

Booklist offers critical reviews of books and audiovisual materials for all ages. A publication of the American Library Association for more than a century, it is a respected resource for librarians, booksellers, and educators.

Choice

Website: www.choice360.org

Part of the Association of College and Research Libraries, a division of the American Library Association, Choice reviews nonfiction books that are likely to be of interest to colleges, and thus covers a wide range of college course topics. It is geared for academic librarians, public librarians, and college educators.

Foreword Reviews

Website: www.forewordreviews.com

Foreword Reviews publishes book reviews and features with authors, promoting books from independent publishers, self-publishers, and university presses, and may be found in print and online versions.

The Horn Book

Website: https://www.hbook.com/

Founded in 1924, this prestigious trade journal is the oldest magazine dedicated to reviewing children's and young adult books published in the United States. The magazine reviews books very selectively, presenting appraisals of approximately one hundred hardcover trade books in each issue. Only commercially published books submitted for review by their publishers are considered.

Kirkus Reviews

Website: www.kirkusreviews.com

Kirkus reviews books submitted by major publishers and independent publishers, including all new adult hardcover or original trade paperback fiction, general-audience nonfiction, and children's and teen books. It is a respected source of critical, comprehensive book reviews.

Library Journal

Website: www.libraryjournal.com

Founded in 1876 by Melvil Dewey, Library Journal highlights books that librarians may wish to add to their collections. A key prepublication trade journal for librarians in public, school, and special interest libraries, it is also read by booksellers, authors, and the media.

PW (Publishers Weekly)

Website: www.publishersweekly.com

Dating back to the late 1800s, PW continues to carry a good deal of weight in the book world, covering all aspects of the book publishing industry, including sales, marketing, author interviews, and book reviews. It also offers a free daily e-newsletter known as PW Daily.

School Library Journal

Website: www.slj.com

Affiliated with Library Journal, but a completely separate publication, School Library Journal offers reviews and articles designed specifically for school librarians, media specialists, and public librarians who work with young people—from preschool through high school. In addition to reviewing children's and young adult books, it presents professional *development titles for educators and school and children's librarians.*

CIP DATA, PCIP DATA, LCCN, AND ISBN INFORMATION

Professionally produced books always include Cataloging-in-Publication (CIP) data (or PCIP data) and International Standard Book Numbers (ISBNs). Contact the following organizations for these important components of your title.

Bowker

Website: www.bowker.com

Bowker is the world's leading provider of bibliographic information and the official ISBN agency of the United States. To learn about getting ISBNs for your book, visit the Bowker website and click on "Author Solutions."

Cassidy Cataloguing Services

Website: https://www.cassidycat. com

Since 1996, this company has been providing Publishers' Cataloging-in-Publication data, or PCIP data, for publishers whose books may not qualify for the Library of Congress Cataloging-in-Publication program. Each PCIP block includes all of the information normally included in CIP data.

Cipblock.com

Website: https://cipblock.com/

Designed for self-publishers, start-up

publishers, and small to medium-sized presses looking for a fast turnaround time, this company—run by a librarian—produces quality PCIP blocks at a reasonable price.

Five Rainbows Cataloging Service

Website: https://fiverainbows.com/

Designed for both self-published authors and publishers, Five Rainbows has been providing PCIP data since 2007.

Library of Congress

Website: https://www.loc.gov/ publish/cip/about/process.html

Librarians need a unique number and other descriptive data to identify and catalog every book they acquire. The Library of Congress provides both Cataloging-in-Publication (CIP) data and Library of Congress Control Numbers (LCCNs). Visit the website provided above to learn about who is eligible for each program and how you can apply.

COMPANIES THAT IMPRINT PROMOTIONAL MATERIALS

Whether you have to produce "rewards" for people who have contributed to your crowdfunding campaign or you want to attract attention to the table you set up at a book fair or convention, you may need imprinted pens and other items, imprinted table covers, and posters.

Compare what the following companies have to offer and choose the one that will meet your needs. Note that some companies require you to order a minimum number of posters or other imprinted items. If you want to print just one or two posters, it may be more cost-effective to visit your local office supply store, such as Staples or a FedEx Office Print & Ship Center, which may have options that better suit your needs.

4Imprint.com

Website: 4imprint.com

4Imprint can provide personalized pens, clothing, tote bags, and many more giveaway items to help promote you and your book. It can also print posters of your book cover.

Crestline

Website: https://crestline.com/

Once on the website, click on "Custom Promotional Products," and you'll find products related to exhibiting at trade shows or book fairs, such as display items, table covers, bags and other giveaways, and more.

Custom Ink

Website: www.customink.com

Custom ink specializes in clothing items such as t-shirts but also imprints drinkware, pens, and other giveaway items.

Vistaprint

Website: www.vistaprint.com

This mail order business card printer also prints posters and other signs, as well as various promotional products such as mugs. Vistaprint prints vertical and horizontal posters in various sizes, and will print just one poster.

CROWDFUNDING PLATFORMS

If you need additional money to produce your book or to promote it, crowdfunding offers a new way of getting the cash you require without taking out loans. The following are all well-known crowdfunding sites. Just be sure that you thoroughly understand the rules and regulations presented on each site before committing to a platform, as there are big differences between the various crowdfunding programs.

GoFundMe

Website: www.gofundme.com

GoFundMe has a simple user interface that makes the process easy for anyone who wishes to raise money through crowdfunding. There are no deadlines or goal requirements, and no penalties if you fall short of your donation goal. Keep in mind, however, that campaigns on this site are more likely to fund emergencies and tragedies rather than book promotion.

Indiegogo

Website: www.indiegogo.com

Indiegogo is committed to raising funds for innovative products from entrepreneurs, inventors, and other creative individuals. This is a good option to consider if you want to raise money for your book campaign or to use the perks part of the campaign to presell your book.

Kickstarter
Website: www.kickstarter.com
Similar to backers on Indiegogo, backers on Kickstarter receive rewards depending on the amount of money they have pledged. Check the site's rules, however, to see what happens to the funds raised if you fall short of your goal.

Patreon
Website: www.patreon.com
Patreon works more like a subscription service than a one-time donation platform. People can support their favorite content creators, including authors and podcasters, by becoming "patrons" and pledging to donate a certain amount of money to them each month.

Publishizer
Website: https://publishizer.com
In addition to being a book crowdfunding platform, Publishizer allows you to pitch your book to one of its scouts. If they like it, you create a proposal, and you and the scout try to generate enough preorders to not just fund the book, but possibly attract the attention of a commercial house.

Unbound
https://unbound.com/
This London-based crowdfunding publisher is specifically focused on obtaining funding for its authors' book projects. You pitch your idea to the company's editors and crowdfund to try to raise the required money for the project. Then Unbound's team produces and promotes your book.

EMAIL MANAGEMENT PROGRAMS FOR SENDING OUT E-BLASTS

E-blasts can send out a promotional piece to a large number of people at the same time. If you would like professional assistance with this form of promotion, consider signing up with one of the following companies.

Campaigner
Website: https://try.campaigner.com
Campaigner offers a free trial. If you decide to subscribe, the per-month charge depends on the number of emails you send out in your e-blasts.

Campaign Monitor
Website: https://www.campaignmonitor.com
Like Campaigner, Campaign Monitor also offers a free trial and per-month fees that depend on the size of your e-blasts.

Constant Contact
Website: https://go.constantcontact.com
Constant Contact offers a free trial for its easy-to-use, all-in-one email marketing platform. After the free trial, per-month prices depend on the number of contacts that will receive your e-blast.

Mailchimp

Website: https://mailchimp.com

Mailchimp offers a free plan with which you can send up to 10,000 emails a month with a daily limit of 2,000 subscribers. It also offers three different paid plans with various options.

MailerLite

Website: https://www.mailerlite.com

MailerLite has a free plan as well as paid plans. Check out the options and compare the features and costs to those of the company's competitors.

FOREIGN RIGHTS AND TRANSLATION

If you want to get your book into the hands of readers who live in other countries and speak different languages, you need to become familiar with the world of foreign rights and translation. Fortunately, there are companies and organizations that provide information on this area of publishing and, in some cases, offer helpful services such as automated rights selling systems.

Babelcube

Website: www.babelcube.com

Babelcube enables self-published authors to audition freelance translators and have their books translated on a royalty-sharing basis with the people who do the translation. The company gets a percentage for distributing the translations.

Drop Cap

Website: www.dropcap.com

DropCap's rights agents will submit an author's title directly to foreign publishers in more than 120 countries for translation consideration or will work through selected co-agents. The company prefers authors who have more than one book but is open to considering one-book authors if the title seems to have strong foreign rights potential.

Pubmatch.com

Website: www.pubmatch.com

A partnership between PW (Publishers Weekly) and the Combined Book Exhibit, Pubmatch is an automated rights selling system that enables authors to make titles available for rights transactions.

Frankfurt Rights

Website: https://frankfurtrights.com

Frankfurt Rights, formerly IPR License, provides an online portal that allows rights holders to complete domestic and international licensing deals.

Publishing Perspectives

Website: https://publishingperspectives.com

Publishing Perspectives offers a daily newsletter that features articles on foreign rights and rights-related events in New York City and internationally.

FREE PR LEADS

Monitoring free PR leads is labor intensive, but it is also a way to learn about media that are actively looking for book authors or experts to interview or feature. Check the following free PR leads regularly, and if something seems like a good fit, submit your pitch as soon as possible, since some of the media outlets get swamped with responses. If your response is what they're looking for and is sent in early enough, you might be contacted for an interview, or you might find that what you wrote in your email is quoted directly. Keep your answers to the point, include your credentials (including the title of your book), and never write anything that you don't want quoted.

Help a Reporter Out (HARO)
Website: www.helpareporter.com
This free service offers a three-times-a-day—Monday through Friday, at 5:30 AM, 12:30 PM, and 5:30 PM—electronic newsletter of media queries and interview opportunities. If you check HARO queries regularly, you may find journalists, bloggers, and other media who are interested in you and your book. You can then reach out to each person by submitting a pitch.

PitchRate
Website: https://pitchrate.com
PitchRate is a free daily e-newsletter of available media opportunities. It is especially strong in bloggers who are looking for books to review and/or to offer as part of giveaways.

ProfNet
Website: https://profnet. prnewswire.com/
Part of Cision, ProfNet is a service that offers journalists the opportunity to post their interview needs, and offers

experts—including book authors—the opportunity to receive e-blasts daily and pitch themselves for coverage. Note that while there is an annual fee for experts to get the full subscription for ProfNet, if you're a journalist, this service will be free for you. If you teach at a college or university, inquire if they have a subscription you can use.

RadioGuestList.com
Website: https://www.radioguestlist. com/
Designed to connect radio interview shows, TV program hosts, and podcasts that need guests with authors and experts, this free online service allows you to sign up for free emails that contain "Guest Requests." (Premium fee-based services are also available.) You can then email hosts and producers to pitch yourself to appear on the show.

FREELANCE EDITORS, PROOFREADERS, AND OTHER PUBLISHING PROFESSIONALS

If you want your book to earn reviews and garner other media attention, it must meet professional standards for writing and be free of spelling, grammar, and style errors. To make sure that your book is as good as it can be, consider hiring editors, proofers, indexers, or other publishing professionals that have experience in producing high-quality books. These professionals may also be helpful if you write your own press releases.

American Society for Indexing
Website: https://www.asindexing. org/
Visit the website and click on "Find an Indexer" to locate a professional with experience in indexing nonfiction books on your subject.

Book Editing Associates
Website: www.book-editing.com
This network connects writers with qualified editors, proofreaders, and other publishing professionals who are available for hire.

Editorial Freelancers Association (EFA)
Website: www.the-efa.org
The EFA is made up of editors, writers, indexers, typesetters, proofreaders, researchers, desktop publishers, translators, and other skilled freelancers. Its directory enables you to find the type of book professional you need. You can also post a job through its job alert membership system, Job List, which should lead to emails from members who want to be considered.

Fiverr
Website: www.fiverr.com

Fiverr is an online marketplace for various freelance book publishing professionals, from editors and designers to typesetters and marketers. Fees for services start as low as five dollars but can reach into the hundreds or thousands.

Independent Editors Group (IEG)
Website: www. independenteditorsgroup.com
The Independent Editors Group is made up of professional freelance editors in New York City who have held senior editorial positions in major publishing houses and are available for hire.

New York Book Editors
Website: nybookeditors.com
Consisting of editors with a wealth of experience working in New York's major publishing houses, New York Book Editors connects authors with well-regarded editors in the industry.

Proofreading Pal
Website: http://proofreadingpal.com
This company includes proofreading and editing as a combined service. Your project is proofread for spelling, grammar, etc., and is also checked by editors for sentence structure, clarity, and style.

Reedsy
Website: https://reedsy.com
Reedsy is a network of publishing professionals—including designers,

typesetters, editors, and marketers—that you can hire to help you complete your project.

MEDIA OUTLETS

If you are not working with a publicist, you will have to put together your own list of media outlets—newspapers, magazines, TV shows, radio shows, and podcasts—that might be interested in reviewing your book, interviewing you, or otherwise introducing you and your title to potential readers. You can, of course, find information on shows, publications, and other media outlets of interest through searches on the Internet. If you belong to a writers association, you might be able to create a more focused media list by posting a request that asks fellow members for media contacts that have helped them in their own book promotion efforts. In addition, the following resources will provide a starting point as you look for promising outlets.

Agilitypr.com
Website: https://www.agilitypr. com/
This website offers two free lists: "Top 10 U.S. Newspapers by Circulation" and "Top 10 Magazines by Circulation." Although you will be in competition with the heavy hitters from the top commercial publishers if you submit your book for review to one of these publications, if your book is of professional quality, you might get coverage.

BookBuzzr
Website: https:// bookbuzzr.com/blog/ best-podcasts-for-authors-list/
This website lists categories of podcasts of interest to authors, including those that feature author interviews, podcasts by book reviewers, and author podcasts.

Cision Connect Database
Website: cision.com
The Cision Connect media database provides 1.4 million journalists, outlets, and opportunities that are vetted by Cision's research team, which makes over 20,000 updates a day. The database also includes 1 billion social influencer profiles. This is an extensive media database, providing detailed contact information for countless newspaper and magazine editors, TV producers or hosts, and radio interviewers and producers. However, this is a fee-based database. Check the website for more information about the annual cost.

Media UK
Website: https://media.info/uk
This is a free listing of media contacts specializing in UK media.

USNPL (United States Newspaper Listing)

Website: https://usnpl.com

This is a free directory of United States newspapers. Click on the state in which you're interested, and you will find a list *of cities and towns, along with their newspapers. Click on the publication of choice, and you will find contact information, including the editor's name, phone and fax numbers, and more.*

ONLINE SERVICES FOR SHARING DIGITAL REVIEW COPIES

Although you'll probably be sending your book out to specific publications or other media for review, you may be able to increase your book's visibility and possibly your chance of getting a review by listing your book on the digital platforms NetGalley or Edelweiss. For a fee, these platforms can make a review copy of your book available to bloggers and other individuals who might not otherwise become aware of your title.

Edelweiss

Website: www.abovethetreeline.com

Edelweiss is a digital cataloging membership-based fee service that allows publishers and authors to make digital or print review copies available to potential reviewers as well as librarians, educators, and booksellers. Once a title is put into the service, you will receive requests for a DRC or a print version, if you select that option. You can then determine if you want to send the review copy or if you prefer to skip the request. There is an annual free, and there may also be nominal download fees for each title.

If you are an IBPA member, you can use Edelweiss at a discount.

NetGalley

Website: www.netgalley.com

Like Edelweiss, NetGalley allows publishers to make digital ARCs available to reviewers for a fee. If you are a member of the IBPA (Independent Book Publishers Association), you can use NetGalley at a discount. The fee-per-title option is suggested for those who have only one title to promote. For those who are publishing more than a few titles annually, there is a subscription option. Remember that most major commercial publishers also use NetGalley, so while this will put your book in good company, it will also give your book a lot of competition.

ONLINE SITES WHERE YOU CAN SELL YOUR BOOKS

Although Amazon may be one of the best-known online book sellers, these days, authors and publishers have many options. The following list will help you get started. Just be aware that for the most part, the focus of the retailers listed below is on authors and publishers that are selling new titles.

Amazon

Website: https://sell.amazon.com/start?ld=SEUSSOAGOOG-B10246B-D

If your books are printed through Amazon and KDP Printing, you already know about that option for selling, and you already have an Amazon account. If not, you can visit the site listed above and learn about your selling options.

Barnes & Noble

Website: https://www.barnesandnobleinc.com/publishers-authors/sell-your-book-at-barnes-noble/

Website: https://press.barnesandnoble.com/

Visit the first website listed above to learn about the Barnes & Noble book selection process so that your book can be considered for sale both in stores and online. Visit the second website to learn how you can create and sell your book through Barnes & Noble Press.

Bookshop.org

Website: https://bookshop.org/affiliate_profile/introduction

Established in 2020, this is a selling alternative to major retailers. By becoming an affiliate, you can sell your own books through Bookshop.org.

eBay

Website: https://www.ebay.com/sellercenter/selling/how-to-sell

EBay was one of the earliest online marketplaces to sell everything from books to clothing. Visit the site listed above and learn about becoming a seller. It is free to set up an account and to offer products for sale. EBay then gets paid a fee out of your sale.

Etsy

Website: https://www.etsy.com

Most people associate handmade or specialized items or crafts with Etsy, but you can sell anything on this site, including books.

Facebook Marketplace

Website: https://www.facebook.com/marketplace/

At Facebook Marketplace, people can discover, buy, and sell items. By listing on this site, you can reach buyers both locally and in other locations.

Shopify

Website: https://www.shopify.com

Shopify allows you to build and customize an online store and sell in multiple places, including web, mobile, in-person, and brick-and-mortar locations. You can try out Shopify for 14 days, no credit card required. After that, there are various selling plans for the online store you can create.

Squarespace

Website: squarespace.com

In addition to being a website-building platform (see page 259), Squarespace's commerce platform enables you to sell your products and grow your business through your own online store.

PRESS RELEASE DISTRIBUTION SERVICES

After you write a good press release for your media kit, you may want to send it out for wider distribution. The following services can help you accomplish that. Each one has its own particular method and fee schedule, so check out each website—and ask questions if you need to—before making a commitment.

Business Wire

Website: www.businesswire.com

Business Wire distributes press releases to news media, databases, bloggers, social networks, and other sources of potential publicity. Fill out their Contact Us form to get information about which distribution service is best for you and your book.

eReleases

Website: www.ereleases.com

This service provides an array of press release options according to fee, and also offers a press release-writing service. Visit this website to find a Book Release Sample: https://www.ereleases.com/ press-release-sample/books/

Newswire

Website: www.newswire.com

Newswire LLC offers a number of distribution plans to meet the needs of a wide variety of publicity campaigns. Customers may opt for a single press release or a monthly subscription service.

PR Newswire

Website: www.prnewswire.com

Owned by Cision, the public relations software platform that operates HARO (see page 251), PR Newswire requires a paid membership to use its services and charges additional fees to send out press releases. It also offers editorial services and analysis of your program's effectiveness.

PR Web

Website: www.prweb.com

Owned by the same parent company as PR Newswire, PR Web focuses on online press release distribution. It offers a variety of service packages to suit different budgets.

SOCIAL MEDIA WEBSITES

Social media has helped level the playing field for all authors, and especially for self-published authors and authors who have been commercially published but are not household names. Through social media websites, you can provide information about your book, about yourself, and about book events, such as launch parties and signings. You can also keep existing readers engaged by offering new reviews, links to videos, and updates, while reaching out to potential readers and reviewers. Although it takes some time and work, the rewards can be great.

Amazon Author Page

Website: https://authorcentral. amazon.com/gp/ help

Amazon Author Pages give readers a chance to learn more about their favorite authors and find (and buy) the authors' books. An author can create an Author Page by signing up for an Author Central account.

Facebook and Facebook Live

Website: www.facebook.com

Facebook Live: https://www.facebook.com/ formedia/blog/create-social-content Facebook is a popular social media platform that connects friends and family members using a simple interface. It is an excellent marketing tool for authors who want to spread the word about their new book. On the Facebook website, you can learn about Facebook Live, which is a free way to connect with your audience in a live streaming video through your smartphone or through the webcam on your computer. You can also host an event on Facebook Live.

Goodreads

Website: www.goodreads.com

Readers post their personal reviews of books on Goodreads as a means of guiding other book lovers to the best titles available. If your book isn't listed on the Goodreads website, you can add it to the database and start the reviewing and rating process.

Instagram

Website: www.instagram.com

A popular social media website, Instagram is used by authors to promote their books and help build their brand. Bookstagrammers, who post book reviews on Instagram, have become part of the book community.

LinkedIn

Website: www.Linkedin.com

This networking site enables authors to keep up with the producers, reviewers, bookers, interviewers, and readers that they already know as well as develop new contacts. Through LinkedIn, you can obtain prepublication blurbs, pitch your book for interviews and reviews, and even seek out speaking engagements in different venues.

Pinterest

Website: www.pinterest.com

Pinterest is an image-sharing and cataloging site on which users create "pinboards," each of which is a collection of images related to a single topic. As an author, your pinboards can provide information about you, your books, your writing process, and so on, thereby stimulating continued interest in you and your titles.

TikTok

Website: www. tiktok.com

This fast-growing social media platform is based on brief videos ranging from fifteen seconds to a maximum of three minutes. Since its release in 2016, TikTok has become a popular way for authors to promote themselves as well as their books. A niche at TikTok of special interest to authors is BookTok. Find it by searching the #BookTok hashtag.

Twitter

Website: www.twitter.com

Twitter provides a quick, easy way for users to share and spread their ideas. By joining Twitter, you can learn more about your audience by engaging with people directly. It is also a free way to follow and communicate with fellow authors or professionals throughout the United States and internationally.

YouTube

Website: www.youtube.com

This popular video-sharing platform allows users to build followings by regularly posting video blogs, or "vlogs," to their own YouTube channels. You will be able to archive the videos that you create, including clips of your TV appearances and/or book trailers.

TRAINING IN MEDIA SKILLS

Most media trainers have been producers or hosts of shows themselves, so they know the skills involved in participating in successful radio, podcast, television, and cable interviews. Consider taking even one session with a media trainer or coach to see if it helps you feel more comfortable in front of the camera.

Dunlop Media

Website: www.dunlopmedia

Steve Dunlop was a correspondent for CBS News for fourteen years as well as anchor/correspondent for Reuters Television and NBC News. He offers customized media training based on your budget and your needs.

Moxie Institute

Website: www.moxienstitute.com

California-based Moxie Institute offers media training as well as training in public speaking.

TRAINING IN SPEAKING SKILLS

Authors who are compelling speakers can help to promote their book, can share their expertise, and—in some cases—can make additional income through speaking fees. If speaking is of interest to you, but you feel that you need to hone your skills, the following resources may prove helpful.

National Speakers Association

Website: www//nsaspeaker.org

The NSA will expose you to excellent speakers and can also provide a speakers' "boot camp"—usually referred to as

the Speakers Academy—for aspiring speakers. This international membership association has several categories of membership, but membership is not required to attend local monthly meetings or the annual summer conference that features some of the top speakers in the field.

Toastmasters International
Website: www.toastmasters.org

Toastmasters offers its members the opportunity to practice speaking in front of other members at its regular meetings. Toastmasters teaches through a network of clubs, and some companies and schools also have Toastmasters chapters.

WEBSITE BUILDERS, DO-IT-YOURSELF

A website created for you and/or your book is a useful tool to generate media attention even with free options such as a Facebook author page. Today, a dedicated author or book website can help both the media and potential readers find you and your book when they put your name or the title of your book into Google or another major search engine. The listings below are mostly DIY options. If you want to find a web designer to create a website for you, ask your author friends for referrals, and be sure to visit their author websites to see which options are especially effective and user-friendly.

Authors Guild
Website: www.authorsguild.com
This association, discussed previously (see page 236), offers its member the opportunity to purchase a website with a reasonable quarterly hosting rate. Authors are able to update their own sites.

Duda
Website: www.duda.co
Duda offers some unique features, such as the ability to create multilingual websites and send visitors customized offers. It offers a free thirty-day trial.

GoDaddy
Website: www.GoDaddy.com
You may already know that GoDaddy is a leading seller of domain names, but GoDaddy also enables you to build a free website. You use a template to build the site, and you can add a shop to it, as well. You can also upgrade to a paid plan

with more premium features. GoDaddy suggests purchasing the Ecommerce plan so you can more easily accept payments at your store.

Jimdo
Website: www.jimdo.com
Using artificial intelligence, Jimdo is a DIY site. You get started for free, but there are four different subscription plans, each with different prices and features, with the ability to pay monthly or annually. You can also sell from your site.

Squarespace
Website: www.squarespace.com
Squarespace is a website-building platform that offers pre-built websites to suit its customers' needs. Users start with a fourteen-day free trial, after which they are charged a monthly fee based on the product they choose. You can also sell from the site.

Weebly

Website: www.weebly.com

Weebly is a web-hosting service that is geared towards the online shopping experience. Basic websites are free of charge, but there are also monthly fee-based options. Weebly also features an app store, which contains a variety of apps that users can add to their websites to enhance functionality.

Wix

Website: www.wix.com

Wix allows users to create professional-looking websites with a range of fee-based services, with four different premium plans. You can also sell from the site.

Sample Filled-in Timeline Table

In Chapter 6, you learned how to set up a timeline for the writing, editing, and production of your book, as well as the promotional tasks that you must take care of before your book is published. The table below lists the different steps that must be taken from the completion of your manuscript to your book's release date, and also indicates how long each step is likely to take and what it is likely to cost. I highly recommend that you create your own timeline table, as it will help ensure that you complete all of the necessary prepublication steps and will also make it easy for you to keep track of the money you spend on your project.

Task	Time Frame	Cost
Complete Manuscript	2 to 12 months or up to several years	No cost if you do it yourself, but you may choose to hire researchers or a ghost writer to help you.
Have Manuscript Copyedited	3 weeks	Costs can range from $1,000 or more.
Find and Secure Rights to Graphics and Excerpts	1 to 6 weeks	You can do the work yourself for no cost, but it can cost from 0 to $25 to $300 per item to purchase the rights. Or you can hire a permissions editor and pay $25 an hour or more per hour. (Check with the Editorial Freelancers Association, or EFA, for rates.)
Apply for CIP data	1 week to 2 months	The government program is free but is not available to self-published authors. Or you can purchase CIP data from private companies. (See page 247 in Resources.)
Apply for LCCN if CIP Data Is Unavailable for You	1 to 2 weeks	No cost.
Have Final Draft of Manuscript Proofread	2 to 6 weeks	There are a wide range of fees, with proofreaders charging by the page, the word, or the project. The price also depends on the complexity of the manuscript and the proofreader's expertise, with nonfiction and technical books often costing more than novels.
Have the Book Typeset	2 to 4 weeks. Expedited projects completed within 1 week cost more.	Prices are normally based on the number of finished pages and the complexity of the project.
Create Index	1 to 4 weeks	You can do it yourself for no cost. Prices charged by professionals range from $500 to $1,000, depending on the length of the book and the complexity of the project.
Have the Typeset Book Proofread	1 to 3 weeks	There are a wide range of fees, with professionals charging by the page, the word, or the hour. Prices also depend on the complexity of the book and the experience of the proofreader.

Task	Time Frame	Cost
Obtain Blurbs	1 to 8 weeks	No cost unless you mail out ARCs.
Design Front Cover	1 to 4 weeks	Prices range from $100 to $1,500.
Design Back Cover and Spine	1 to 3 weeks	If you hire a freelance writer to create the copy, fees will be based on an hourly rate per project ($50 to $200). The person who designed the front cover should also design the back cover and spine.
Determine the Formal Release Date.	1 day	No cost because you do it yourself.
Create a Sales Sheet	1 day	No cost unless you hire someone else to do it and pay an hourly or project fee.
Create ARCs and a List of Places That Will Receive Them	1 to 3 weeks	Make ARCs through Kinko's, Amazon, Staples, or Lightning Source for $5 to $15 per book. Alternatively, use copies of your completed book as ARCs.
Create a Media Kit, including: • Press Release • Author Bio • Interview Questions • Blurbs and Excerpts	1 to 3 weeks	Do it yourself for no cost, or hire a publicist for $1,500 to $5,000 on a monthly basis, usually with a 3-month minimum.
Create List of Potential Media Outlets	1 to 4 weeks	Do it yourself for no cost, or hire a publicist for $1,500 to $5,000 on a monthly basis, usually with a 3-month minimum. (Note that publicists will rarely share their media lists even for a one-time fee.)
Begin PR Campaign	Upon finishing your manuscript for at least a year and a half.	Do it yourself for no cost, or hire a freelance publicist for $1,500 to $5,000 a month for a minimum of 3 or 4 months, including sending out ARCs in advance, doing prepublication publicity, working the month of publication, and working for at least 1 month afterwards.
Purchase Imprinted Publicity Materials (pens, pencils, t-shirts, mugs, posters, bookmarks, etc.)	1 to 3 weeks	Set a $150 to $500 budget, and stick to it. (To put things in context, 500 imprinted stick pens can cost about $150 and up.)

About the Author

Dr. Jan Yager received her BA in fine arts from Hofstra University, her MA in criminal justice from Goddard College, and her PhD in sociology from CUNY Graduate Center. She has taught at many colleges and universities, including the University of Connecticut, The New School, and the New York Film Academy, and now teaches at John Jay College of Criminal Justice, CUNY, where she is an Adjunct Associate Professor in the Sociology Department.

Over the course of her extensive career in publishing, which included full-time jobs at Macmillan Publishers and Grove Press, Dr. Yager has been a Book Publicist, Director of Foreign and Subsidiary Rights, Acquisitions Editor, Book Coach, Permissions Editor, Event Planner, and more. Her award-winning fifty-plus books include *Foreign Rights and Wrongs, Effective Business and Nonfiction Writing, Victims, When Friendship Hurts,* and *Business Protocol,* and she has been published by Simon & Schuster, Scribner, Wiley, and other houses. She has also self-published through the publishing company she founded more than twenty-five years ago, Hannacroix Creek Books, Inc.

The author has appeared on many major TV and radio shows, including *Today, Good Morning America, CBS Sunday Morning, Oprah,* and *The View.* She is also a popular speaker on book promotion, foreign rights, and getting published, and is the author of *How to Self-Publish Your Book.* For more information, visit https://www.drjanyager.com or https://www.publishersmarketplace.com/members/hannacroixcreek/.

Index

A

Academic books, 28
Academic publishing
   authors and, 11–12
   working with, to obtain book
     reviews, 142
Accommodations, choosing, for trade
   shows and book fairs, 211
Adult books, 24–28
   academic, 28
   fiction, 24–26
   nonfiction, 26–28
   professional, 27
   textbooks, 28
Advance endorsements. *See* Blurbs.
Advance reading copies (ARCs). *See*
   ARCs.
Altshuler, Michael, 77
Amazon, obtaining book reviews from,
   146
Applications for trade shows and fairs,
   completing, 203
ARCs (advance reading copies)
   digital (PDFs), 115, 119
   paper, 115
   paper versus digital, 124
   using, in press kits, 177
   using, to obtain blurbs, 115, 119
   using, to obtain book reviews, 124
   when to prepare, 101, 104–105
Audience for book, identifying, 21–29
   academic, 28
   adult, 24–28
   children, 22–23
   fiction, 24–26
   middle grade, 23–24
   nonfiction, 26
   poetry, 27
   professional, 27
   textbook, 28
   young adult, 24
Audience for author events, attracting,
   193
Author bio and photo, 168–170
   sample, 169–170
Author talks. *See* Speaking engagements
   as means of selling books.
Authors
   academically published, 11–12
   commercially published, 10–11, 74
   hybrid-published, 11
   self-published, 12–13
   understanding role of, 73–84

B

Bach, Richard, 80
Backlist books, 10
Barnes & Noble, obtaining book reviews
   from, 147
Bayron, Kalynn, 74
Bea, Aisling, 82
BISAC subject listings, choosing, 98, 104
Blogs
   creating your own, 56
   obtaining book reviews from, 148–149
   using, for promotion, 55–56
BlueInk Review, obtaining book reviews
   from, 153

Blurbs, obtaining, 97, 109–120
  ARCs and, 115, 119
  best sources of, 111–113
  from old book reviews, 118
  how to request, 113–119
  how to use, 119–120
  importance of, 109–110
  including, in press kits, 175
  sample letters for requesting, 116–118
  unpublished versus published, 110
  use of, when requesting book
    reviews, 127
  when to gather, 110–111
Board books, 22
Book categories
  academic, 28
  adult, 24–28
  board, 22
  bridge, 22
  chapter, 23
  children's, 22–23
  early readers, 22
  fiction, adult, 24–26
  graphic novels, 24
  middle grade, 23
  nonfiction, adult, 26
  picture, 22
  poetry, 27
  professional, 27
  specialized adult, 27–28
  textbooks, 28
  young adult (YA), 24
Book events, speaking at, 196–197. See
    also Speaking engagements as
    means of selling books.
Book fairs and trade shows
  applications for, completing, 203
  books to bring to, 209–210
  choosing location for table or booth
    at, 204
  definitions of, 201
  exhibiting books at, 201–217
  following up leads after, 216
  guidelines for success at, 212–217

having your books exhibited for you
    at, 216
how publishing houses prepare for,
    202–203
making travel arrangements for,
    210–211
practical items to bring to, 204–210
preparing for, 203–212
promotional materials and books to
    bring to, 208–210
setting up space at, 204–208
shipping materials to, 211–212
See also Speaking engagements as
    means of selling books.
Book Industry Standards and
    Communications (BISAC). See
    BISAC subject listings.
Book reviews. See Reviews, book.
Book signings. See Bookstores, signings
    at; Libraries, signings at; Speaking
    engagements as means of selling
    books.
Book stands for trade shows, 206
BookBuzzr, 53
BookLife Reviews, obtaining book reviews
    from, 153
Booklist, obtaining book reviews from,
    131–132
Bookstagram accounts, 70
Bookstores
  signings at, 187–190
  speaking engagements at, 187–190
  specialty, as marketplace, 15
  trade, as marketplace, 14
Booktubers, 148
Bound galleys, 104. See also ARCs.
Bridge books, 22
Broadcast media, 42–48
  obtaining contact information for,
    144–145
  radio, 42–44
  television, 44–48
Business cards for trade shows, 210
Business Wire, 180

C

Campaigner, 60
Cataloging-in-Publication data. *See* CIP data.
Catalogues for use at trade shows, 214
Chapter books, 23
Children's books, 22–24
    board books, 22
    bridge books, 22
    chapter books, 23
    early readers, 22
    fiction and nonfiction, 23
    graphic novels, 24
    middle grade books, 23
    picture books, 22
    young adult (YA) books, 24
Choice, obtaining book reviews from, 132
CIP data, obtaining, 93–94
Cision media database, 144
Clarion Reviews, obtaining book reviews from, 154
Coaches, book marketing, 76
Commercial publishing
    authors and, 10–11
    production schedules and, 88–89, 91
    working with, to obtain book reviews, 142
Community Relations Managers (CRMs), 188
Connections, making, importance of in promotion, 82–83
Constant Contact, 60
Contact information for media, obtaining and recording, 144–145
Conventions and conferences
    speaking engagements at, 193–196
    See also Book fairs and trade shows.
Copyediting manuscript, 92
Copyeditors, professional, 92
Costs, estimating and documenting, 90
Cover design, creating, 97–100
Credit card readers for trade shows, 207
Crowdfunding, 78–79

D

Developmental editors, professional, 92
Direct mail as means of selling books, 18–19
Dyer, Wayne, 74

E

Early readers, 22–23
Easy readers. *See* Early readers.
E-blasts, using for promotion, 58–59
Edelweiss, 126
Electronic press kits (EPK), 176
Email and e-blasts, using for promotion, 58–59
    professionals that send out, 60
E-newsletters, 57–58
    creating your own, 57–58
EPK. *See* Electronic press kits.
eReleases, 180
Excerpts of book, including, in press kits, 175
Exhibiting books at book fairs and shows, 201–217

F

Facebook, using for promotion, 64–67
Facebook Live, 66
Fault in Our Stars, The (Green), 151
Fiction, adult, 24–26
    genres of, 25
Font. *See* Typeface style, choosing.
Foreword Reviews, obtaining book reviews from, 133
Format of book, choosing, 95–96
Franklin, Benjamin, 75
Frontlist books, 11
Funding book promotion. *See* Crowdfunding.

G

Gardner, Erle Stanley, 76
Getty Images, 93
Godek, Gregory J.P., 74
GoFundMe, 79

Goodreads, obtaining book reviews
    from, 147
Google, online tools provided by, 55
Graphic novels, 24
Graphics, finalizing, 92–93
Green, John, 151
Guadalajara International Book Fair,
    201–202

H
Haley, Alex, 197
Hepworth, Amelia, 151
Honorariums for speaking at libraries,
    192
Horn Book Magazine, obtaining book
    reviews from, 133–134
Hybrid publishing, authors and, 11

I
I Love You to the Moon (Hepworth), 151
Illustrations. *See* Graphics, finalizing.
Independent readers. *See* Early readers.
Indexers, professional, 96
Indexing book, 96
Indiegogo, 79
IndieReader, obtaining book reviews
    from, 154
Influencers, obtaining book reviews
    from, 150–151
Instagram, using for promotion, 70
Intelligence for Your Life, 143
International Standard Book Number
    (ISBN). *See* ISBNs.
Internet, origins of, 50–51
Internet-based book review platforms,
    146–152
Internet-based media platforms, 49–72
    nonsocial media platforms, 51–63
    obtaining book reviews from,
        146–152
    social media platforms, 63–72
Interview questions, suggested, 171–175
    sample, 172–174
ISBNs, obtaining, 98, 99

J
Journals
    association-related, 39
    compared with magazines, 36
    obtaining contact information for,
        144–145
    obtaining post-publication book
        reviews from, 138–141
    obtaining prepublication book
        reviews from, 130–137
    specialty, 38, 139–140
Journals, trade, obtaining prepublication
    book reviews from, 130–137

K
Kickstarter, 79
Kirkus Indie, obtaining book reviews
    from, 154–155
Kirkus Reviews, obtaining book reviews
    from, 134–135

L
LCCN, obtaining, 94
Lead box, 62
Lee, Bruce, 81
Libraries
    as marketplace, 16–17
    signings at, 16–17, 191–193
    speaking engagements at, 16–17,
        191–193
Library Journal, obtaining book reviews
    from, 135
Library of Congress Cataloging-in-
    Publication data. *See* CIP data.
Library of Congress Control Number,
    obtaining, 94
LinkedIn, using for promotion, 67–69

M
Magazines
    association-related, 39
    compared with journals, 36
    international, 39–40
    local, 37

obtaining book reviews from, 138–141
obtaining contact information for,
144–145
popular, 37–38
regional, 37
specialty, 38
Magazines and journals, 36–40
difference between, 36
obtaining book reviews from, 138–141
Mail campaigns. *See* Direct mail as
means of selling books; Email and
e-blasts, using, for promotion.
Mailchimp, 60
Mailing materials to trade shows, 211–212
Mailing out press kits, 179–181
Marketplaces for books, 13–20
direct mail, 18–19
libraries, 16–17
non-bookstores that sell books, 15–16
online marketplaces, 19–20
speaking engagements, 17–18. *See also*
Speaking engagements as means of
selling books.
special sales, 18
specialty bookstores, 15
trade bookstores, 14
Maron, Mark, podcast of, 52
Media, Internet-based, 49–72
Internet, the, 50–51
nonsocial media platforms, 51–63
social media platforms, 63–72
Media, making friends with, 82–83
Media, traditional, 31–48
magazines and journals, 36–40
newsletters, 40–41
newspapers, 32–35
obtaining book reviews from, 130–145
obtaining contact information for,
144–145
radio, 42–44
television, 44–48
Media kits
author bio and photo for, 168–170
book reviews, blurbs, and excerpts
for, 175–176

choosing media outlets to receive,
177, 179
components of, 105, 164
creating, 161–177
electronic, 176
mailing out, 179–181
press releases for, 164–168
sending ARCs with, 177
sending cover letter with, 177, 178
sending out, through distribution
services, 180
suggested interview questions for,
171–175
timing of mailing, 180–181
using, at trade shows, 208
when to prepare, 105
Media Mail
using, to send materials to trade
shows, 212
using, to send out press kits, 179
Media outlets
creating list of appropriate, 105–106
obtaining contact information for,
144–145
Media platforms, nonsocial online,
51–63
blogs, 55–56
email and e-blasts, 58–59, 60
e-newsletters, 57–58
online videos, 59–61
podcasts, 51–55
websites, 61–63
Media platforms, social, 63–72
Facebook, 64–67
Instagram, 70
LinkedIn, 67–69
Pinterest, 70–71
TikTok, 71–72
Twitter, 67
Metadata, 101
importance of, 104
Middle grade books, 23
Money, use of, in promotion, 77–80.
See also Costs, estimating and
documenting; Crowdfunding.

N

Name tags for trade shows, 207
National Speakers Association (NSA),
  197
NetGalley, 126
Newsletters
  association-related, 40
  company-related, 41
  electronic, 57–58
  obtaining book reviews from, 140–141
  obtaining contact information for,
    144–145
  specialty, 41
Newspapers
  hiring publicist with connections in,
    34
  international, 35
  local, 32–33
  national, 33–34
  obtaining book reviews from, 141–143
  obtaining contact information for,
    144–145
  regional, 33
  specialty, 34–35
Newswire, 180
Non-bookstores as marketplace, 15–16
Nonfiction, adult, 26–28
  genres of, 26

O

123RF, 93
Online Book Club, obtaining book reviews
  from, 155
Online book reviewing platforms,
  146–152. *See also* Pay book review
  platforms.
Online book reviews, encouraging,
  151–152
Online marketplaces, 19–20
Online videos, using for promotion,
  59–61

P

Password-protected PDFs. *See* PDFs, use
  of, for advance reading copies.

Patience, importance of, in promotion,
  81–82
Pay book review platforms, 152–155
PCIP data, obtaining, 94
PDFs, use of, for advance reading copies,
  115, 119
Permissions editors, professional, 93
Persistence, importance of, in promotion,
  80–81
Photograph services, 93
Photographs. *See* Graphics, finalizing.
Physical format of book, choosing, 95–96
Picture books, 22
Pindor, Dominika, 72
Pinterest, using for promotion, 70–71
Pitch, creating, 160–161
Podcasts, using for promotion, 51–55
  author-friendly, 53
  being interviewed on, 52–53
  creating your own, 54–55
  true crime, 52
Poetry books, 27
Posters for trade shows, 208–209
PR Newswire, 180
PR Web, 180
Preparation, importance of, in book
  promotion, 75. *See also* Timelines for
  book production and promotion.
Prepublication book reviews from trade
  journals, obtaining, 130–137
Press kits. *See* Media kits.
Press release, 164–168
  sample, 165–167
Press release distribution services, 180
Price of book, on cover, 98–99
Print media, 32–41
  magazines and journals, 36–40
  newspapers, 32–35
  newsletters, 40–41
  obtaining contact information for,
    144–145
Print on demand (POD), 11
Production schedules, commercial, 88
Professional books, 27
Promotion plan, creating, 100–106

Proofreading manuscript, 95
Proofreading typeset book, 97
Publicists
  hiring, for newspaper publicity, 34
  hiring, for publicity campaign,
    181–183
Publishers Weekly. See PW.
PW *(Publishers Weekly)*, obtaining book
    reviews from, 135–136

R
Radio, 42–44
  local, 43
  national, 43
  obtaining book reviews from, 143
  obtaining contact information for,
    144–145
  specialty, 44
Rand, Ayn, 77
Readers, identifying potential. *See*
    Audience for book, identifying.
Release date, choosing, 88–89, 100–101
Reprint permission, obtaining, 92–93
Reviews, book
  cover letters for obtaining, 125, 126,
    127, 128–129
  difficulty of obtaining, 121–123
  encouraging good reviews online,
    151–152
  including, in press kits, 175
  making review copies available
    online, 126
  obtaining from Internet-based
    platforms, 146–152
  obtaining from pay platforms,
    152–155
  obtaining from prepublication trade
    journals, 130–137
  obtaining from traditional media,
    137–145
  professional versus nonprofessional,
    123
  sending out copies of book when
    requesting, 124–125
  use of blurbs and, 127

working with a publisher to obtain,
  142
Reward-based crowdfunding. *See*
  Crowdfunding.
Rodin, Auguste, 83
Rogan, Joe, podcast of, 52
Rolling carts for trade shows, 206
Rouff, Brian, 140
R.R. Bowker LLC, 99

S
Sales pitch. *See* Pitch, creating.
Sales seasons, 88–89
Sales sheets
  creating, 101–103
  samples of, 102, 103
  using, at trade shows, 208
Salesmanship, importance of in
  promotion, 76
School Library Journal, obtaining book
  reviews from, 136–137
Seasons, sales, 88–89
Self-published authors, responsibilities
  of, 12–13
Self-Publishing Review, obtaining book
  reviews from, 155
Shipping materials to trade shows and
  book fairs, 211–212
Shows. *See* Book fairs and trade shows.
Shutterstock, 93
Signs for use at trade shows, 209
Social media influencers. *See* Influencers.
Social media platforms. *See* Media
  platforms, social.
Speakers bureaus, 187
Speaking engagements as means of
  selling books, 17–18, 185–200
  attracting audience to, 193
  attracting media to, 195
  at bookstores, 187–191
  at conventions and conferences,
    193–196
  at libraries, 191–193
  at special book events, 196–197
  remote, 189

securing, 186–187
Speaking skills, improving, 197–200
Special sales as means of selling books,
    18
Specifications (specs). *See* Metadata.
Style Factory, 58
Subject headings for books. *See* BISAC
    subject listings, choosing.
Suggested interview questions. *See*
    Interview questions, suggested.

T

Table covers for trade shows, 205
Talking points, 160–161
    sample, 162–163
Television, 44–48
    local, 46–47
    local news, 47
    national, 45–46
    obtaining book reviews from, 143
    obtaining contact information for,
        144–145
    regional, 46
    specialty, 48
Tesh, John, radio show of, 143
Testimonials. *See* Blurbs.
Textbooks, 28
TikTok
    obtaining book reviews from, 147–148
    using for promotion, 71–72
Time, management of, in promotion, 77
Timelines for book production and
        promotion, 87–107
    choosing BISAC subject heading, 98
    copyediting, 92
    cover design, 97–100
    creating advance reading copies
        (ARCs), 104–105. *See also* ARCs.
    creating media kit, 105
    creating media list, 105–106
    creating promotion plan, 100–106
    creating sales sheets, 101–104
    finalizing graphics, 92–93
    finalizing manuscript, 92–93
    getting blurbs, 97

getting ISBN, 98, 99
getting reprint permission, 92–93
indexing, 6
obtaining CIP data, 93–94
production schedules in commercial
    publishing, 88, 89, 91
proofreading, 95, 97
release date, choosing, 88–89, 100–101
seasons, sale, 88–89
timeline table, filled in, 261–263
typesetting, 95–97
writing, 91–92
Toastmasters, 197
Trade journals that provide
        prepublication book reviews,
        130–137
Trade shows. *See* Book fairs and trade
    shows.
Traditional media. *See* Media,
    traditional.
Travel arrangements for trade shows
    and fairs, making, 210–211
Trim size of book, 95, 96
Trolls, dealing with, 69
Twain, Mark, 185
Twitter, using for promotion, 67
Typeface style, choosing, 96
Typesetting book, 95–97

U

Unbound crowdfunding, 79

V

Videoconferencing events, 189
Videos, online, 59–61

W

Websites, creating, 61–63
Writing, length of process of, 91–92

Y

Young adult (YA) books, 24
YouTube
    obtaining book reviews from, 148
    videos, using for promotion, 59–61

OTHER SQUAREONE TITLES OF INTEREST

How to Self-Publish Your Book

A Complete Guide to Writing, Editing, Marketing & Selling Your Own Book

Dr. Jan Yager

A new world has opened to writers who wish to have their words turned into finished books. With technological advances in typesetting, printing, distribution, and sales, self-publishing has become a reality. But while converting your writing into a commercially available title may sound relatively easy—based upon the claims of some companies that offer this service—there are many important considerations you should be aware of before going to press. Publishing expert Dr. Jan Yager has created an easy-to-follow guide that will take you from a book's conception and writing to its production and sales. Whether your work is fiction or nonfiction, *How to Self-Publish Your Book* offers sound and proven advice at every turn, enabling you to avoid common pitfalls along the way to becoming a self-published author.

The book is divided into three parts. Part One takes you through the initial manuscript preparation—setting your goals, writing, sequencing, editing, and proofing, as well as creating a business plan for your book's eventual release. Part Two focuses on the actual production of your book. It explains the importance of cover and interior design, what you need to know about producing physical books and e-books, and how to turn your title into an audiobook. Part Three provides key information on how to market and sell your book—subjects that are crucial to a title's success, but of which most writers have very little understanding. Also included is a valuable resource section that guides you to websites which offer essential information on self-publishing service providers, including complete self-publishing companies as well as freelance editors, proofreaders, printers, distributors, marketers, and publicists.

Today, self-publishing workshops and lecturers charge hopeful writers hundreds of dollars, promising to turn their self-published books into bestsellers. The fact is that your book's chance of success starts at its origin, not with the finished product. However you choose to produce your book, whether through a self-publishing company or through separate services, here is a complete road map to what lies ahead—based not on hype or wishful thinking, but on Dr. Jan Yager's lifetime of experience in the world of publishing.

$19.95 US • 272 pages • 7.5 x 9-inch paperback • 2-color • Reference/Writing
ISBN 978-0-7570-0465-0 (pb) • ISBN 978-0-7570-5465-5 (eb)

How to Publish Your Nonfiction Book, SECOND EDITION

A Complete Guide to Making the Right Publisher Say Yes

Rudy Shur

So, you have a great idea for a nonfiction book, but you don't know a thing about how to get it published. Where do you start? What should you send? Are some book publishers better than others? So many questions—but where do you find the answers? The fact is that most

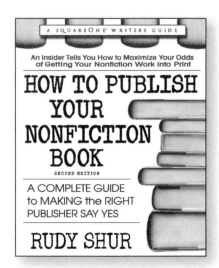

budding writers are in the dark when it comes to the publishing world—as are many published authors. *How to Publish Your Nonfiction Book* was written to provide you with an insider's knowledge of how publishing companies operate. Now, in response to a rapidly changing industry, author Rudy Shur has revised and updated this complete guide to making the right publisher say yes to your nonfiction book.

This edition of *How to Publish Your Nonfiction Book* starts off by helping you define your book's category, audience, and marketplace so that you know exactly where your book "fits in." It then guides you in choosing the best publishing companies for your project and teaches you how to write a winning submission package. Once you've learned how to take these steps, the Square One System tells you exactly how to submit your package so that you optimize success while minimizing your time, cost, and effort. Also included is a special section on contracts that will turn legalese into plain English, allowing you to be a savvy player in the publishing game. Most importantly, this book will help you avoid the most common errors that so often prevent writers from reaching their goal.

Dreaming of seeing your book in print is easy. Getting it published can take some work. With *How to Publish Your Nonfiction Book* in hand, you have a proven system of getting your book from the desk drawer to the bookstore.

$18.95 US • 256 pages • 7.5 x 9-inch paperback • 2-Color • Reference/Writing
ISBN 978-0-7570-0430-8 (pb) • ISBN 978-0-7570-5430-3 (eb)

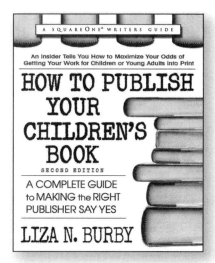

How to Publish Your Children's Book, SECOND EDITION

A Complete Guide to Making the Right Publisher Say Yes

Liza N. Burby

It is the place where wizards live, forests are enchanted, and things are often not what they seem. It is also the home of editors, agents, marketers, and art directors. It is the world of children's book publishing. Until the first edition of this book was released, it was one of the most confusing places for hopeful writers to navigate as well. Now, in response to a rapidly changing industry, award-winning writer Liza N. Burby has revised and updated this complete guide to making the right children's book publisher say yes to your book for children or young adults.

This edition of *How to Publish Your Children's Book* begins by helping you define your book's category, audience, and marketplace so that you know exactly where your book "fits in." You are then taught how to choose the best publishing companies for your book proposal, as well as coached in how to write a winning submission package. Then the Square One System tells you exactly how to submit your package so that you optimize your chance of success while minimizing your time, cost, and effort. Also included is a special section on contracts that will turn legalese into plain English, allowing you to be a savvy player in the publishing game. Most important, this book will help you avoid the most common errors that so often prevent writers from reaching their goal. Throughout each chapter, you will gain valuable insight into the typical thought processes of children's book editors, agents, and publishers, as well as practical advice from popular children's authors such as Jane Yolen and Johanna Hurwitz.

Whether you're just thinking about writing a YA or children's book, or are already a published author, you're sure to find *How to Publish Your Children's Book* a solid reference guide you can use time and time again.

$19.95 US • 320 pages • 7.5 x 9-inch paperback • 2-Color • Reference/Writing
ISBN 978-0-7570-0409-4 (pb) • ISBN 978-0-7570-0409-9 (eb)

How To Make Real Money Selling Books (Without Worrying About Returns),
SECOND EDITION

A Complete Guide to the Book Publishers' World of Special Sales

Brian Jud

Do you want to sell more books—with no returns? No matter what size publisher you are—even if you self-publish—you have the ability to sell hundreds of thousands of your books to markets that are entirely outside the bookstore environment. For years, large publishing houses (and savvy independent publishers) have zeroed in on these lucrative markets, satisfied their constant need for new books, and quietly profited from these "special sales" venues. In this updated edition of *How to Make Real Money Selling Books (Without Worrying About Returns)*, book-marketing expert Brian Jud unlocks the secret to navigating the world of special sales.

This comprehensive and easy-to-follow guide provides everything a book publisher needs to know about taking advantage of marketing opportunities beyond the bookstore. It opens your eyes to a wealth of solid, often surprising outlets—from book fairs and specialty shops to specialized libraries and companies that offer premium sales. Unlike bookstores, these are markets that never or rarely return titles. But that's only the beginning. You will also learn how each market works, how to locate key contacts, and how to successfully negotiate a deal. Rounding out this book is invaluable information on print runs, discounts, contracts, and distributors, as well as a "heads-up" on common marketing pitfalls and how to avoid them. By the time you finish reading this book, you will wonder how you ever managed without it.

Each year, many millions of books are sold through these valuable outlets. Isn't it time you took advantage of these special opportunities? With *How to Make Real Money Selling Books* in hand, you can widen your horizon to success.

$24.95 US • 496 pages • 6 x 9-inch paperback • Business/Marketing/Publishing
ISBN 978-0-7570-0513-8 (pb) • 978-0-7570-5513-3 (eb)

Editing Made Easy

Simple Rules for Effective Writing

Bruce Kaplan

"Longtime newspaper editor Kaplan offers no-frills advice to self-editors. . . . VERDICT: This affordable, bare-bones guide will appeal to writers (and others who have to write)— especially those who like referring to a handy list of do's and don'ts."

—LIBRARY JOURNAL

As the title states, this book is designed to be easy to use for all writers. It offers straightforward, practical guidelines for editing, without getting into the weeds of advanced English grammar. You will find no lofty technical grammatical terms here, such as "present perfect progressive," "correlative conjunctions," "imperative mood," or "interrogative adjective." However, much of the advice in this book is not to be written in stone. English is a flexible language, and writing a creative calling. As you will see, there are many acceptable ways for writers to express themselves.

What you will find in this book is:

- How to avoid the most common errors of grammar and spelling.
- How to spot typographical and factual errors.
- Understanding the styles of print and online media.
- How to make your writing more exciting and dynamic.
- Improving your odds of having your work published.

The goals of this book are simple: to put the odds on the writer's side and increase your chances of being published or finding success as a reporter, feature writer, novelist, freelance writer, blogger, Web developer, Web editor, communications consultant, advertising copywriter, speechwriter, or public relations consultant—in fact anything involving the written word.

$9.95 US • 112 pages • 5.5 x 8.5-inch paperback • Language & Disciplines
ISBN 978-0-942679-36-6 (pb) • ISBN 978-0-942679-36-6 (eb)

How to Read a Person Like a Book
REVISED EDITION

Observing Body Language to Know What People Are Thinking

Gerard I. Nierenberg, Henry H. Calero, and Gabriel Grayson

Imagine meeting someone for the first time, and within minutes—without a word being said—having the ability to accurately know what that person is thinking. Magic? Not quite. Whether we are aware of it or not, our body movements clearly express our feelings, attitudes, and motives. The simple gestures that we normally pay so little attention to can communicate key information—information that can be useful in so many situations. How to Read a Person Like a Book is designed to teach you how to read and reply to the nonverbal signals from business associates, friends, loved ones, and even strangers. Best-selling authors Gerard Nierenberg, Henry Calero, and Gabriel Grayson have collaborated to put their working knowledge of body language into this practical guide to recognize and understand body movements.

In this book, you will find the authors' proven techniques for gaining control of negotiations, detecting lies, and recognizing signals of sexual attraction. By correctly reading body movements, you will dramatically improve your understanding of others, giving you the advantage of added insight into all social and business situations.

With How to Read a Person Like a Book you will learn how to tell if someone is not being truthful, when to push forward or back off during a negotiation, how to interpret an aggressive or weak handshake, when someone has lost interest in what you are saying, how to put someone at ease by mirroring gestures, and what to look for as signals of affection and attraction.

By mastering the simple techniques of reading body language, you will be able to head off problems before they actually become problems, as well as take advantage of meaningful opportunities when the moments are right. Whether on a date, in an office, or on a family outing, your ability to read other people will be a unique skill that will always come in handy.

$13.95 US • 128 pages • 6 x 9-inch paperback • Communications
ISBN 978-0-7570-0314-1 (pb) • ISBN 978-0-7570-5314-6 (eb)